S0-AXJ-215

French Verb Workbook

Jeffrey T. Chamberlain, Ph.D.
George Mason University, Virginia

Lara Finklea Mangiafico, Ph.D.
Montgomery County Public Schools, Maryland

BARRON'S

Copyright © 2006 by Barron's Educational Series, Inc.

All rights reserved. No part of this book may be reproduced in
any form, by photostat, microfilm, xerography, or any other
means, or incorporated into any information retrieval system,
electronic or mechanical, without the written permission
of the copyright owner.

All inquiries should be addressed to:
Barron's Educational Series, Inc.
250 Wireless Boulevard
Hauppauge, New York 11788
http: //www.barronseduc.com

ISBN-13: 978-0-7641-3241-4
ISBN-10: 0-7641-3241-5

Library of Congress Control Number 2006902014

Printed in the United States of America

9 8 7 6 5 4 3 2 1

Contents

Part Four
The Subjunctive Tenses

Part Five
Additional Topics

Appendix

Introduction

For many students of a foreign language, verbs seem to be the most complicated part. Present, past, or future? First person, second, or third? Singular or plural? Formal or informal forms of address? Indicative, subjunctive, or imperative? What about the conditional? So many concepts, so little time!

We've written this book to make learning how to use French verbs effortless and enjoyable. There is still no magic button, no good short cut that we've ever found, but we present the French verb system one concept at a time, concentrating on the forms and the uses of verbs with clear, uncomplicated explanations and plenty of opportunity to practice both speaking and writing. As the French proverb says, **Paris ne s'est pas fait en un jour:** Paris wasn't built in a day. Or, as we say in English, "Rome wasn't built in a day." All this says that it takes time and practice to learn a language well—but you'll get there!

This book can be used profitably by

- those who know some French, but who wish to improve their knowledge of French verbs in a comprehensive and intensive, but user-friendly way

- students enrolled in a French course in high school, college, or university who feel that they need more practice with French verbs

- students enrolled in continuing education classes

- people anticipating a business, study, or pleasure trip to a French-speaking country

- beginners in the language

Although we have specifically concentrated on French verbs and their forms and uses, you will also find occasional references to other grammatical points that will help you study and review. We didn't want to duplicate the grammar that you can find in, for example, a first-year French textbook. We did want to make sure that our presentations of verb conjugations (their different forms) and verb uses were as clear as we could make them, and we've given you many examples as models to help you conjugate and use all the verbs in this book and other similar verbs. An excellent source of more detailed information is *501 French Verbs*, also available from Barron's Educational Series, Inc.

As you work through this book, you should not skip any chapters, especially if you're a beginner. This workbook is designed to be sequential and coherent. It builds on concepts and vocabulary introduced in previous chapters. By the end, you will be in a position to grasp the fundamentals of the French verb system. You can also use this book as a review and reference manual, referring to any chapter when you find that you need to check up on one of the verb tenses. We have also provided a short *Pronunciation Guide* at the beginning of the book. It explains some of the basics of French pronunciation and spelling.

We want to say a special thanks to our colleague Walter Mircea-Pines for his expert and invaluable help in putting the glossaries together. **Un grand merci, Walter!**

Whether you are just beginning your study of French or have had some training and experience in the language, this book is for you. **Amusez-vous bien!** (Have fun!)

How to Use This Book

French Verb Workbook is divided into five parts, each consisting of a number of chapters that present different aspects of the main theme. Part One covers the present tense, Part Two the past tenses, Part Three the future and conditional tenses, Part Four the subjunctive (past and present), and Part Five the imperative and other constructions.

Overviews

Before starting to read the chapters and complete the exercises of a particular unit, read the overview at the beginning, especially if you are unsure about grammatical terms or concepts. The overview will explain the technical terms used in the following chapters in a non-technical and easy-to-follow way: what is a conjugation, what is a verb tense, what is a past participle, what is the subjunctive, and so on.

Grammar Presentations

Each chapter begins with a brief description of the topic followed by a few examples shown in French sentences. We then present all the main verb forms and conjugation patterns you will need to understand and use French verbs correctly.

Using French Verbs

At the end of each chapter, or in some cases at the end of a major chapter section, we give you the opportunity to practice what you have learned through different kinds of exercises. The exercises concentrate on using French verbs, and we have tried to make them interesting and fun. Some of the exercises involve translating from English to French. It's always interesting and very helpful to compare how two languages express things, and you will find that in most cases, French and English use not only different words (of course!), but also different constructions and even sometimes different verb tenses, to express similar ideas. Remember the proverb we mentioned in the Introduction: **Paris ne s'est pas fait en un jour.** As you complete these exercises, focus on the verb forms and tenses from the chapter, but remember that there may be more than one way to express the same idea in translating from English to French. So you can check your work, we've provided the answers to the exercises in the back of the book.

Perspective Personnelle

Throughout this book, you will find sections that involve your personal perspective. In these exercises, we will ask you to respond according to your own experience and ideas. Because each person's responses will be different, we have provided no answers for these sections.

Crossword Puzzle *(Les mots croisés)*

Almost every chapter ends with a crossword puzzle designed to provide an entertaining format for reinforcing what you have learned in the chapter. We think you will have fun doing these. The clues will vary in nature and in level of difficulty. This puzzle section will keep you on your mental toes throughout!

Some Final Words

At the back of the book, you will find a French-English and an English-French glossary. The glossaries contain all the French words we've used in the grammar explanations and the exercises. Our goal has been to create a workbook for you that is clearly presented, easy and fun to use, and as complete as possible, allowing you to learn and practice all the major tenses, forms, and uses of French verbs.

Pronunciation Guide

Here are some basic features of French pronunciation and spelling.

The French vowel sounds

Letters	Sounds like . . .	As in . . .	Examples
a, à, â	ah	bah	ça (that)
è, ê, e, ë, ai, ei	eh	bet	le père (father)
é	ay (without the *y* sound)	bay	l'été (summer)
e	euh (unstressed)	book	je (I)
eu, oeu	euh	sir (without the *r*)	le feu (fire)
i, î	ee	see	si (if)
o	uh	bug	donne (give)
ô, au, aux, eau	oh (without the *w* sound)	go	hôtel (hotel)
ou, où	ooh	who	où (where)
u	[no English vowel]	tee (but with lips rounded like *oo*)*	tu (you)

*To make this sound, say a word like *tee*. Then, keeping everything else still, move your lips to a rounded position (as in the word *too*).

Note, though, that *no* French vowel ever sounds exactly like a vowel in English. These are only rough approximations—in some cases, very rough ones!

There are also three *nasal vowels* in French. English doesn't have these vowels at all, so again, we can only suggest rough approximations.

Letters	As in . . .	Examples
am, an, em, en	song (without the *n*)	le blanc (white)
im, in, ain, ein	sang (without the *n*)	le vin (wine)
om, on, um, un	don't (without the *n*)	bon (good)

The French consonants

Letters	Sounds like . . .	As in . . .	Examples
b	b	book	**bien** (well)
c (before **a**, **o**, **u**)	k	car	**copie** (copy)
c (before **e**, **i**)	s	cell	**cinq** (five)
ç	s	façade	**français** (French)
ch	sh	chic	**le chien** (dog)
d	d	dime	**donner** (give)
f, ph	f	French	**la fille** (girl)
g (before **a**, **o**, **u**, or consonant)	g	go	**la gare** (train station)
g (before **e**, **i**)	zh	azure	**rouge** (red)
gn	ny	canyon	**espagnol** (Spanish)
h	(silent in French)	honor	**l'homme** (man)
j	zh	azure	**jeu** (game)
k	k	kiss	**le kilogramme** (kilogram)
l	l	light	**le livre** (book)
m	m	might	**la main** (hand)
n	n	night	**la Noël** (Christmas)
p	p	pen	**le pont** (bridge)
qu	k	lacquer	**quinze** (fifteen)
r	(no English equivalent)*		**rue** (street)
s	s (beginning of a word, or before another consonant)	sip	**le sac** (bag)
s	z (between vowels)	pose	**rose** (pink)
ss	s	pass	**la tasse** (cup)
t	t	ten	**la tête** (head)
-t̲ion-	s	(not like English)	**national** (national)
after s: -st̲ion-	t	(not like English)	**le question** (question)
v	v	verb	**vide** (empty)
w	w (but *v* in *wagon*)	water	**le week-end** (weekend)
x	ks (before a consonant)	extra	**le texte** (text)
x	gz (before a vowel)	example	**l'examen** (exam)
y	y	year	**les yeux** (eyes)
z	z	zap	**zut!** (darn it!)

*The French (Parisian) *r* is a slight and quick vibration in the back of your throat. It's like saying a *k* or a *g* but not closing off your throat entirely to make the sound.

Final consonants

Here are some notes concerning final consonants:

- Many consonants are silent when they appear at the end of a word.

- The final consonants **c**, **r**, **f**, and **l** (think of the word *careful*) are often pronounced.

- The final **r** of infinitives that end in **-er** (**parler**, **étudier**, **habiter**, and so on) is *not* pronounced.

- The third person verb ending **-ent** is not pronounced.

Liaison

Sometimes, silent consonants are pronounced when they are linked (*liaison* = linking) to a following word that begins with a vowel sound. Two frequent cases of *liaison* occur with the plural articles **les** and **des** and with the plural subject pronouns **nous**, **vous**, **ils**, and **elles**. In liaison, the otherwise silent final **s** is pronounced like a *z*. Here are examples of verbs with and without liaison.

Liaison: before a vowel or vowel sound	Sounds like . . .	No *liaison*: before a consonant	Sounds like . . . (no *z* sounds)
nous avons	"nouzavons"	**nous savons**	"nou[ ]savons"
vous apprenez	"vouzapprenez"	**vous comprenez**	"vou[ ]comprenez"
ils habitent*	"ilzabitent"*	**ils visitent**	"il[ ]visitent"
elles ont	"ellezont"	**elles sont**	"elle[ ]sont"

*Remember that **h** is silent in French, so pronunciation of words like **habiter** starts with a vowel sound.

Part One

The Present Indicative

Verbs and the Present Tense: an Overview

What are verbs?

Verbs are words that indicate the action performed by the subject of a sentence. For this reason, they agree with the *person* (first, second, third) and the *number* (singular or plural) of the subject. By "they agree with," we mean that each verb has different forms that are used with subjects in each person and number.

Subject	Verb	Translation
Elle	**chante**	She sings
3rd person singular subject pronoun	3rd person singular form of the verb **chanter** (to sing)	
Mes amis	**chantent**	My friends sing
3rd person plural subject pronoun	3rd person plural form of the verb **chanter**	

Infinitives and conjugations

The *infinitive* is the form of the verb not inflected (modified) for a person or number. In English, it is commonly preceded by *to: to sing, to eat,* and so on. In dictionaries, French verbs are listed in the infinitive form, which ends in either **-r** *or* **-re**.

French verbs are divided into three conjugations according to their infinitive endings. A *conjugation* is the systematic arrangement of the verb forms according to person and number and according to tense and mood. The infinitive endings for most French verbs are **-er** (like **parler**), **-ir** (like **dormir**), and **-re** (like

lire). As we will show you in Chapter 1, the infinitive ending is the key to how to conjugate a verb. In other words, how to find the patterns for the verb endings for the first, second, and third persons, singular and plural.

Tense

A verb *tense* indicates the time an action occurred: now (present tense), at an earlier time (past tense), at a later time (future tense).

Conjugation	Translation	Tense
Je mange le gâteau maintenant.	I'm eating the cake now.	present tense
J'ai mangé le gâteau hier.	I ate the cake yesterday.	past tense
Je mangerai le gâteau demain.	I'll eat the cake tomorrow.	future tense

Mood

Not only do verbs allow you to express the time an action takes place, but they also allow you to convey manner of thinking, point of view, and so on. This aspect of verbs is known as *mood*.

Conjugation	Translation	Mood
Marie lit ce roman.	Mary is reading that novel.	indicative mood (a statement)
Marie, lis ce roman!	Mary, read that novel!	imperative mood (a command or request)
Il faut que Marie lise ce roman.	It is necessary that Marie read that novel.	subjunctive mood (an expression of necessity)

Regular and irregular verbs

A *regular verb* is one that is conjugated according to a recurring and predictable pattern. Most French verbs fall into this category. A verb that is not conjugated in this way is known as *irregular*. Think of the English irregular verb *to be*: I *am*, you *are*, he/she/it *is* . . .

Subject pronouns

To conjugate verbs, you will need to know (or review) the *subject pronouns*. In this chart, *fam.* means *familiar*, and *pol.* means *polite*.

Singular		Plural	
first person	**je, j'*** (I)	first person	**nous** (we)
second person	**tu** *fam.*, **vous** *pol.* (you)	second person	**vous** *fam. and pol.* (you)
third person	**il** (he, it)	third person	**ils** (they) (masc.)
	elle (she, it)		**elles** (they) (fem.)
	on (one)		

*****je** before a consonant, **j'** before a vowel sound: **je parle**, **j'écoute**, **j'habite** (**h** is silent).

There are both familiar and polite pronouns to use when you are speaking or writing to someone in French. Be sure to use these forms correctly, as using the wrong forms of address can be taken as rudeness—or worse!

The familiar form **tu** is used to address a person with whom you are on familiar terms: a member of your family, a friend, a fellow student, and so on. If you call someone by a first name, then you are usually on familiar terms. Otherwise, you must use the polite form **vous**, whether you are speaking or writing to one person or to more than one. **Vous** is always used to address more than one person, whether you are using the familiar or polite form.

What are sentences?

A *sentence* is an organized sequence of words that allows you to make a statement, ask a question, express a thought, offer an opinion, and so on. In writing, a sentence is easily identified because it starts with a capitalized letter and ends with a period, a question mark, or an exclamation point.

Sentence	Type of Sentence
Marc est français. / Mark is French.	declarative
Qui est cette femme? / Who is that woman?	interrogative
Je viens aussi! / I'm coming too!	emphatic

Subjects and predicates

Sentences have two basic parts: a subject and a predicate. A *subject* is "who" or "what" the sentence is about. In French, it is usually the first element in a simple sentence.

Marie parle français.	Mary speaks French.
Elle est française.	She is French.

A *predicate* is the remaining part of the sentence, and it includes the verb. It provides information about the subject. In most simple sentences, you will find it after the subject.

Céline parle français.	Céline speaks French.
Elle est québécoise.	She is from Quebec.

1
The Present Indicative of Regular Verbs

The present tense expresses actions and events that are taking place right now, as you are speaking or writing (**nous parlons**; **vous écrivez**). It also expresses habitual actions (**J'étudie tous les soirs**). The present tense also expresses continuing or permanent actions or states (**Je parle français**), as well as general statements or facts: **Paris est la capitale de la France.**

French verbs can be grouped according to the infinitive ending, usually **-er**, **-re**, or **-ir**. The infinitive often corresponds to the meaning "to do." Here are some examples: **étudier** (to study), **attendre** (to wait), **partir** (to leave). The infinitive is the form of the verb that is listed in dictionaries.

Verbs are conjugated, which means that they have different forms, depending on the subject of a sentence. The subject can be in the first person (I, we), the second person (you), or the third person (he, she, it, they). Verb charts list the conjugations in this order: first, second, and third person singular; then first, second, and third person plural.

Verbs with infinitives ending in *-er*

This is the largest group of French verbs. The present tense endings for **-er** verbs look like this:

je	-e	nous	-ons
tu	-es	vous	-ez
il/elle/on	-e	ils/elles	-ent

These endings are added to the present stem, which comes from the infinitive. To find the present stem, drop the infinitive ending **-er**.

parler (to speak): stem **parl-**

je parle	I speak; I'm speaking; I do speak
tu parles	you [singular, informal] speak; you're speaking; you do speak
il/elle/on parle	he/she/one speaks; he/she/one is speaking; he/she/one does speak
nous parlons	we speak; we're speaking; we do speak
vous parlez	you [plural or formal] speak; you're speaking; you do speak
ils/elles parlent	they speak; they're speaking; they do speak

travailler (to work): stem **travaill-**

je travaille	I work; I'm working; I do work
tu travailles	you [singular, informal] work; you're working; you do work
il/elle/on travaille	he/she/one works; he/she/one is working; he/she/one does work
nous travaillons	we work; we're working; we do work
vous travaillez	you [plural or formal] work; you're working; you do work
ils/elles travaillent	they work; they're working; they do work

In present tense verbs, only the endings **-ons** and **-ez** are pronounced. All the other endings are silent, so that **je parle; tu parles; il/elle/on parle; ils/elles parlent** are pronounced in the same way, as are **je travaille; tu travailles; il/elle/on travaille; ils/elles travaillent**. But the endings, while not pronounced, are always written.

In verbs like **étudier** (such as **apprécier, copier, crier, se marier**), the present stem ends in **-i**, which comes before the ending in all forms: **je crie; j'apprécie; je copie; je me marie**.

étudier (to study): stem **étudi-**	
j'étudie	**nous étudions**
tu étudies	**vous étudiez**
il/elle/on étudie	**ils/elles étudient**

Speaking and writing in the present tense

Three different kinds of present tense statements in English are expressed with the French present tense. For example, "I study French, I'm studying French," and "I do study French" are all expressed with a single French present tense: **J'étudie le français.**

Tu and vous

Remember that in French, there are two different words for *you*: **tu** and **vous**. Use the subject pronoun **tu** when you are speaking to one person you know well: a family member (including pets), a close friend, a child, or a fellow student. Always use **vous** when you are speaking to more than one person. Also, use **vous** when you are speaking to only one person you don't know, or don't know well, a person to whom you would show politeness and respect.

tu parles; tu étudies: the familiar form, when you are speaking to one person

vous parlez; vous étudiez: the polite form, when you are speaking to one person

vous parlez; vous étudiez: familiar and polite, when you are speaking to more than one person

On parle français . . .

French uses the subject pronoun **on** for general statements, such as: **on parle français** ("One speaks French. French is spoken.") In informal use, **on** can also mean *we*. **Mes amis et moi, on mange souvent au restaurant** (My friends and I often eat out). The subject **on** is always used with the third person singular (**il/elle**) verb form.

Making a sentence negative

You can make a French sentence negative by placing **ne** before the verb and **pas** after it. **Ne** becomes **n'** before a verb beginning with a vowel sound.

Je ne parle pas.	I don't speak. I'm not speaking.
Nous n'étudions pas.	We don't study. We're not studying.

Sometimes, two verbs are used together. In this case, the first verb is conjugated, and the second verb is left in the infinitive form (sometimes introduced by à or de): **Je désire partir.** (I want to leave.) **Nous commençons à étudier.** (We're starting to study.)

Examples of -er verbs

adorer*	to love, to adore		**écouter***	to listen to
aimer*	to like/love		**entrer***	to enter
arriver*	to arrive		**étudier***	to study
chanter	to sing		**jouer**	to play
chercher	to look for		**laver**	to wash
danser	to dance		**parler**	to speak
déjeuner	to have lunch		**préparer**	to prepare
détester	to hate		**regarder**	to look at
discuter	to discuss, have a discussion, to argue		**travailler**	to work
			trouver	to find
dîner	to have dinner			

*Note that **je** becomes **j'** when it precedes a word beginning with a vowel sound.

Using -er verbs

Perspective personnelle

Vrai ou faux? Indicate whether each sentence is true (**vrai**) or false (**faux**) for you. As French is a spoken language, we want you to speak it! Read each sentence aloud to practice.

_____ **J'adore les chats.**

_____ **Mes parents discutent beaucoup la politique.**

_____ **Mes amis dansent bien.**

_____ **Pour me détendre** (to relax), **je joue de la guitare.**

_____ **Mes amis et moi, nous aimons travailler.**

_____ **Je déteste le football.**

_____ **Mes collègues travaillent beaucoup.**

_____ **Mon époux / épouse adore le chocolat.**

A. **What is the correct form?** Conjugate the verb in parentheses to agree with the subject. Then read the completed sentence aloud.

1. **Ma mère _____ (adorer) les pêches.**

2. **Louis et Rachel _____ (jouer) au football.**

3. **Daniel _____ (préparer) la nourriture.**

4. **Je n'_____ (aimer) pas les petits pois.**

5. **Les adolescents _____ (écouter) la musique.**

6. **Mes parents n'_____ (étudier) pas le français.**

7. **Vous _____ (déjeuner) au restaurant?**

8. **Tu _____ (détester) les films d'horreur?**

9. **Mon père _____ (laver) la voiture.**

10. **Alex et Chloë _____ (inviter) leurs amis au restaurant.**

B. **Now, write sentences of your own!** For each box, create one or two sentences by choosing one expression from each column and conjugating the verb accordingly. Hint: You can turn any sentence into an informal yes/no question just by placing a question mark at the end. Read your sentences aloud for practice.

Modèle:

ma mère mon frère tu	aimer	la glace la chimie la musique classique les légumes

Tu aimes la glace?
Ma mère aime la musique classique.

je vous mon meilleur ami	écouter	la radio le rock le professeur

1. _____

   _____

mes amis nous tu	travailler	à la maison au bureau à la bibliothèque au café

2. _____

   _____

ma collègue ma sœur je vous	détester	les mathématiques la télévision les oranges la musique classique

3. _____

   _____

-er verbs with spelling changes

Verbs ending in **-cer** and **-ger** have a spelling change in the **nous** form of the present tense. In **-cer** verbs, we change **c** to **ç** before the **-ons** ending of the **nous** form. We do this because a **c** before an **o** (or an **a**) has a hard "k" sound (as in the English word *cat*). Changing the **c** to **ç** maintains the "soft c" sound (as in **français**) of the verb so that the verb stem is pronounced the same way in all forms.

   Likewise, in **-ger** verbs, we add an **e** before the **-ons nous** ending. A **g** before an **o** (or an **a**) has the "hard g" sound (as in *gorille*). Adding an **e** before the **nous** ending maintains the "soft g" (as in *gentil*) of the verb so that the verb stem is pronounced the same way in all forms.

commencer (to start)		*manger* (to eat)	
je commence	nous commençons	je mange	nous mangeons
tu commences	vous commencez	tu manges	vous mangez
il/elle/on commence	ils/elles commencent	il/elle/on mange	ils/elles mangent

Verbs like **commencer** : avancer, lancer, placer, remplacer.

Verbs like **manger** : changer, nager, ranger, voyager.

Many -er verbs have *two stems*: one for the **nous** and **vous** forms, based on the infinitive, and another for the other forms in the present tense. In the **je**, **tu**, **il/elle/on** and **ils/elles** forms where the endings are silent, the infinitive stem vowel changes from -e- to -è- or from -é- to è. The two stems are pronounced differently because e without an accent is most often silent: **nous achetons** is pronounced **nous ach'tons**, **vous achetez** as **vous ach'tez**.

acheter (to buy): stems *achèt-*, *achet-*		*préférer* (to prefer): stems *préfèr-*, *préfér-*	
j'achète	nous achetons	je préfère	nous préférons
tu achètes	vous achetez	tu préfères	vous préférez
il/elle/on achète	ils/elles achètent	il/elle/on préfère	ils/elles préfèrent

Verbs like **acheter**:

acheter	to buy	lever	to lift, to put up, to raise
achever	to complete	peser	to weigh
élever	to bring up, to rear (as a child)	promener	to take (someone) for a walk
emmener	to take (a person) along		

Verbs like **préférer**:

célébrer	to celebrate	précéder	to precede
compléter	to complete	régner	to reign
considérer	to consider	répéter	to repeat
coopérer	to cooperate	révéler	to reveal
espérer	to hope	rouspéter	to grumble, grouch
exagérer	to exaggerate	sécher	to dry
intégrer	to integrate	suggérer	to suggest
interférer	to interfere	tolérer	to tolerate
interpréter	to interpret		
posséder	to own		

Some -er verbs, instead of changing the stem vowel from é to è, double the stem consonant l or t.

appeler (to call): stems *appell-, appel-*		*jeter* (to throw): stems *jett-, jet-*	
j'appelle	nous appelons	je jette	nous jetons
tu appelles	vous appelez	tu jettes	vous jetez
il/elle/on appelle	ils/elles appellent	il/elle/on jette	ils/elles jettent

Verbs like **appeler** and **jeter**:

appeler	to call	**jeter**	to throw
ensorceler	to bewitch	**projeter**	to plan, to project
épeler	to spell	**rappeler**	to recall, to call back
feuilleter	to leaf through (a book, for example)	**renouveler**	to renew

Verbs that end in -yer also have two stems: one in y for the **nous** and **vous** forms, based on the infinitive, and another in i for the other forms in the present tense *where the endings are silent*. The letter *y* is written only between two pronounced syllables.

payer (to pay): stems *pai-, pay-*		*essayer* (to try): stems *essai-, essay-*	
je paie	nous payons	j'essaie	nous essayons
tu paies	vous payez	tu essaies	vous essayez
il/elle/on paie	ils/elles paient	il/elle/on essaie	ils/elles essaient

Verbs like **payer**:

aboyer	to bark	**essuyer**	to wipe
balayer	to sweep	**nettoyer**	to clean
effrayer	to frighten	**rayer**	to cross out
employer	to use	**tutoyer**	to address someone as "tu" (instead of "vous")
ennuyer	to bore		
envoyer	to send	**vouvoyer**	to address someone as "vous"
essayer (de)	to try		

Using -er verbs with spelling changes

Perspective personnelle

Vrai ou faux? Indicate whether each sentence is true (**vrai**) or false (**faux**) for you. Remember to read each sentence aloud to practice.

_____ **En voyage à Paris, j'emmène mes parents.**

_____ **Le samedi matin (On Saturday mornings), nous nettoyons la maison.**

_____ **Quelquefois, mes parents interfèrent dans ma vie.**

_____ **Mais d'autres fois (other times) mes parents essaient de m'aider.**

_____ **Pour me détendre (to relax), je feuillette des magazines.**

_____ **Pour se détendre, mon meilleur ami ensorcelle une jeune femme.**

C. Au centre commercial. Imagine you are people-watching at a shopping mall. Look at the pictures below. Using the model as your guide, describe what the following people prefer, what they buy, and how much they pay.

le compact disc

le ballon

le dvd

le jouet

la glace

le téléphone

les chaussons de danse

la poêle

le livre

Modèle:

Sandrine (la musique)

Sandrine préfère la musique. Elle achète un disc compact. Elle paie 18 euros.

    1. **Le professeur (faire la cuisine)**

    _____

    _____

    2. **Les enfants (jouer)**

    _____

    _____

    3. **Sébastien (le football)**

    _____

    _____

    4. **Julie et Thérèse (la danse)**

    _____

    _____

    5. **Nous (le cinéma)**

    _____

    _____

    6. **M. et Mme Robin (manger)**

    _____

    _____

    7. **Vous (lire)**

    _____

    _____

D. What is the correct form? Conjugate the verb in parentheses so that it agrees with the subject. Then read the completed sentence aloud.

  1. **Le chien du voisin** _____ **(aboyer) toute la nuit.**

  2. **Nous** _____ **(commencer) à préparer le dîner.**

  3. **Les Dupont** _____ **(célébrer) leur anniversaire de mariage ce weekend.**

  4. **Ces tomates** _____ **(peser) 5 kilos.**

  5. **Nous** _____ **(vouvoyer) le professeur.**

  6. **On** _____ **(tutoyer) ses amis.**

  7. **Le professeur** _____ **(rayer) les réponses incorrectes.**

  8. **Cet agriculteur** _____ **(élever) des vaches.**

  9. **Sylvie** _____ **(répéter) toujours la même histoire.**

10. **Le matin** (in the morning), **j'**_____ (appeler) **le chien. Puis je le** _____ (promener).

11. **Mes chaussettes** (my socks) **ne** _____ (secher) **pas!**

12. **Toi et ta famille, vous** _____ (projeter) **de faire du camping ce weekend?**

13. **L'université ne** _____ (tolérer) **pas la discrimination.**

14. **Nous** _____ (nager) **dans la piscine tout l'été.**

E. **Now, write sentences of your own!** For each box, create one or two sentences by choosing one expression from each column and conjugating the verb accordingly. Remember: You can turn any sentence into an informal yes/no question just by placing a question mark at the end. Read your sentences aloud for practice.

je mes collègues vous	acheter	un livre une radio des vêtements

1. _____
   _____

ma mère tu nous	nettoyer	la maison la cuisine la salle de bains

2. _____
   _____

nous mes enfants mon patron	jeter	la poubelle des pierres une balle

3. _____
   _____

Verbs with infinitives ending in -re

These verbs have two patterns in the present tense: one with one stem and another with three stems. The endings for the singular forms are different from the endings for -er verbs.

To find the present stem, drop the infinitive ending -re.

rendre (to give back, to turn in): stem *rend-*		*attendre* (to wait for): stem *attend-*	
je rends	nous rendons	j'attends	nous attendons
tu rends	vous rendez	tu attends	vous attendez
il/elle/on rend	ils/elles rendent	il/elle/on attend	ils/elles attendent

Examples of -re verbs:

attendre	to wait for	**perdre**	to lose
confondre	to confuse, to mix up	**prétendre**	to claim
défendre	to defend	**rendre**	to give back, turn in
descendre	to go down(stairs), to take down	**répondre (à)**	to answer
entendre	to hear	**vendre**	to sell

Using -re verbs

Perspective personnelle

Vrai ou faux? Indicate whether each sentence is true (**vrai**) or false (**faux**) for you. Remember to read each sentence aloud to practice.

_____ **Je ne perds jamais mes clés.**

_____ **J'attends souvent mes amis.**

_____ **Chez moi, on entend souvent le train.**

_____ **Quand on téléphone chez moi, le répondeur répond toujours.**

_____ **Mes amis vendent leurs livres sur e-bay.**

F. **What is the correct form?** Conjugate the verb in parentheses to agree with the subject. Then read the completed sentence aloud.

1. **Une mère _____ (défendre) toujours ses enfants.**

2. **Je _____ (revendre) la voiture de ma mère.**

3. **Le fromage _____ (fondre) quand on le chauffe** (when one heats it)

4. **Nous _____ (attendre) le bus depuis 20 minutes!**

5. **Les étudiants _____ (rendre) leurs devoirs au professeur.**

6. **_____ (entendre)-vous ce bruit?**

7. **Tu ne _____ (perdre) jamais tes clés?**

8. **Il _____ (prétendre) être un expert en géologie.**

9. **Patrick et Sylvie _____ (répondre) à la question de leur mère.**

G. **Now, write sentences of your own!** For each box, create one or two sentences by choosing one expression from each column and conjugating the verb accordingly. Remember: You can turn any sentence into an informal yes/no question just by placing a question mark at the end. Read your sentences aloud for practice.

mes collègues		**la voiture**
tu	**vendre**	**l'ordinateur**
mon fils		**du citron pressé**

1. _____

    _____

je vous mes amis	attendre	le bus mon époux / mon épouse le professeur

2. _____

_____

mes parents ma femme / mon mari nous	perdre souvent	la clé de la maison la voiture les devoirs

3. _____

_____

Verbs with infinitives ending in -ir

The plural forms include -iss- as part of their verb ending, and the singular endings are like those of most -re verbs.

finir (to finish): stems *fini-, finiss-*		*choisir* (to choose): stems *choisi-, choisiss-*	
je finis	nous finissons	je choisis	nous choisissons
tu finis	vous finissez	tu choisis	vous choisissez
il/elle/on finit	ils/elles finissent	il/elle/on choisit	ils/elles choisissent

Examples of -ir verbs:

agir	to act	guérir	to heal
chérir	to cherish	maigrir	to lose weight
choisir	to choose	nourrir	to feed
désobéir (à)	to disobey	obéir (à)	to obey
établir	to establish	réfléchir (à)	to think about
finir	to finish	remplir	to fill
grandir	to grow (up)	réussir	to succeed
grossir	to gain weight	rougir	to blush

A few -ir verbs have two stems, but they don't include -iss in the plural forms. The plural stem maintains the consonant preceding the -ir infinitive ending.

dormir (to sleep) : stems *dor-, dorm-*		*partir* (to leave): stems *par-, part-*	
je dors	nous dormons	je pars	nous partons
tu dors	vous dormez	tu pars	vous partez
il/elle/on dort	ils/elles dorment	il/elle/on part	ils/elles partent

Verbs like **dormir**:

dormir: je dors, nous dormons	to sleep
partir: je pars, nous partons	to leave, to depart
sentir: je sens, nous sentons	to feel
servir: je sers, nous servons	to serve
sortir: je sors, nous sortons	to leave, to go out, to take out

Verbs that end in **-vrir** and **-frir** have only one stem, and they are conjugated like regular **-er** verbs with singular endings **-e, -es, -e**.

ouvrir (to open): stem *ouvr-*		*offrir* (to offer): stem *offr-*	
j'ouvre	**nous ouvrons**	**j'offre**	**nous offrons**
tu ouvres	**vous ouvrez**	**tu offres**	**vous offrez**
il/elle/on ouvre	**ils/elles ouvrent**	**il/elle/on offre**	**ils/elles offrent**

Verbs like **ouvrir** and **offrir**:

couvrir	to cover
découvrir	to discover
offrir	to offer
ouvrir	to open
souffrir	to suffer

Using -ir verbs

Perspective personnelle

Vrai ou faux? Indicate whether each sentence is true (**vrai**) or false (**faux**) for you. Remember to read each sentence aloud to practice.

_____ **Comme dessert, je choisis toujours de la glace.**

_____ **D'habitude, mon chien obéit.**

_____ **Mon époux (mon épouse) rougit facilement.**

_____ **Je nourris le chat.**

_____ **Je pars pour le gymnase très tôt le matin.**

_____ **Quand nous avons des invités, nous leur offrons** (offer them) **notre meilleur vin.**

H. **What is the correct form?** Conjugate the verb in parentheses so that it agrees with the subject. Then read the completed sentence aloud.

1. **Les meilleurs étudiants _____ (réussir) toujours.**

2. **Tu _____ (finir) ton travail bientôt?**

3. **Mme Noël est (is) malade. Elle _____ (souffrir) beaucoup récemment.**

4. **Je _____ (choisir) toujours des films policiers.**

5. **Nous _____ (réfléchir) beaucoup à nos problèmes.**

6. **Les adolescents _____ (dormir) tard le weekend.**

7. **Joëlle _____ (rougir) quand elle est embarrassée.**

8. Les arbres _____ (fleurir) en avril.

9. Mon frère _____ (agir) comme un clown devant les filles.

10. Nous _____ (partir) en voyage la semaine prochaine.

11. Vous _____ (maigrir). Vous êtes au régime? (Are you on a diet?)

12. Les parents _____ (punir) les enfants qui n'_____ (obéir) pas.

13. Qui _____ (nourrir) le chien en ton absence?

14. Cécile et Marc _____ (sortir) ensemble souvent.

I. Now, write sentences of your own! For each box, create one or two sentences by choosing one expression from each column and conjugating the verb accordingly. Remember: You can turn any sentence into an informal yes/no question just by placing a question mark at the end. Read your sentences aloud for practice.

les enfants Maman vous	choisir	la meilleure solution le saumon un nouveau restaurant

1. _____

_____

tu le président nous	partir	en vacances samedi avec Philippe

2. _____

_____

le médecin je les professeurs	réfléchir	au problème de Maman à la philosophie de Descartes le soir (in the evening)

3. _____

_____

Reviewing regular verbs

J. Which verb? For each sentence, choose a verb that makes the most sense, and conjugate it to agree with the subject. More than one verb may fit. When you've completed each sentence, read it aloud!

parler	appeler	écouter
épeler	guérir	travailler
réussir	regarder	attendre

1. Les étudiants consciencieux _____ beaucoup.

2. Je ne _____ jamais la télévision.

3. Tu _____ à tous tes examens?

4. Nous _____ souvent la musique rock.

5. Vous _____ français, n'est-ce pas?

6. Ma sœur Charlotte est véterinaire. Elle _____ beaucoup d'animaux.

7. Les nouveaux parents _____ le bébé Paul. On _____ ça P-a-u-l.

vendre	choisir	perdre	employer
effrayer	maigrir	grossir	partir
détester	manger	réfléchir	découvrir

8. Paul et Amélie _____ les mathématiques.

9. Nous _____ souvent du chocolat. C'est pour ça que (That's why) nous _____ .

10. Tu _____ ta voiture? Pourquoi? Tu ne l'aimes pas?

11. Le jeune professeur _____ de la technologie dans sa classe.

12. Ma mère _____ une nouvelle voiture.

13. Je _____ au problème.

14. Vous _____ du poids! Il est évident que vous _____ .

15. Mon grand-père dit (says) qu'on _____ quelque chose de nouveau (something new) tous les jours (every day).

K. Change each sentence from singular to plural.

EXAMPLES: J'adore les légumes!   →   Nous adorons les légumes!
                 Tu parles français.   →   Vous parlez français.
                 Elle finit le livre.   →   Elles finissent le livre.

1. Tu rougis facilement, n'est-ce pas?

_____

2. Si je mange beaucoup de desserts, je grossis.

_____

3. Tu regardes la télé le soir?

_____

4. J'obéis au professeur.

_____

5. L'étudiante tutoie son camarade de classe.

_____

6. Tu descends l'escalier; puis, tu tournes à gauche.

_____

7. Le Parisien part en vacances le premier août.

   _____

8. Le soldat confond l'ennemi.

   _____

L. Change each sentence from plural to singular.

EXAMPLES: Ils guérissent les malades.   →   Il guérit les malades.

Nous cherchons un bon médecin.   →   Je cherche un bon médecin.

Vous vendez les livres?   →   Tu vends les livres?

1. Elles arrivent toujours en retard.

   _____

2. Nous défendons les droits des femmes.

   _____

3. Ils agissent comme des animaux.

   _____

4. Nous répondons tout de suite aux courriels.

   _____

5. Vous jouez aux échecs?

   _____

6. Les professeurs vouvoient les étudiants.

   _____

7. Nous appelons la police quand il y a un problème.

   _____

8. Vous obéissez au code de la route?

   _____

Les mots croisés 1

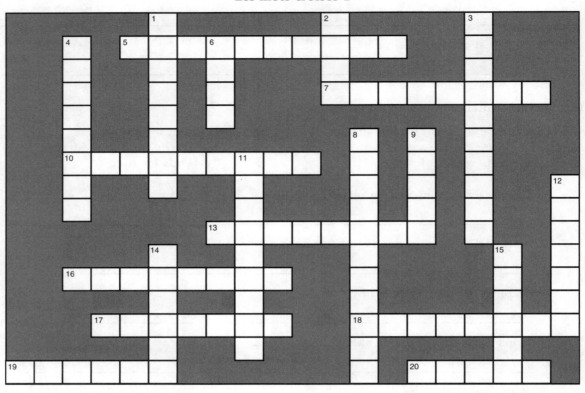

Complete the clues by conjugating the verbs in the present tense.

Horizontal

5   Les enfants fatigués ___ (rouspéter) souvent.

7   Je ___ (découvrir) de nouvelles choses chaque jour.

10   Cécile et Valérie ___ (détester) les légumes.

13   Vous ___ (préférer) chanter ou danser?

16   Cette fille ___ (désobeir) à ses parents.

17   À la plage, nous ___ (nager) dans la mer.

18   Nous ___ (essayer) de danser.

19   Nicolas ___ (chérir) sa collection de vieilles cartes postales.

20   Je ne ___ (perdre) jamais mes enfants.

Vertical

1   Vous ___ (souffrir)?

2   On ___ (vendre) des vêtements dans ce magasin?

3   Tu ___ (travailler) dans un restaurant?

4   Tu ___ (regarder) beaucoup la télé?

6   Quand on a des invités, on ___ (servir) toujours un bon vin.

8   Mes collègues sont au régime. Ils ___ (maigrir) vite!

9   ___ (aimer)-vous les mots croisés (crossword puzzles)?

11   Mes chiens ___ (effrayer) parfois mes amis.

12   Tu ___ (entendre) le chien?

14   Paul ___ (rougir) quand il est nerveux.

15   Quand on téléphone chez moi, ma mère ___ (répondre) toujours.

2
Irregular Verbs

Verbs that do not conform to a conjugation pattern are called irregular verbs. For example, in English, the verb *to be* is irregular. Let's compare *to be* to a regular verb, *to walk*.

to be		to walk	
I am	we are	I walk	we walk
you are	you are	you walk	you walk
he/she/it is	they are	he/she/it walks	they walk

French has many irregular verbs, and they can be grouped according to similarities in their patterns.

Five of the "most irregular" verbs

There are five important and very frequently-used irregular verbs in French. They are irregular both in their stems and their endings. Note the similarities in the **vous** and **ils/elles** forms underlined below.

aller to go	*avoir* to have	*être* to be	*faire* to do, to make	*dire* to say
je vais	j'ai	je suis	je fais	je dis
tu vas	tu as	tu es	tu fais	tu dis
il/elle/on va	il/elle/on a	il/elle/on est	il/elle/on fait	il/elle/on dit
nous allons	nous avons	nous sommes	nous faisons	nous disons
vous allez	vous avez	vous êtes	vous faites	vous dites
ils/elles vont	ils/elles ont	ils/elles sont	ils/elles font	ils/elles disent

Some notes about using these verbs :

- **Aller**, *to go*: **je vais à Paris** = "I'm going to Paris." **Aller** is also used with an infinitive to express something you will do in the near or foreseeable future: **Je vais partir** = "I'm going to leave." See Chapter 4, "Special Constructions."

- **Avoir**, *to have*, but "I have to do my homework" = **Je dois travailler**. Use the verb **devoir** with an infinitive to express that someone must do something.

- **Être:** Adjectives with **être** agree with the subject of the sentence. The form of the adjective can be masculine or feminine, singular or plural. An adjective that describes a mixed group (masculine and feminine) is expressed in the masculine plural.

> **Marc** (masculine singular) **est français** (masculine singular).
>
> **Jeanne** (feminine singular) **est française** (feminine singular).
>
> **Robert et Bill** (masculine plural) **sont américains** (masculine plural).
>
> **Rita et Barbara** (feminine plural) **sont américaines** (feminine plural).
>
> **Giorgio et Carla** (masculine and feminine) **sont italiens** (masculine plural).

- **Dire**, *to say*, can be followed by a *noun object*: **Je dis toujours la vérité** (I always tell the truth). **Dire** can also be followed by **que** *and a subject + verb*: **La météo dit qu'il va faire beau demain** (The weather report says that it will be nice tomorrow).

- **Avoir** and **faire** are used in many idiomatic expressions in French.

avoir faim	to be hungry
avoir soif	to be thirsty
avoir les yeux bleus, verts, marron	to have blue, green, brown eyes
avoir les cheveux blonds, roux, bruns, noirs	to have blond, red, brown, black hair
avoir mal à la tête, aux dents, au dos	to have a headache, a toothache, a backache
avoir envie de + infinitif	to feel like (doing something)
avoir chaud	to be hot
avoir froid	to be cold
avoir peur (de)	to be afraid (of)
avoir besoin de	to need
il y a	there is / there are
avoir + (number) + ans	to be x years old
faire la vaisselle	to do the dishes
faire la lessive	to do the laundry
faire la fête	to party
faire la tête	to pout, to sulk
faire le lit	to make the bed
faire la cuisine	to cook
faire le ménage	to do housework
faire une promenade	to take a walk

Using *aller, avoir, être, dire,* and *faire*

Perspective personnelle

Vrai ou faux? Indicate whether each sentence is true (**vrai**) or false (**faux**) for you. Remember to read each sentence aloud to practice speaking.

_____ **Je vais souvent au centre commercial.**

_____ **Mes amis et moi, nous n'avons pas beaucoup de temps libre.**

_____ **Je fais souvent la fête.**

_____ **Mes collègues sont rouspéteurs.**

_____ **Je dis toujours la vérité.**

_____ **Le soir** (at night), **j'ai souvent peur.**

A. What is the correct form? Conjugate the verb in parentheses so that it agrees with the subject. Then read the completed sentence aloud.

1. Vous _____ (dire) toujours la bonne réponse en classe?

2. En hiver (In winter) je/j' _____ (avoir) froid si je ne _____ (mettre) pas mes chaussettes.

3. M. et Mme Capoulade _____ (aller) au cinéma tous les dimanches (every Sunday).

4. Ton copain _____ (être) beau et intelligent?

5. Il _____ (avoir) les cheveux noirs et les yeux bleus.

6. Nous _____(être) très aimables.

7. Jacqueline et Henri _____ (faire) une promenade ensemble.

8. Tu _____ (aller) dîner au restaurant ce soir (tonight)?

9. Mes amis _____(dire) que je _____ (être) pénible. Je _____ (dire) que ce n'est pas vrai (it's not true)!

10. Vous _____(faire) la lessive le samedi (on Saturdays)?

11. Les enfants _____ (avoir) envie de jouer.

12. Qu'est-ce que tu _____ (faire) ce soir ? Moi, je _____ (aller) à la discothèque.

B. Now, write sentences of your own! For each box, create one or two sentences by choosing one expression from each column and conjugating the verb accordingly. Hint: You can turn any sentence into an informal yes/no question just by placing a question mark at the end. Read your sentences aloud to practice.

on vous je	aller	à l'école au restaurant à la discothèque

1. _____

_____

tu mes parents mon professeur	être	sympathique(s) méchant(e)(s) intelligent(e)(s)

2. _____

_____

<table>
<tr><td>nous
mes amis
mon patron</td><td>faire</td><td>la cuisine
la vaisselle
une promenade</td></tr>
</table>

3. _____

_____

<table>
<tr><td>je
l'homme idéal
la femme idéale
vous</td><td>avoir</td><td>les yeux verts
besoin de travailler
les cheveux noirs</td></tr>
</table>

4. _____

_____

Les mots croisés 2.1

Complete the crossword puzzle with present tense forms of **être**, **avoir**, **faire**, **aller**, or **dire**.

Horizontal

2   Tu ___ à l'église le dimanche?

4   Vous ___ souvent des randonnées?

8   Elles ___ envie de sortir.

9   Nous ___ la fête après un grand examen.

12   Je/J' ___ 56 ans.

13   Je/J' ___ polie.

14   Nous ___ les cheveux noirs.

16   Les enfants ___ qu'il y a des monstres sous leur lit.

19   Nous ___ à la piscine pour nager.

20   Elle ___ véterinaire.

21   Ils ___ gentils.

Vertical

1   Thomas ___ qu'il aime les tomates.

2   Cédric et Thérèse ___ au cinéma ensemble.

3   Je/J' ___ chez ma grand-mère le samedi.

5   Nous ___ américains.

6   Miriam ___ jouer au tennis cet après-midi.

7   Tu ___ intelligent.

9   La vieille femme ne ___ pas la cuisine.

10   Nous ___ que le français est une belle langue.

11   Tu ___ une belle voiture.

15   Vous ___ libre vendredi soir?

16   Je/J' ___ toujours la vérité.

17   Je/J' ___ le lit tous les jours.

18   Les filles ___ la tête quand leur mère dit non.

Irregular verbs with one present tense stem

These forms are irregular because -re and -ir verbs usually have two stems (one in the singular and one in the plural): **je rends**, but **nous rendons**, **je finis**, but **nous finissons**, **je dors**, but **nous dormons**. The following verbs have only one stem. It is always pronounced the same way.

courir (to run): stem *cour-*		*rire* (to laugh): stem *ri-*	
je cours	nous courons	je ris	nous rions
tu cours	vous courez	tu ris	vous riez
il/elle/on court	ils/elles courent	il/elle/on rit	ils/elles rient

Conjugated like **rire**: **sourire** (to smile)

Irregular verbs with two present tense stems

The following verbs have an *added consonant sound* in the plural stem.

mettre (to put): stems *met-* (t is silent), *mett-* (tt sound pronounced)		*conduire* (to drive): stems *condui-, conduis-*	
je mets	nous mettons	je conduis	nous conduisons
tu mets	vous mettez	tu conduis	vous conduisez
il/elle/on met	ils/elles mettent	il/elle/on conduit	ils/elles conduisent

écrire (to write): stems *écri-, écriv-*	
j'écris	nous écrivons
tu écris	vous écrivez
il/elle/on écrit	ils/elles écrivent

lire (to read): stems *li-, lis-*	
je lis	nous lisons
tu lis	vous lisez
il/elle/on lit	ils/elles lisent

suivre (to follow): stems *sui-, suiv-*	
je suis	nous suivons
tu suis	vous suivez
il/elle/on suit	ils/elles suivent

vivre (to live): stems *vi-, viv-*	
je vis	nous vivons
tu vis	vous vivez
il/elle/on vit	ils/elles vivent

connaître (to know): stems *connai-, connaiss-*	
je connais	nous connaissons
tu connais	vous connaissez
il/elle/on connaît	ils/elles connaissent

paraître (to appear): stems *parai-, paraiss-*	
je parais	nous paraissons
tu parais	vous paraissez
il/elle/on paraît	ils/elles paraissent

Note the circumflex (î) in **il/elle/on connaît, il/elle/on paraît**. An official spelling reform published in 1990 makes the circumflex in these conjugations optional.

The following verbs, in addition to requiring the addition of a consonant sound to the plural stem, have *different vowels* in the singular and plural stems.

savoir (to know): stems *sai-, sav-*	
je sais	nous savons
tu sais	vous savez
il/elle/on sait	ils/elles savent

valoir (to be worth): stems *vau-, val-*	
(This verb is normally used only in the third person.)	
il/elle/on vaut	ils/elles valent

plaindre (to pity): stems *plain-, plaign-*	
je plains	nous plaignons
tu plains	vous plaignez
il/elle/on plaint	ils/elles plaignent

joindre (to join together): stems *join-, joign-*	
je joins	nous joignons
tu joins	vous joignez
il/elle/on joint	ils/elles joignent

The following verbs also have two stems, but the stem changes *when the endings are not silent.*

croire (to believe): stems *croi-, croy-*		*voir* (to see): stems *voi-, voy-*	
je crois	nous croyons	je vois	nous voyons
tu crois	vous croyez	tu vois	vous voyez
il/elle/on croit	ils/elles croient	il/elle/on voit	ils/elles voient

mourir (to die): stems *meur-, mour-*	
je meurs	nous mourons
tu meurs	vous mourez
il/elle/on meurt	ils/elles meurent

Irregular verbs with three present tense stems

These verbs always have one stem in the present and two in the plural.

tenir (to hold): stems *tien-, ten-, tienn-*		*venir* (to come): stems *vien-, ven-, vienn-*	
je tiens	nous tenons	je viens	nous venons
tu tiens	vous tenez	tu viens	vous venez
il/elle/on tient	ils/elles tiennent	il/elle/on vient	ils/elles viennent

devoir (to have to, to owe): stems *doi-, dev-, doiv-*		*recevoir* (to receive): stems *reçoi-, recev-, reçoiv-*	
je dois	nous devons	je reçois*	nous recevons
tu dois	vous devez	tu reçois*	vous recevez
il/elle/on doit	ils/elles doivent	il/elle/on reçoit*	ils/elles reçoivent*

*ço : soft c, as in nous commençons

vouloir (to wish, to want): stems *veu-, voul-, veul-*		*pouvoir* (to be able to): stems *peu-, pouv-, peuv-*	
je veux*	nous voulons	je peux*	nous pouvons
tu veux*	vous voulez	tu peux*	vous pouvez
il/elle/on veut	ils/elles veulent	il/elle/on peut	ils/elles peuvent

*je veux, tu veux, je peux, tu peux: Note the special ending: -x.

prendre (to take): stems prend-, pren-, prenn-		boire (to drink): stems boi-, buv-, boiv-	
je prends	nous prenons	je bois	nous buvons
tu prends	vous prenez	tu bois	vous buvez
il/elle/on prend	ils/elles prennent	il/elle/on boit	ils/elles boivent

Verbs conjugated like **prendre**:

apprendre	to learn
comprendre	to understand
surprendre	to surprise

Remember that **rendre** is a *regular -re verb* that is not conjugated like **prendre**.

Using irregular verbs

Perspective personnelle

Vrai ou faux? Indicate whether each sentence is true (**vrai**) or false (**faux**) for you. Remember to read each sentence aloud to practice.

_____ Souvent, quand j'ai du temps libre, j'écris des courriels.

_____ Mes parents vivent près de chez moi.

_____ Je veux apprendre le français.

_____ Ma famille et moi, nous connaissons tous les bons restaurants de notre ville.

_____ Au dîner, je bois du vin.

C. **What is the correct form?** Conjugate the verb in parentheses so that it agrees with the subject. Then read the completed sentence aloud.

1. **La compagnie** _____ **(recevoir) beaucoup de courrier.**

2. **Vous** _____ **(croire) aux fantômes (ghosts)?**

3. **Les enfants dans la classe de Mme Joliot** _____ **(rire) beaucoup.**

4. **La petite fille** _____ **(mettre) la table avant le dîner.**

5. **Ce tableau** _____ **(valoir) un million d'euros.**

6. **Les étudiants** _____ **(écrire) beaucoup de dissertations.**

7. **Nous** _____ **(connaître) bien la ville de Paris.**

8. **Tu** _____ **(savoir) l'adresse de l'ambassade américaine?**

9. **Michel** _____ **(vivre) avec sa sœur.**

10. **Les Richard** _____ **(venir) du Canada.**

11. **Nous** _____ **(devoir) apprendre nos verbes!**

12. **Les enfants** _____ **(ne pas pouvoir) comprendre les problèmes des adultes.**

13. **Martine et Vivianne** _____ **(tenir) les clés.**

14. **Sa femme** _____ **(paraître) très sympathique.**

D. **Now, write sentences of your own!** For each box, create one or two sentences by choosing one expression from each column and conjugating the verb accordingly. Remember: You can turn any sentence into an informal yes/no question just by placing a question mark at the end. Read your sentences aloud for practice.

je les enfants mon copain ma copine	vouloir	voyager du chocolat regarder la télé

1. _____

   _____

tu un de mes collègues nous	connaître	le français Paris le président

2. _____

   _____

vous le professeur mes amis	écrire	un livre une lettre des courriels

3. _____

   _____

Les mots croisés 2.2

Use verbs in the present tense to complete this puzzle.

Horizontal

1   Marthe et Joëlle ___ (écrire) beaucoup de courriels.
3   Tu ___ (pouvoir) m'aider?
6   Mon amie ___ (courir) cinq kilomètres par jour.
7   I am dying: je/j' ___.
10   Les garçons ___ (mettre) la table pour le dîner.
11   Nous ___ (savoir) toutes les réponses!
12   He is reading: Il ___.
13   Ça ___ (valoir) la peine!
16   Tu ___ (conduire) bien?
18   Nous ___ (vivre) dans un monde merveilleux!
19   Are you coming?: Vous ___?

Vertical

2   I believe: je/j' ___.
3   It seems: Il ___.
4   Au restaurant, je/j' ___ (prendre) toujours un dessert.
5   Les enfants ___ (vouloir) manger des bonbons avant le dîner.
8   Ma famille et moi, nous ne ___ (recevoir) pas beaucoup de lettres.
9   Vous ___ (connaître) les Portet?
11   Elle ___ (sourire) beaucoup.
14   Vous ___ (boire) du vin rouge?
15   I see: je/j' ___.
17   On ne ___ (devoir) pas fumer.

Reviewing irregular verbs

E. Which verb? For each sentence, choose a verb that makes sense, and conjugate it to agree with the subject. More than one verb may fit. When you've completed each sentence, read it aloud!

venir	être	vivre
croire	rire	pouvoir
avoir	écrire	conduire

1. Quand ils entendent une plaisanterie, ils _____.

2. Les bons étudiants _____ toujours en classe.

3. Nous _____ aux Etats-Unis.

4. Je _____ que Marc _____ très beau!

5. Ma mère _____ sa nouvelle voiture très prudemment.

6. Tu _____ envie de manger?

7. On ne/n' _____ plus beaucoup de lettres.

boire	devoir	comprendre
être	plaindre	valoir
apprendre	faire	suivre

8. Vous _____ la petite fille pauvre?

9. Ma mère et moi, nous _____ du thé le matin.

10. Je/j' _____ très bien le problème.

11. Tu _____ un cours de psychologie?

12. Ce bracelet _____ 500 euros.

13. Vous _____ voir le médecin: vous _____ malade!

14. Nous _____ le français!

F. Change each sentence from singular to plural.

EXAMPLES: J'adore les légumes!   →   Nous adorons les légumes!
             Tu parles français.   →   Vous parlez français.
             Elle finit le livre.   →   Elles finissent le livre.

1. Elle connaît Irène.

   _____

2. Si je bois beaucoup de vin, je deviens bête.

   _____

3. Tu peux conduire la voiture de Thomas?

   _____

4. Je fais toujours les devoirs.

   _____

5. **Tu vois que j'ai des ennuis.**

_____

6. **Le médecin sait guérir les malades.**

_____

G. Change each sentence from plural to singular.

EXAMPLES:	Ils guérissent les malades.	→	Il guérit les malades.
	Nous cherchons un bon médecin.	→	Je cherche un bon médecin.
	Vous vendez les livres?	→	Tu vends les livres?

1. **Elles doivent aller en prison.**

_____

2. **Nous sourions quand nous sommes contents.**

_____

3. **Ils lisent un livre chaque semaine.**

_____

4. **Vous avez de l'argent?**

_____

5. **Nous ne pouvons pas trouver le chat.**

_____

6. **Vous savez la réponse?**

_____

3
Pronominal Verbs

Pronominal verbs, sometimes called reflexive verbs, appear frequently in French. They are conjugated with a *reflexive pronoun* that refers to the same person or thing as the subject pronoun. The reflexive pronouns are shown in *italics* in the conjugations below. In the third person, **se** is the reflexive pronoun for both the singular and the plural. The reflexive pronoun immediately precedes the verb. Note that **me**, **te**, and **se** become **m'**, **t'**, and **s'** when they appear before a vowel sound.

se réveiller (to wake up)		*s'amuser* (to have fun)	
je *me* réveille	nous *nous* réveillons	je *m'*amuse	nous *nous* amusons
tu *te* réveilles	vous *vous* réveillez	tu *t'*amuses	vous *vous* amusez
il/elle/on *se* réveille	ils/elles *se* réveillent	il/elle/on *s'*amuse	ils/elles *s'*amusent

Examples of pronominal verbs

s'amuser	to have fun
s'appeler	to be called, to be named
s'endormir	to fall asleep
s'habiller	to get dressed
se baigner	to bathe
se brosser les dents (les cheveux)	to brush one's teeth (hair)
se coucher	to go to bed
se déshabiller	to get undressed
se détendre	to relax
se doucher	to take a shower
se laver (le visage, les mains)	to wash (one's face, hands)
se lever	to get up
se maquiller	to put on makeup
se peigner	to comb one's hair
se préparer	to get ready
se raser	to shave
se reposer	to rest
se réveiller	to wake up
se spécialiser (en)	to major (in)

In negative sentences, **ne** precedes the reflexive pronoun, and **pas** follows the verb: **je ne me réveille pas, tu ne t'amuses pas**, and so on.

In affirmative imperative sentences (those that give a suggestion or a command), the reflexive pronoun *follows* the verb: **Reveille-toi!** (Wake up!), **Amusez-vous!** (Have a good time!). When the reflexive pronoun follows the verb, **te** becomes **toi**. In negative commands, pronouns remain in their usual place before the verb. We present the imperative in more detail in Chapter 19.

Pronominal verbs frequently describe a "reflexive" action in which the subject and the object of the verb are the same. In English, the reflexive pronoun is usually—and almost always preferably—not expressed.

Phrase	Literal Translation	Clearer Translation
je m'amuse	"I amuse myself"	I have fun, I'm having fun
je m'appelle	"I call myself"	My name is…
je me baigne	"I bathe myself"	I take a bath
je me couche	"I lay myself down"	I go to bed
je me demande	"I ask myself"	I wonder
je m'endors	"I put myself to sleep"	I go to sleep, I fall asleep
je m'habille	"I dress myself"	I get dressed
je me lève	"I get myself up"	I get up
je me peigne	"I comb myself"	I comb my hair
je me repose	"I rest myself"	I'm resting, I rest
je me réveille	"I awaken myself"	I wake up
je me rase	"I shave myself"	I shave

When a part of the body is mentioned with a pronominal verb, it is preceded by a *definite article* (**le**, **la**, or **les**), not by a possessive adjective, as in English.

Je me brosse les dents.	I brush my teeth.
Tu te brosses les cheveux.	You brush your hair.
Elle se lave les mains.	She washes her hands.

Verbs become *pronominal* when they describe a reciprocal action in which two or more people do things for one another. These "reciprocal" verbs are always stated in the plural, as two or more people are involved. In these cases, the reflexive pronoun (each other, one another) is expressed in English, as well.

Nous nous téléphonons souvent.	We call each other often.
Vous vous parlez tous les jours.	You talk to each other every day.
Ils se rendent visite tous les étés.	They visit one another every summer.
Elles s'écrivent des courriels.	They send each other e-mails.

Examples of reciprocal verbs

s'aimer	to like each other, love each other
s'embrasser	to kiss, kiss each other
se disputer	to quarrel
se parler	to talk to each other
se rencontrer	to meet each other

These verbs may also be used non-reciprocally, when the subject and the object are not the same. In this case, they are *not* pronominal verbs.

Nous te téléphonons souvent.	We call you often.
Vous me parlez tous les jours.	You talk to me every day.
Ils nous rendent visite tous les étés.	They visit us every summer.
Elles vous écrivent des courriels.	They send you e-mails.

Many French verbs can be used as *pronominal* and as *non-pronominal* verbs. The meaning is different in each instance. When the verbs are pronominal, their meaning is *idiomatic*. This means that the reflexive pronoun is not interpreted, nor is it translated literally.

Non-pronominal Verb	Meaning	Pronominal Verb	Meaning
agir	to act	**il s'agit de***	it is a question of, it is about
aller	to go	**s'en aller**	to go away
arrêter	to stop (someone), to arrest	**s'arrêter de**	to stop doing something
attendre	to wait for	**s'attendre à**	to expect
détendre	to calm, slacken	**se détendre**	to relax, take it easy
douter	to doubt	**se douter de**	to suspect (the opposite meaning!)
ennuyer	to bore	**s'ennuyer**	to be bored (the opposite meaning!)
entendre	to hear	**s'entendre (avec)**	to get along (with)
faire	to make, do	**s'en faire**	to be worried
intéresser	to interest	**s'intéresser à**	to be interested in
marier	to unite in marriage, marry off	**se marier**	to get married
mettre	to place, put	**se mettre à**	to begin (to do something)
occuper	to occupy	**s'occuper de**	to take care of, be busy with
passer	to pass, to spend (time)	**se passer**	to happen
		se passer de	to do without
rappeler	to call back	**se rappeler**	to recall, remember
servir	to serve	**se servir de**	to use
tromper	to deceive	**se tromper**	to make a mistake, be mistaken

***Dans ce film/livre/roman, il s'agit de . . .** This film/book/novel is about . . .

Some idiomatic verbs are used *only* as pronominal verbs. These include:

> **s'évanouir:** to faint
>
> **se méfier (de):** to be wary, suspicious (of)
>
> **se moquer de:** to make fun of, not to care anything about
>
> **se soucier (de):** to worry (about)
>
> **se spécialiser en:** to specialize in, major in
>
> **se souvenir:** to remember

Using and reviewing pronominal verbs

Perspective personnelle

Vrai ou faux? Indicate whether each sentence is true (**vrai**) or false (**faux**) for you. Remember to read each sentence aloud to practice.

_____ **Le matin, je m'habille. Puis, je me douche.**

_____ **Le soir, juste avant de me coucher, je me brosse les dents.**

_____ **Mes amis et moi, nous nous disputons souvent.**

_____ **Je m'entends bien avec mon patron.**

_____ **Mes parents s'embrassent souvent.**

A. Que fait-on? Using the picture as a guide, describe what the following people are doing. After writing your responses, read them aloud, pretending to explain what is happening in the house.

Modèle: Raymond *se rase*.

1. **Valérie et Pierre** _____.

2. **Rosalie** _____.

3. **Marc** _____.

4. **Ludovic** _____.

5. **Sabine et Hélène** _____.

6. **Jean-Philippe** _____.

7. **Rachel et Catherine** _____.

B. Pronominal? Based on the context of the sentence, decide whether the verb should be pronominal. Choose the correct form.

Modèles: Michèle (se lave / *lave*) la voiture.
           Yannick (*se lave* / lave).

1. **Le prêtre (se marie / marie) le jeune couple.**

2. **Nous (nous détendons / détendons) à la plage.**

3. **Yves et Thérèse (se couchent / couchent).**

4. **La mère (se couche / couche) la petite fille.**

5. **Ce film (s'intéresse / intéresse) les adolescents.**

6. **Les mauvais professeurs (s'ennuient / ennuient) les étudiants.**

7. **Les enfants (s'habillent / habillent) leurs poupées.**

8. **Je/j' (m'appelle / appelle) mon amie Charlotte.**

9. **Vous (vous baignez / baignez) le matin (in the morning)?**

10. **Nous (nous promenons / promenons) tous les jours (every day).**

11. **Je/j' (m'amuse / amuse) avec mes amis.**

12. **Cécile (se sert / sert) d'un ordinateur pour faire ses devoirs.**

C. What is the correct form? Conjugate the verb in parentheses to agree with the subject. Then read the completed sentence aloud.

1. **Dans ce film, il _____ (s'agir) d'un homme qui veut être assassin.**

2. **Je _____ (s'appeler) Brigitte. Tu _____ (s'appeler) comment?**

3. **Monique _____ (ne pas se maquiller) en été.**

4. **Ssssh! Les enfants _____ (se reposer)!**

5. **Vous _____ (se brosser) les dents deux fois par jour (twice a day)?**

6. **Robert n'est pas bien (is not well). Il _____ (s'évanouir) chaque fois qu'il _____ (se lever).**

7. **Michel et Dominique _____ (se marier) en juin. Quel beau couple! Ils _____ (s'aimer) beaucoup, _____ (s'embrasser) tout le temps (all the time), et _____ (se disputer) rarement.**

8. **Tu _____ (s'intéresser) à la philosophie?**

9. **Je _____ (ne pas s'entendre) bien avec mes beaux-parents (in-laws).**

10. **Les étudiants _____ (s'ennuyer) dans la classe de M. Reynaud.**

11. Thomas _____ (ne pas pouvoir) venir ce soir. Il _____ (s'occuper) de ses frères.

12. Nous _____ (se moquer) de nos parents.

13. Vous _____ (se tromper) constamment!

14. Je _____ (se spécialiser) en biologie.

15. Nicole _____ (se souvenir) bien du jour de leur mariage.

D. **Now, write sentences of your own!** For each box, create one or two sentences by choosing one expression from each column and conjugating the verb accordingly. Remember: You can turn any sentence into an informal yes/no question just by placing a question mark at the end. Read your sentences aloud for practice.

| je
mes amis
vous | s'amuser | tout le temps (all the time)
à la maison
au musée |

1. _____

   _____

| nous
le professeur
les vieux (old people) | se détendre | rarement
à la plage
avec un bon livre |

2. _____

   _____

| mon frère
ma sœur
tu | se brosser | les dents
les cheveux |

3. _____

   _____

E. **Which verb?** For each sentence, choose a verb that makes sense and conjugate it to agree with the subject. More than one verb may fit. When you've completed each sentence, read it aloud!

se détendre	se réveiller	se parler
s'arrêter	se déshabiller	se passer
se préparer	s'amuser	se rencontrer

1. **Thierry est au régime** (on a diet). **Alors, il _____ de desserts.**

2. **Nous _____ à 7h du matin parce que nous avons cours à 8h.**

3. **D'habitude, je _____ en regardant la télé.**

4. **Vous _____ pour votre examen de chimie?**

5. **Tu _____ de fumer? Bravo!**

6. **Les sœurs _____ au téléphone tous les soirs** (every night).

se servir	se disputer	se lever
se spécialiser	se moquer	se coucher
s'aimer	s'en aller	se baigner

7. On ne _____ jamais du professeur!

8. Tu _____ à quelle heure (at what time)?

9. Vous _____ en quoi?

10. Les enfants _____ puis _____ .

11. Mon époux et moi, nous _____ , mais nous _____ quelquefois.

12. Pour écrire sa dissertation, Vincent _____ de l'ordinateur.

F. Change each sentence from singular to plural.

EXAMPLES: J'adore les légumes!   →   Nous adorons les légumes!
              Tu parles français.   →   Vous parlez français.
              Elle finit le livre.   →   Elles finissent le livre.

1. À mon avis (in my opinion), elle se maquille trop.
   _____

2. Si je me couche en retard, je rouspète le jour suivant.
   _____

3. Tu te spécialises en mathématiques?
   _____

4. Je ne m'endors jamais en classe.
   _____

5. Tu t'habilles vraiment bien.
   _____

6. Il se rase tous les jours.
   _____

G. Change each sentence from plural to singular.

EXAMPLES: Ils guérissent les malades.   →   Il guérit les malades.
              Nous cherchons un bon médecin.   →   Je cherche un bon médecin.
              Vous vendez les livres?   →   Tu vends les livres?

1. Elles s'en vont rapidement.
   _____

2. Nous nous intéressons au yoga.
   _____

3. Ils s'occupent du chien abandonné.
   _____

4. Vous vous moquez de moi?
   _____

5. Nous ne nous trompons jamais.
   _____

6. Vous vous levez à quelle heure?
   _____

Les mots croisés 3

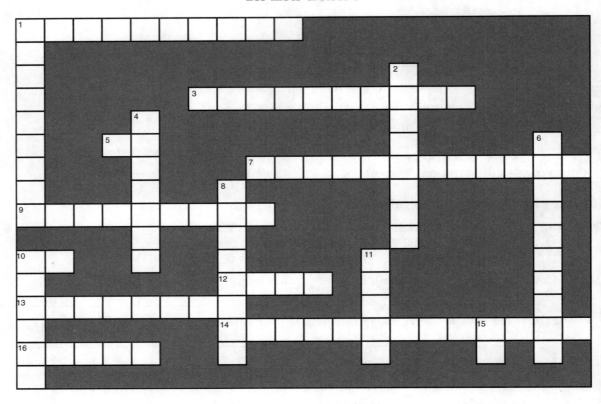

Complete this puzzle with a reflexive verb or reflexive pronoun.

Horizontal

1   **Madeleine ___ (se maquiller) un peu trop à mon avis.**
3   The kids brush their teeth: **Les enfants ___ les dents.**
5   **Il ne ___ douche pas assez!**
7   **Vous ___ (se souvenir) du problème?**
9   What time do you go to bed?: **Tu ___ à quelle heure?**
10 **Je/j' ___ rase tous les matins.**
12 **Vous ___ spécialisez en chimie?**
13 My name is Lydie: **Je/j' ___ Lydie.**
14 **Nous ___ (se disputer) souvent avec nos parents.**
16 He's going away: **Il ___.**

Vertical

1   They are getting married: **Ils ___.**
2   I never make a mistake: **Je ne ___ jamais.**
4   **On ___ (s'ennuyer) dans le cours de philsophie.**
6   **Thomas et son père ne ___ (s'entendre) pas très bien.**
8   They get up at 7:00: **Elles ___ à 7h.**
10 I'm having fun: **Je/j ___.**
11 **Dans ce film, il ___ (s'agir) d'un couple amoureux qui a beaucoup de problèmes.**
15 **Tu dois ___ reposer.**

4
Special Constructions

Weather and time

Quel temps fait-il?	How's the weather?
Il fait beau.	It's nice out, it's nice weather.
Il fait mauvais.	It's terrible out, it's bad weather.
Il fait chaud, froid, frais.	It's hot, cold, cool.
Il pleut.	It's raining.
Il pleut à verse.	It's pouring.
Il neige.	It's snowing.
Il fait du soleil.	It's sunny.
Il fait du vent.	It's windy.
Il fait du brouillard.	It's foggy.
Il gèle.	It's freezing.
Il fait un temps de chien!	It's really awful!

Quelle heure est-il ?	What time is it?
Il est 4 heures.	It's 4 o'clock.
Il est 20 heures.	It's 8 pm.

Remember that the French language expresses the time in two ways: through a 12-hour clock and a 24-hour clock. In the examples below, the 24-hour clock times, when they are different from the 12-hour clock times, are in *italics*. These are used in official contexts and in time schedules for airlines, trains, television listings, movies, theater, and concerts.

Il est minuit.
Il est zéro heure.

Il est minuit et quart.
Il est zéro heure quinze.

Il est minuit et demi.
Il est zéro heure trente.

Il est une heure moins le quart.
Il est zéro heure quarante-cinq.

Il est une heure.

Il est deux heures.

Il est trois heures.

Il est quatre heures.

Il est huit heures.

Il est huit heures dix.

Il est huit heures et demie.
Il est huit heures trente.

Il est neuf heures moins dix.
Il est huit heures cinquante.

Il est midi.
Il est douze heures.

Il est midi et quart.
Il est douze heures quinze.

Il est midi et demi.
Il est douze heures trente.

Il est une heure moins le quart.
Il est douze heures quarante-cinq.

Il est une heure.
Il est treize heures.

Il est deux heures.
Il est quatorze heures.

Il est trois heures.
Il est quinze heures.

Il est quatre heures.
Il est seize heures.

Il est neuf heures.
Il est vingt et une heures.

Il est neuf heures dix.
Il est vingt et une heures dix.

Il est neuf heures et demie.
Il est vingt et une heures trente.

Il est dix heures moins dix.
Il est vingt et une heures cinquante.

Using weather and time expressions

Perspective personnelle

Vrai ou faux? Indicate whether each sentence is true (**vrai**) or false (**faux**) for you. Remember to read each sentence aloud for practice.

_____ **Je suis heureux / heureuse quand il neige.**

_____ **Je n'aime pas quand il pleut à verse.**

_____ **Je me sens énergique quand il fait du soleil.**

_____ **Je n'ai pas beaucoup d'énergie quand il fait mauvais.**

_____ **Actuellement** (currently), **il fait beau.**

A. Quel temps fait-il? Based on the picture, give a description of the weather. Don't limit yourself to just one sentence, make your description as complete as possible!

1.

_____
_____
_____
_____
_____
_____

2.

_____
_____
_____
_____
_____
_____

3.

_____
_____
_____
_____
_____
_____

Perspective personnelle

Vrai ou faux? Indicate whether each sentence is true (**vrai**) or false (**faux**) for you. Remember to read each sentence aloud for practice.

_____ **Le matin, je me réveille à sept heures et quart.**
_____ **Dans ma famille, on dîne normalement vers six heures.**
_____ **Je commence à travailler (ou je commence mes cours) à dix heures.**
_____ **Je finis de travailler (ou je finis mes cours) à 17 heures.**
_____ **Normalement, je me couche à minuit.**

B. Quelle heure est-il? Imagine that you are traveling in a Francophone country. People keep asking you what time it is. Look at your watch and answer aloud. Then write your answer. Use the 12-hour version of the time.

Modèle: **Il est trois heures et quart.**

First, you are out during the day:

1. _____

2. _____

3. _____

4. _____

Now you are out at night:

5. _____

6. _____

7. _____

8. _____

Other expressions with **il:**

il faut + infinitive	it is necessary to; one must
il s'agit de + infinitive	it is a question of; it's about
il vaut mieux + infinitive	it's better to
il y a	there is; there are

Il faut étudier avant l'examen.	One must study before the exam.
Dans ce film, *il s'agit de* petits extraterrestres.	This movie is about little creatures from outer space.
Il vaut mieux arriver à l'aéroport en avance.	It's better to arrive at the airport early.
Il y a un bon restaurant près d'ici?	Is there a good restaurant nearby?
Il y a beaucoup de cafés à Paris.	There are a lot of cafés in Paris.

Remember that these impersonal verbs are always conjugated in the third person singular with **il.** They do not have any other forms.

Using impersonal expressions

Perspective personnelle

Vrai ou faux? Indicate whether each sentence is true (**vrai**) or false (**faux**) for you. Remember to read each sentence aloud for practice.

_____ **Chez moi, il y a un chat.**
_____ **Pour réussir à l'école, il faut poser des questions au professeur.**
_____ **Dans mon livre préféré, il s'agit d'une histoire d'amour.**
_____ **A mon avis, il vaut mieux faire la cuisine que manger au restaurant.**

C. Idées incomplètes. Complete each sentence using one of the following expressions:

il faut	**il vaut mieux**
il y a	**il s'agit de (d')**

1. **Dans mon livre préféré, _____ une femme malheureuse qui s'appelle Emma.**

2. **Pour réussir dans la vie, _____ être sympathique et débrouillard(e).**

3. **Dans une salle de classe, _____ des pupitres, un tableau noir, un professeur, et des étudiants.**

4. **Pour réussir à l'école, _____ étudier et faire ses devoirs.**

5. **Dans mon émission préférée à la télé, _____ un hôpital où les médecins essaient de guérir les malades.**

6. **Chez moi, _____ une télevision, un ordinateur, des meubles, deux chiens, et cinq personnes.**

Savoir and connaître

The French language includes two verbs that express "to know." Here they are in the present tense:

savoir		connaître	
je sais	nous savons	je connais	nous connaissons
tu sais	vous savez	tu connais	vous connaissez
il/elle/on sait	ils/elles savent	il/elle/on connaît	ils/elles connaissent

Savoir means *to know a fact*—something that you have learned or that someone has told you.

Je sais que tu parles français.	I know that you speak French.
Tu sais mon numéro de téléphone?	Do you know my telephone number?
Nous ne savons pas quel temps il fait.	We don't know how the weather is.
Elles savent toujours la réponse.	They always know the answer.

Savoir followed by an *infinitive* means *to know how to do something*.

Lance sait vraiment faire du vélo.	Lance really knows how to ride a bike.
Savez-vous nager?	Do you know how to swim?

Connaître means *to know* in the sense of *being familiar* with someone, something, or a place you've been to.

Je connais un excellent café près d'ici.	I know an excellent café nearby.
Tu connais mon frère Julien?	Do you know my brother Julien?
Nous ne connaissons pas ce quartier.	We're not familiar with this neighborhood.
Mes parents connaissent très bien Paris.	My parents know Paris very well.

Using *savoir* and *connaître*

Perspective personnelle

Vrai ou faux? Indicate whether each sentence is true (**vrai**) or false (**faux**) for you. Remember to read each sentence aloud for practice.

_____ Mes parents connaissent Paris.

_____ Je sais qu'Elvis est toujours en vie (alive).

_____ Je connais un homme qui s'appelle John.

_____ Mon copain / ma copine sait faire la cuisine.

_____ Moi et mes collègues, nous connaissons un restaurant bon marché.

D. Quel verbe? Which verb would you use? For each item, indicate if you would use **savoir** or **connaître** to express "knowing."

1. a girl in your French class
2. the name of a girl in your French class
3. a good French restaurant in your city
4. the address of the best French restaurant in your city
5. Charles Baudelaire's year of birth
6. the work of Charles Baudelaire
7. how to ski
8. a good ski resort
9. Dakar, Sénégal
10. that Dakar is the capital of Sénégal

E. Savoir ou connaître? This time, choose the correct verb (**savoir** or **connaître**), and supply the correct form.

1. Paulette _____ que Jean sort avec Jocelyne.
2. Vous _____ mon frère, n'est-ce pas?
3. Yves et Étienne _____ le numéro de téléphone de Mme Grimaud.
4. Je _____ que mes parents m'aiment.
5. Nous _____ les romans de Balzac.
6. Tu ne _____ pas l'exportation la plus importante de Haïti?
7. Je _____ un bon magasin de chaussures à Grenoble.
8. Vous _____ faire la cuisine?
9. Richard ne _____ pas très bien le Québec.
10. Tu ne _____ pas Thomas?
11. Nous _____ faire du patinage.
12. Sophie et Chloë _____ bien les plages de la Côte d'Azur.

Special constructions with the present tense: present, past, and future actions

In the present

To emphasize that something is going on in the present or that someone is busy doing something (at this moment), use **être en train de** + infinitive.

Je suis en train de faire mes devoirs.	I'm (busy) doing my homework.
Ils sont en train de réparer la voiture.	They're (in the middle of) fixing the car.

This construction is used only to emphasize that the action is going on right this minute, as we speak. To say something such as: "I'm studying French" (not just right now, but in general), you would say: **J'étudie le français**.

In the past

To say that you have just done something, you can use the expression **venir de**, in the present tense, with an infinitive. (For verbs in the past tenses, see Part II, Chapters 6–10.)

Je viens d'arriver.	I've just arrived.
Désolé, elle vient de partir.	Sorry, she has just left.
Nous venons de terminer nos devoirs.	We've just finished our homework.

Even though this expression refers to the past (what has just happened), be sure to use the *present tense* of **venir!**

In the future

To say that you are going to do something, you can use the present tense of **aller** with an infinitive. This construction refers to something you're going to do in the near or foreseeable future. (For verbs in the future tense, see Chapter 11.)

Je vais aller en Europe cet été.	I'm going to go to Europe this summer.
Qu'est-ce que tu vas faire ce week-end?	What are you going to do this weekend?
Ce soir, nous allons manger au restaurant.	Tonight, we're going to eat out.

Using present, past, and future constructions

Perspective personnelle

Vrai ou faux? Indicate whether each sentence is true (**vrai**) or false (**faux**) for you. Remember to read each sentence aloud for practice.

_____   **Demain, je vais sortir avec mes amis.**

_____   **Je suis en train d'étudier les verbes français.**

_____   **Mon ami vient d'acheter une nouvelle voiture.**

_____   **Pour nous amuser, mes amis et moi, nous allons faire une randonnée.**

_____   **Mon père est malheureux. Il est en train de payer les factures.**

F. Que fait-on? Using the picture as a guide, describe what the following people are doing right this minute. After writing your responses, read them aloud, pretending to explain to someone what is happening in the house.

Modèle: Marc *est en train d'écrire*.

1. **Julien et Quentin** _____.

2. **Joëlle** _____.

3. **Véronique** _____.

4. **Gabrielle et Gérard** _____.

5. **Hugo** _____.

6. **Paul** _____.

7. **Estelle** _____.

8. **Bernard et Béatrice** _____.

G. Qu'est-ce qu'on vient de faire? Based on the statements below, what have these people just finished doing? Choose the logical verb; then write the appropriate sentence, using the **venir de** construction.

Modèle: Quentin est fatigué. (courir, se détendre, manger)
            Quentin vient de courir.

1. **Je n'ai pas d'argent. (gagner à la loterie, acheter une voiture très chère, travailler)**

2. **Tu n'as pas faim. (prendre un grand dîner, voir un film français, lire le journal)**

_____

3. **Elise et Odile sont surprises. (nager, se lever, voir leur mère avec un homme inconnu)**

_____

4. **Nous sommes rouspéteurs. (se réveiller, recevoir une bonne note, voir un ami)**

_____

5. **Vous êtes heureux. (s'endormir au travail, se disputer avec le patron, recevoir un compliment)**

_____

6. **Les enfants sont très propres. (revenir de la plage, se baigner, jouer dans le jardin)**

_____

7. **Nous avons mal à la tête** (a headache). **(voir un concert de rock, se brosser les dents, jouer au football)**

_____

8. **Victor n'a pas soif. (manger, boire de l'eau, trouver une pièce d'un euro)**

_____

9. **Vous êtes triste. (être licencié(e), rencontrer des amis, acheter de nouveaux vêtements)**

_____

10. **Le chien est très sale. (se baigner, se mettre sur le canapé, jouer dans de la boue)**

_____

H. Qu'est-ce qu'on va faire? Based on the drawings, tell what the following people are probably _going to do_. Use **aller** + _infinitive._

Modèle: Lise _va jouer au tennis._

1. **Romain et Vincent** _____.

2.   **Nous** _____ .

3.   **Vous** _____ .

4.   **Je** _____ .

5.   **Tu** _____ .

6.   **Denise** _____ .

7.   Je _____.

8.   Vous _____.

Reviewing special constructions

I. **Des questions!** Imagine you are staying with a French-speaking family in Belgium. The six-year-old son has many questions for you. Answer his questions aloud; then write your answers.

1.   **Qu'est-ce que (what) tu es en train de faire?**

    _____

2.   **A quelle heure est-ce que tu te lèves normalement?**

    _____

3.   **A quelle heure est-ce que tu te couches normalement?**

    _____

4.   **A quelle heure est-ce que tu vas sortir ce soir?**

    _____

5.   **A quelle heure est-ce que tu vas rentrer?**

    _____

6.   **Qu'est-ce qu'il y a (what is there) dans ton sac?**

    _____

7.   **Quelle saison préfères-tu—l'hiver, le printemps, l'été, ou l'automne?**

    _____

8.   **Qu'est-ce que tu vas faire demain?**

    _____

J. La météo. Based on the map, write to tell the weather each city *will have* tomorrow.

Modèle: *À Brest, il va faire du soleil.*

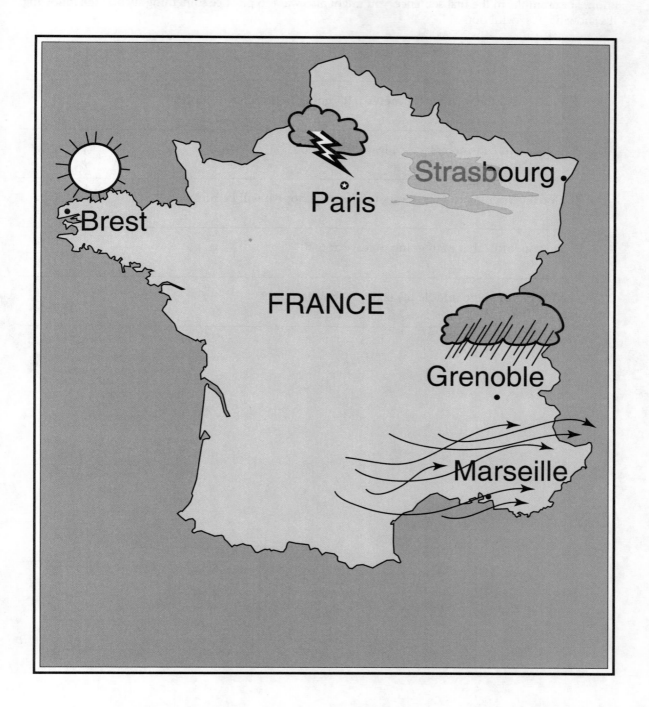

1. À Paris, _____.

2. À Marseille, _____.

3. À Grenoble, _____.

4. À Strasbourg, _____.

K. **Comment dit-on?** How would you translate the following sentences into French? Practice saying the sentences aloud and writing them. Also, practice variations of these sentences that reflect your personal situation. For example, in the first sentence, you might also want to practice something such as the following: It's snowing. It's awful out.

1. It's better to stay inside. It's raining.

_____

2. I just heard the weather **(la météo)**. It's going to be windy tomorrow.

_____

3. We have to (it is necessary to) leave at **(à)** 4:00.

_____

4. Chrisine is going to take a walk tomorrow. I hope it will be nice out.

_____

5. Do you know that I am going to leave at 6:30?

_____

6. Victoria is (in the middle of) taking a shower.

_____

Les mots croisés 4

Complete clues by translating into French or completing with appropriate words.

Horizontal

2   It's freezing.

5   **Mes collègues ___ (connaître/savoir) utiliser le nouveau logiciel.**

7   **Vous ___ manger bientôt?**

9   It's raining.

13 I just got here: **Je ___'arriver.**

14 It's 6:45. **Il est sept heures ___.**

15 It's 12:30 p.m. **Il est ___.**

16 We're going out tonight. **On va ___ ce soir.**

17 It's foggy. **Il fait du ___.**

Vertical

1   There is a cat on the bed. **___ un chat sur le lit.**

3   **Tu ___ (connaître/savoir) Philippe?**

4   It is necessary to study. **___ étudier.**

6   It's 1:10. **Il est ___.**

8   It's midnight: **Il est ___.**

10 **Nous ___ en train de discuter.**

11 It's 3:00. **___ heures.**

12 It's sunny. **Il fait ___.**

5
Asking Questions

In French, as in English, there are two kinds of questions. Some questions can be answered with *yes, no, I don't know*, or *I'm not sure*. These are referred to as yes-or-no questions. Other questions ask for additional unknown information: Who? What? Where? When? Why? How? How much? How many? Which one? This chapter explains how to ask each of these two question types in French.

Yes-or-no questions

You can ask a yes-or-no question in French in four ways. As in English, yes-or-no questions end with rising intonation. This means that you raise the pitch of your voice at the end of the question.

Rising intonation

The simplest way to ask a yes-or-no question is just to raise the intonation of your voice at the end of a statement. This is the way questions are asked in casual and informal conversation.

Vous parlez français?	Do you speak French? (You speak French?)
On est déjà arrivé?	Are we there yet?
Tu veux prendre un verre?	Would you like to go out for a drink?

Est-ce que

A statement can be turned into a question by adding **est-ce que** at the beginning of the sentence. This way of asking questions is used in informal conversation and writing.

Est-ce que vous parlez français?	Do you speak French?
Est-ce qu'on est déjà arrivé?	Are we there yet?
Est-ce que tu veux prendre un verre?	Would you like to go out for a drink?

Remember that **est-ce que** becomes **est-ce qu'** before a vowel sound, as you see in the second example above.

N'est-ce pas?

To ask someone to agree that what you say is true or correct, add the expression **n'est-ce pas** to the end of your question.

Tu parles français, n'est-ce pas?	You speak French, don't you?
Il fait très beau, n'est-ce pas?	Lovely weather, isn't it?
Mireille chante bien, n'est-ce pas?	Mireille sings well, doesn't she?

Although English uses different expressions for these questions ("don't you? isn't it? doesn't she?"), French uses the same expression: **n'est-ce pas?**

Inversion of the subject and the verb

In French questions, the subject pronoun may come after the verb, rather than before. Questions with subject-verb inversion are more formal than those with rising intonation or with **est-ce que**, although the meaning is still the same.

Parlez-vous français?	Do you speak French?
Est-on déjà arrivé?	Are we there yet?
Veux-tu prendre un verre?	Would you like to go out for a drink?

The inverted subject is connected to the verb with a hyphen. The pronoun **je** is almost never inverted. Instead, simple rising intonation or **est-ce que** is used with **je**.

Usually, only a *pronoun subject* (**tu, il, elle, on, nous, vous, il,** or **elle**) is placed after the verb. If there is a *noun subject*, it stays at the beginning of the question, and the pronoun that corresponds to the subject (always the third person: **il, elle, ils, elles**) is added after the verb. This is different from English, where, as you see in the translations below, the question begins with a verb. The noun subject and the corresponding inverted subject pronoun are italicized in these French questions:

Michelle est-*elle* française?	Is Michelle French?
Vos parents habitent-*ils* ici?	Do your parents live here?
Ce magasin vend-*il* beaucoup de CD?	Does this store sell a lot of CDs?

In the third person singular, if the verb does not end in *t* or *d*, you add -*t*- before the inverted subject pronoun (**il/elle/on**).

Jean-Marc a-t-*il* tous ses livres?	Does Jean-Marc have all his books?
Votre soeur habite-t-*elle* chez vous?	Does your sister live at your house?

This spelling change shows that, when these subject pronouns are inverted, a pronounced *t* *always* precedes them, even **vend-il**, which is pronounced (but not written!) like **"vent-il."**

"Information" questions: Who? What? Where? When? Why? How? How much? How many? Which one?

Some questions do not expect a "yes" or "no" answer, but require more information. In French, as in English, when spoken these questions do not have rising intonation. So, you can't use rising intonation to ask these kinds of questions. Information questions you may know already are as follows:

Comment allez-vous?	How are you?
Comment ça va?	How are you doing?
Comment vous appelez-vous?	What's your name?
Quelle heure est-il?	What time is it?
Quel temps fait-il?	How's the weather?

Information questions may be asked in two ways. The important thing to remember about information questions is that *they always begin with the question word or expression.*

Here are some examples of words or expressions that can begin a question:

Qui?	Who?	**Quel? Quelle?**	Which?
Que? Quoi?	What?	**Quels? Quelles?**	
Où?	Where?	**Avec qui?**	With whom?
Quand?	When?	**A qui?**	To whom?
Pourquoi?	Why?	**De quoi?**	About what?
Comment?	How?	**Combien?**	How much? How many?

Est-ce que?

Like yes-or-no questions, information questions may be formed with the expression **est-ce que**, which *follows the question word or phrase*, italicized in the examples below:

Où est-ce que tu habites?	Where do you live?
Pourquoi est-ce que tu étudies le français?	Why are you studying French?
Quand est-ce que l'avion arrive?	When does the plane arrive?
Comment est-ce qu'on écrit un bon essai?	How does one write a good essay?
Quel genre de musique est-ce que tu préfères?	What kind of music do you like?
Combien de CD est-ce que tu vas acheter?	How many CDs are you going to buy?

In simple questions that begin with **où, quand, combien**, or **comment**, a noun subject may exceptionally be inverted. This is even *required* in questions with **où + être: Où est mon ordinateur? Où sont mes clés?** Remember that noun subjects are not inverted in other questions.

Où habitent tes parents?	Where do your parents live?
Où se trouve le musée Rodin?	Where is the Musée Rodin located?
Combien coûte un billet pour Nice?	How much is a ticket to Nice?
Quand part le train pour Nice?	When does the train for Nice leave?
Comment va ton père?	How's your father doing?

Quel is an interrogative adjective that agrees with the noun it modifies: **Quel genre? Quelle chanson? Quels disques? Quelles femmes?**

Use the phrase **combien coûte** to ask how much something costs, but note that when **combien** asks how much or how many *of* something, it is followed by **de: Combien de CD? Combien de livres? Combien d'argent?**

In very casual spoken French (*only* spoken!), **est-ce que** is sometimes omitted, and in spite of our rule that the question word or phrase always starts the question, you may find the word or phrase at the end instead. You may hear questions like these:

> *Où* tu habites? Tu habites *où*?
>
> *Pourquoi* tu étudies le français? Tu étudies le français *pourquoi*?
>
> *Quand* l'avion arrive? L'avion arrive *quand*?
>
> *Comment* on écrit un bon essai? On écrit un bon essai *comment*?
>
> *Quel genre de musique* tu préfères? Tu préfères *quel genre de musique*?
>
> *Combien de CD* tu vas acheter? Tu vas acheter *combien de CD*?

Subject-verb inversion

Like yes-or-no questions, information questions may also be formed with subject-verb inversion. This style is more formal than that of questions with **est-ce que**. The inverted subject pronoun and verb follow the question word or phrase as italicized in the examples below:

Où habites-tu?	Where do you live?
Pourquoi étudies-tu le français?	Why are you studying French?
Quand l'avion arrive-t-il?	When does the plane arrive?
Comment écrit-on un bon essai?	How does one write a good essay?
Quel genre de musique préfères-tu?	What kind of music do you like?

Questions about persons: *qui?*

To ask a question about a person (who? or whom?), always use the interrogative pronoun **qui**. **Qui** refers to a person or persons whether the word serves as the *subject*, the *direct object*, or the *object of a preposition*. As usual, the question word, **qui**, begins the question. If there is a preposition, the whole question phrase (**à qui, avec qui, de qui, pour qui**) begins the sentence.

When **qui** is the subject, there is no subject-verb inversion (because the subject is the question word and has to come first!), but a longer form, **qui est-ce qui**, may be used with no difference in meaning.

Qui parle français? *Qui est-ce qui* parle français?	Who speaks French?
Qui veut aller à la plage aujourd'hui? *Qui est-ce qui* veut aller à la plage aujourd'hui?	Who wants to go to the beach today?
but:	
Qui est ce monsieur-là? (**Qui est-ce qui** is not used with the verb **être**.)	Who is that man over there?

When **qui** is the direct object, it comes first, and the question may be formed with subject-verb inversion or with **est-ce que**.

Qui veux-tu inviter ce soir? *Qui est-ce que* tu veux inviter ce soir?	Who(m) do you want to invite tonight?
Qui allons-nous rencontrer au bistro? *Qui est-ce que* nous allons rencontrer au bistro?	Who are we going to meet at the bistro?

When **qui** is the object of a preposition, the entire phrase comes first, and the question may be formed with subject-verb inversion or with **est-ce que**. Note that in English, but not in French, the preposition may come at the end of the question.

A qui écris-tu souvent des courriels? *A qui* est-ce que tu écris souvent des courriels?	Who(m) do you often send e-mails to?
De qui Marie parle-t-elle? *De qui* est-ce que Marie parle?	Who is Marie talking about?

Questions about things: *que? quoi?*

To ask a question about a thing (what?), use the interrogative pronoun **que**, or use **quoi** after a preposition. The question word or phrase begins the question, and the question may be formed with subject-verb inversion or with **est-ce que**. **Que** becomes **qu'** before a word beginning with a vowel sound.

Que vas-tu faire ce week-end? *Qu'est-ce que* tu vas faire ce weekend?	What are you going to do this weekend?
Que pensez-vous de notre classe de français? *Qu'est-ce que* vous pensez de notre classe de français?	What do you think about our French class?
À quoi penses-tu? *À quoi* est-ce que tu penses?	What are you thinking about?
De quoi cette journaliste parle-t-elle? *De quoi* est-ce que cette journaliste parle?	What is that reporter speaking about?

A *special case: que as the subject of a question*

When **que** is the subject of a question, the special form **qu'est-ce qui** is used. There is no subject-verb inversion.

Qu'est-ce qui est important dans la vie?	What is important in life?
Qu'est-ce qui se passe?	What's going on?

When *what is* asks for a *definition,* the form **Qu'est-ce que** or **Qu'est-ce que c'est que** is used. As usual, **que** (but never **qui**!) becomes **qu'** when it is followed by a word that begins with a vowel sound.

*Qu'est-ce qu'*un objet direct?	What is a direct object?
Qu'est-ce que c'est que le bonheur?	What is happiness?
Qu'est-ce que c'est?	What is it?

Asking questions

Perspective personnelle

Jeopardy! Imagine that each response is your answer to a question. Read each question aloud. Then choose the question that (for you) would elicit the response.

1. **Votre réponse: parce que ça me rend** (it makes me) **heureux/se**
   a. **Pourquoi est-ce que vous faites du sport?**
   b. **Pourquoi est-ce que vous allez au cinéma?**
   c. **Pourquoi est-ce que vous lisez?**

2. **Votre réponse: l'après-midi** (in the afternoon)
   a. **Quand faites-vous vos devoirs?**
   b. **Quand faites-vous de l'exercice?**
   c. **Quand allez-vous au travail?**

3. **Votre réponse: mon meilleur ami/ma meilleure amie**
   a. **Qui aime sortir avec vous?**
   b. **Qui vous téléphone souvent?**
   c. **Qui vous prête de l'argent?**

4. **Votre réponse: chez moi**
   a. **Où est-ce que vous dormez?**
   b. **Où est-ce que vous mangez d'habitude?**
   c. **Où est-ce que vous regardez la télé?**

5. **Votre réponse: très bien**
   a. **Comment allez-vous?**
   b. **Comment est-ce que vous chantez?**
   c. **Comment est-ce que vous dansez?**

6. **Votre réponse: deux**
   a. **Combien de frères avez-vous?**
   b. **Combien d'heures est-ce que vous étudiez le français par jour?**
   c. **Combien de films voyez-vous chaque semaine?**

A. **Quelle question?** Based on the answer, complete each question with the appropriate question word. Choose from the following: **qui**, **que**, **qu'**, **quand**, **où**, **comment**, **pourquoi**, **quel(le)(s)**, **combien**.

Question	Réponse
1. _____ sont tes parents?	dans la cuisine
2. _____ est-ce que Claude et Gisèle étudient autant?	parce qu'elles veulent réussir à leurs examens
3. _____ allez-vous au travail?	le matin
4. _____ Jean passe-t-il ses vacances?	à Tahiti
5. _____ coûte cette robe?	200 euros
6. _____ dort en classe?	les cancres
7. _____ est-ce que Martine fait?	Elle réfléchit ou elle dort.
8. _____ film est-ce que tu veux voir?	Godzilla

B. **Plus formel, s'il vous plaît!** How would you ask the questions below by using the (more formal) style of inversion?

Modèle: Pourquoi est-ce que Patrick porte cette cravate?
          Pourquoi Patrick porte-t-il cette cravate?

1. **Comment est-ce que vous trouvez la poésie de Nerval?**

   _____

2. **Qu'est-ce que tu fais?**

   _____

3. **Pourquoi est-ce que Rémy et Sylvie habitent à la campagne?**

   _____

4. **Avec qui est-ce que tu vas au cinéma ce soir?**

   _____

5. **Quand est-ce qu'elle part?**

   _____

6. **Qui est-ce que vous regardez?**

   _____

7. **Qu'est-ce que vous regardez?**

   _____

8. **Combien de pièces est-ce que tu vois chaque mois?**

   _____

9. **Est-ce que tu aimes cette jupe?**

   _____

C. Détendez-vous! How would you ask the following questions using the (less formal) **est-ce que** form?

Modèle: **Pourquoi Juliette aime-t-elle ce voyou?**
    Pourquoi est-ce que Juliette aime ce voyou?

1. **Que disent ses parents à propos de** (about) **leur mariage?**
   _____

2. **Que va-t-il porter à la cérémonie?**
   _____

3. **Qui vient aux noces** (wedding) **de son côté** (his side)**?**
   _____

4. **A quel hôtel descendent les invités?**
   _____

5. **Quel genre de musique jouent-ils à la réception?**
   _____

6. **Les invités apportent-ils des cadeaux?**
   _____

D. Mauvaise connection! Imagine you are talking to a Francophone friend on a cell phone. The connection is not always strong, so you keep missing important pieces of information. Below, you see her statements (xxx will indicate words you couldn't make out). Ask questions to get the information you missed.

Modèle: **Ce matin, je vais xxx.**
    Où vas-tu ce matin? or Où est-ce que tu vas ce matin?

1. **Je veux acheter xxx.**
   _____

2. **Je le voudrais** (I want it) **parce que xxx!**
   _____

3. **Le problème, c'est que ça coûte xxx.**
   _____

4. **Après, je vais xxx.**
   _____

5. **J'ai rendez-vous avec xxx.**
   _____

6. **Nous allons xxx. Nous adorons faire ça!**
   _____

7. **Et puis, nous allons déjeuner xxx.**
   _____

8. **Je vais manger xxx.**
   _____

Les mots croisés 5

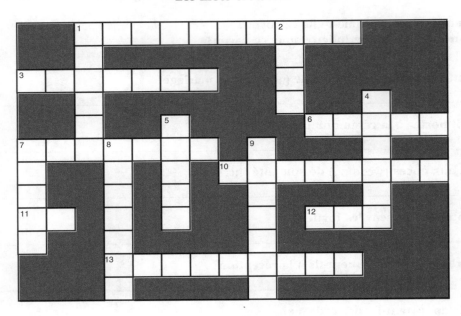

Complete the clues with interrogative words and expressions.

Horizontal

1	What are you doing?: ___ **vous faites?**
3	___ **équipes de football sont les meilleures? (celles de France et d'Italie)**
6	**À** ___ **amis est-ce que tu envoies des lettres? (a ceux qui n'ont pas de courriel)**
7	___ **est-ce que Quentin sort? (avec Lina)**
10	___ **est-ce que vous n'aimez pas votre travail? (parce que c'est ennuyeux)**
11	___ **sont tes parents? (à la maison)**
12	___ **aime le chocolat? (moi!)**
13	We like French, right?: **Nous aimons le français, ___?**

Vertical

1	___ **chemise (f.) préfères-tu? (la rouge)**
2	___ **pays (m.) a le plus d'habitants? (la Chine)**
4	___ **parlent ces femmes? (de leur travail)**
5	___ **est-ce que tu vas à la bibliothèque? (demain matin)**
7	___ **est-ce que David s'intéresse? (à l'anthropologie)**
8	___ **allez-vous? (très bien, merci!)**
9	___ **coûte cet ordinateur? (750 euros)**

Part Two
The Past Indicative Tenses

The Past: an Overview

What is a past tense?

A *past tense* indicates time gone by or some former action or state. There are three main indicative past tenses in French:

Le passé composé

Marie *a téléphoné* hier.	Mary phoned yesterday.
Nous *avons fini* nos devoirs.	We have finished our homework.

The **passé composé**, also called the *compound past*, expresses events and states that happened at a specific time in the past, as well as actions and states that have been completed at the time of speaking or writing.

L'imparfait

Quand j'*étais* au lycée, je *recevais* toujours de bonnes notes.	When I was in high school, I always got good grades.
Mes parents nous *emmenaient* à la plage tous les étés.	My parents used to take us to the beach every summer.

The **imparfait**, or *imperfect tense*, indicates actions and conditions in the past that were ongoing, continued, or customary, actions that occurred over an indefinite period of time. The **imparfait** corresponds (often, but not always) to constructions in English such as *we were eating, we would go*, and *we used to study*.

Le plus-que-parfait

Ils *avaient* déjà *téléphoné* quand tu es rentré.	They had already telephoned when you got back.
Jean m'a dit qu'il t'*avait rencontré* la semaine dernière.	Jean told me that he had met you last week.

The **plus-que-parfait**, or pluperfect, shows that an event had (already) happened before a given past event. It is equivalent to the English compound tense forms *I had spoken, you had written*, and so on.

There are also two literary past tenses in French:

Le passé simple

Napoléon Bonaparte *naquit* en Corse en 1769 et *mourut* à l'île de Sainte-Hélène en 1821.	Napoleon Bonaparte was born in Corsica in 1769 and died on the island of St. Helena in 1821.
François Mitterrand *fut* Président de la France de 1981 à 1995.	François Mitterrand was President of France from 1981 to 1995.

Le passé antérieur

Quand Meursault *eut lu* le télégramme, il demanda deux jours de congé à son patron.	When Meursault had read the telegram, he asked his boss for two days off.
Dès qu'il *fut arrivé* à l'asile, il rencontra le directeur.	As soon as he had arrived at the asylum, he met the director.

You will find these two tenses in very formal written style, as in literary and historical texts.

Compound Tenses

The **passé composé**, the **plus-que-parfait**, and the **passé antérieur** are compound tenses. *Compound tenses* have two parts, an *auxiliary verb* followed by the *past participle* of the verb.

Marie	*a*	*téléphoné*	hier.	Mary telephoned yesterday.
	auxiliary verb	past participle		

In French, the auxiliary verb in a compound tense is either **avoir** or **être**, as you will see in the next chapter.

6
Le Passé Composé

The **passé composé**, or compound past tense, expresses events that happened in the past. Verbs in the **passé composé** tell what happened or changed (or didn't), and a specific moment or duration of time is stated or implied in the context.

Hier, j'*ai télephoné* à mes parents.	I called my parents yesterday.
Pardon, qu'est-ce que tu *as dit*?	I'm sorry; what did you say?
Je n'*ai* jamais *visité* le Canada.	I've never been to Canada.

How to form the *passé composé*

The **passé composé** is a compound tense. The compound tenses have two parts: an *auxiliary verb*, **avoir** or **être**, and the *past participle* of the verb. In the **passé composé**, the auxiliary verb is conjugated in the **présent**. Most verbs are conjugated with **avoir**. To form the past participle of an **-er** verb, replace the infinitive ending **-er** with the past participle ending **-é**.

parler: The past participle is **parlé**.

J'ai parlé.	I spoke. I have spoken. I did speak.
Tu as parlé.	You spoke. You have spoken. You did speak.
Il/Elle/On a parlé.	He/She/One spoke, has spoken, did speak. We spoke. We have spoken. We did speak.*
Nous avons parlé.	We spoke. We have spoken. We did speak.
Vous avez parlé.	You spoke. You have spoken. You did speak.
Ils/Elles ont parlé.	They spoke. They have spoken. They did speak.

*Remember that **on** is used in *informal* French for **nous**: **On a parlé. = Nous avons parlé.**

Here are some common **-er** verbs in the **passé composé**. Note that their past participles end in **-é**.

chanter	**j'ai chanté, tu as chanté, il/elle/on a chanté, etc.**
étudier	**j'ai étudié, tu as étudié, il/elle/on a étudié, etc.**
regarder	**j'ai regardé, tu as regardé, il/elle/on a regardé, etc.**
travailler	**j'ai travaillé, tu as travaillé, il/elle/on a travaillé, etc.**

The past participles of **-re** verbs frequently end in **u**, and those of **-ir** verbs frequently end in **i**. There are many exceptions, though, that must be memorized.

-re verbs: *-re* becomes *-u*

attendre	**j'ai attendu**
entendre	**j'ai entendu**
perdre	**j'ai perdu**
rendre	**j'ai rendu**
vendre	**j'ai vendu**

Exceptions (The past participle has a different stem):

boire	**j'ai bu**
connaître	**j'ai connu**
lire	**j'ai lu**
vivre	**j'ai vécu**

-ir verbs: *-ir* becomes *-i*

choisir	**j'ai choisi**
dormir	**j'ai dormi**
finir	**j'ai fini**
réussir	**j'ai réussi**

Some exceptions:

couvrir	**j'ai couvert**
offrir	**j'ai offert**
ouvrir	**j'ai ouvert**
courir	**j'ai couru**
tenir	**j'ai tenu**

Verbs with irregular past participles

avoir	**j'ai eu**
devoir	**j'ai dû**
dire	**j'ai dit**
écrire	**j'ai écrit**
être	**j'ai été**
faire	**j'ai fait**
mettre	**j'ai mis**
pouvoir	**j'ai pu**
prendre (apprendre, comprendre, surprendre)	**j'ai pris (j'ai appris, j'ai compris, j'ai surpris)**
recevoir	**j'ai reçu**
savoir	**j'ai su**
suivre	**j'ai suivi**

Even the most irregular verbs that you know, like **avoir** and **être**, are conjugated regularly when they are used in the **passé composé**. The past participle may be irregular, but the conjugation is not.

avoir: past participle *eu*		*être*: past participle *été*	
j'ai eu	nous avons eu	j'ai été	nous avons été
tu as eu	vous avez eu	tu as été	vous avez été
il/elle/on a eu	ils/elles ont eu	il/elle/on a été	ils/elles ont été

Using *passé composé*: verbs conjugated with *avoir*

Perspective personnelle

Vrai ou faux? Indicate whether each sentence is true (**vrai**) or false (**faux**) for you. Remember to read each sentence aloud for practice.

_____ Le weekend passé, j'ai regardé la télévision.

_____ Hier soir, mes collègues ont fêté l'anniversaire de notre patron.

_____ Ma grand-mère a reçu le prix Nobel en 1990.

_____ La semaine dernière, j'ai entendu une nouvelle chanson à la radio.

_____ Pour fêter mon anniversaire l'année dernière, mes amis et moi avons bu du champagne.

A. What is the correct form? Conjugate the verb in parentheses in the **passé composé**. Then read the completed sentence aloud.

Modèle: Le week-end dernier, j'ai vu (voir) un nouveau film français.

1. Ma mère _____ (apprécier) son cadeau d'anniversaire.

2. Je/j' _____ (attendre) une heure pour le bus ce matin.

3. Tu _____ (réussir) à trouver une place dans le parking?

4. Ma collègue _____ (travailler) tard hier soir.

5. En évitant (by avoiding) les desserts, mon frère _____ (perdre) dix kilos.

6. Jean-Paul et Sébastien _____ (jouer) tout l'après-midi.

7. Vous _____ (rendre) les livres à la bibliothèque?

8. Je/j' _____ (offrir) des bonbons à mon patron pour Noël.

9. Mon fiancé _____ (vivre) en Égypte pendant dix ans avant de venir au Canada.

10. Nous _____ (inviter) les Martin à dîner avec nous ce soir.

B. Now, write sentences of your own! For each box, create one or two sentences to tell what people did yesterday. Choose one expression from each column, and conjugate correctly. Remember: You can turn any sentence into an informal yes/no question just by placing a question mark at the end. Read your sentences aloud for practice.

une de mes collègues	lire	une longue lettre
tu	écrire	une histoire amusante
nous		des courriels

1. _____

_____

ma mère mon copain / ma copine vous	perdre acheter	de l'aspirine un imperméable de nouvelles bottes

2. _____

_____

vous mes amis je	faire	la cuisine la lessive de l'autostop

3. _____

_____

Verbs conjugated with *être* in the *passé composé*

Some verbs are conjugated with the auxiliary verb **être** in the **passé composé**. These verbs are often verbs of motion or change, and they never have direct or indirect objects. With these verbs, the past participle agrees, like an adjective, in gender (masculine or feminine) and number (singular or plural) with the subject of the sentence. In the example below, you see that the past participle can take the masculine singular form (**allé**), feminine singular form (**allée**), masculine plural form (**allés**), or feminine plural form (**allées**) to agree with the subject.

aller: to go

je *suis* allé/allée	nous *sommes* allés/allées
tu *es* allé/allée	vous *êtes* allé/allée/allés/allées
il *est* allé	ils *sont* allés
elle *est* allée	elles *sont* allées
on *est* allé	

Notice that the past participle with **je**, **tu**, and **nous** will take one of the two forms shown, depending on whether **je**, **tu**, or **nous** is masculine or feminine. With **vous**, there are four choices, since **vous** may be one person (masculine or feminine) or more than one (also masculine or feminine). Look to the context of the sentence to determine the correct form. In this book, we will list possible endings when the past participles agree with their subjects in the compound tenses.

These are the verbs that are conjugated with **être** in the **passé composé**. Most of the past participles are regular, but five (**venu, revenu, devenu, né, mort**) are irregular.

aller (to go)	**je suis allé/allée**
venir (to come)	**je suis venu/venue**
arriver (to arrive)	**je suis arrivé/arrivée**
partir (to leave)	**je suis parti/partie**
monter (to go up, come up, get on [a bus/train/plane])	**je suis monté/montée (dans)**
descendre (to go down, come down, get off [a bus/train/plane])	**je suis descendu/descendue (de)**
entrer (to come in)	**je suis entré/entrée**

sortir (to go out)	**je suis sorti/sortie**
rentrer (to come back)	**je suis rentré/rentrée**
revenir (to come back)	**je suis revenu/revenue**
retourner (to go back)	**je suis retourné/retournée**
passer (to come by, go by)	**je suis passé/passée**
rester (to stay)	**je suis resté/restée**
devenir (to become)	**je suis devenu/devenue**
tomber (to fall)	**je suis tombé/tombée**
naître (to be born)	**je suis né/née**
mourir (to die)	**il est mort, elle est morte**

Six of these verbs may have a direct object. When this happens, they have a different meaning, and they are conjugated with **avoir**. (We recommend that you think of them as totally different verbs.) In the following examples, the *direct objects* are italicized.

monter (to bring up, take up, mount)	**J'ai monté *les photos* dans l'album.**
descendre (to bring down, take down)	**J'ai descendu *les valises*.**
sortir (to take out)	**J'ai sorti *deux billets* de mon portefeuille.**
rentrer (to put back)	**J'ai rentré *mon portefeuille* dans mon sac.**
retourner (to turn over, turn around)	**J'ai retourné *la pièce* pour voir la date.**
passer (to spend [time])	**J'ai passé *deux mois* en France.**

Using *passé composé*: verbs conjugated with *être*

Perspective personnelle

Vrai ou faux? Indicate whether each sentence is true (**vrai**) or false (**faux**) for you. Remember to read each sentence aloud for practice.

_____ **Après le travail hier, je suis sorti(e) avec des collègues prendre un pot** (to have a drink).

_____ **Quand j'ai demandé une augmentation, mon patron est mort de rire.**

_____ **Le weekend passé, mes amis et moi, nous sommes allés au musée.**

_____ **Avant d'aller en classe aujourd'hui, je suis passé par le supermarché.**

_____ **Je suis né(e) aux États-Unis.**

C. **What is the correct form?** Conjugate the verb in parentheses in the **passé composé**. Since these verbs are all conjugated with **être**, don't forget to make the past participle agree with the subject. When you finish, read the completed sentences aloud.

1. **Patricia et Isabel _____ (naître) au Brésil.**

2. **Nous _____ (rester) cinq semaines en Israël.**

3. **Vous _____ (partir) trop tôt hier soir.**

4. **Est-ce que tes parents _____ (venir) chez toi pour la Saint Sylvestre** (New Year's Eve)**?**

5. **Marcel Proust _____ (naître) en 1871 et _____ (mourir) en 1922.**

6. **Ma sœur _____ (devenir) médecin après de longues années d'études.**

7. **Tu _____ (ne pas monter) dans un avion?**

8. Je _____ (partir) à 7h30, et je _____ (revenir) à 9h00.

9. Audrey _____ (sortir) avec Marc vendredi soir, n'est-ce pas?

10. A quelle heure est-ce que votre bus _____ (arriver) ce matin?

D. **Être** or **avoir?** Choose the appropriate conjugation for each sentence. Be careful! These verbs can all be conjugated with **être** *or* **avoir**! Consider the context of the sentence to determine which is correct. When you finish, read the completed sentences aloud.

1. **Est-ce que tu (es / as) sorti la poubelle?**

2. **Bernard (est / a) retourné chez lui.**

3. **(Je suis / J'ai) passé mes vacances à Tahiti.**

4. **Tu (es / as) monté dans la Tour Eiffel?**

5. **Philippe (est / a) descendu à la cuisine à 7h ce matin.**

6. **Martin (est / a) sorti avec Michelle samedi.**

7. **Tu (es / as) rentré la voiture dans le garage?**

8. **(Je suis / J'ai) monté la valise dans le grenier.**

9. **Pierre (est / a) passé par la bibliothèque après son cours.**

10. **(Je suis / J'ai) retourné le livre pour lire le titre.**

11. **Tu (es / as) descendu l'escalier très vite!**

12. **(Je suis / J'ai) rentré tard.**

E. **Now, write sentences of your own!** For each box, create one or two sentences about what people did yesterday by choosing one expression from each column and conjugating the verb accordingly. Remember: You can turn any sentence into an informal yes/no question just by placing a question mark at the end. Read your sentences aloud for practice.

mon patron mes collègues tu	aller à* entrer dans revenir de*	le musée le magasin de jouets l'hôpital

*Note that à + le = au, à + les = aux, de + le = du, and de + les = des.

1. _____

   _____

je nous mes parents	arriver partir venir	à 8h avec une amie à l'heure (on time)

2. _____

   _____

mon grand-père **vous** **une de mes cousines**	**naître** **mourir**	**en Suisse** **en 1945** **récemment**

3. _____

_____

Agreement of the past participle with a preceding direct object

When a verb in the **passé composé** (or in any other compound tense) has a direct object that precedes the verb, the past participle agrees in gender and number, like an adjective, with the direct object. This happens with every verb in a compound tense that has a preceding direct object. If the direct object *follows* the verb, though, there is no gender/number agreement. So:

J'ai monté *les photos*.	no agreement: The phrase *les photos* follows the verb.
Où sont les photos *que* tu as montées?	agreement: The word **montées** is feminine plural to agree with the direct object, (**les photos**) *que*, which comes before the verb.
J'ai descendu *les valises*.	no agreement: The phrase *les valises* follows the verb.
***Quelles valises* est-ce que tu as descendues?**	agreement: The word **descendues** is feminine plural to agree with the direct object, **quelles valises**, which precedes the verb.
Tes valises? Je ne *les* ai pas vues.	agreement: The word **vues** is feminine plural to agree with the direct object, *les* (=**les valises**), which precedes the verb.
J'ai perdu *mon portefeuille*.	no agreement: The phrase *mon portefeuille* follows the verb.
C'est le portefeuille *que* tu m'as offert.	agreement: The word **offert** is masculine singular to agree with the direct object, *que* (=**mon portefeuille**), which precedes the verb.

In addition to the **passé composé**, the other compound tenses we will study in this book are **le plus-que-parfait** (Chapter 9), **le passé antérieur** (Chapter 10), **le futur antérieur** (Chapter 12), **le conditionnel passé** (Chapter 14), **le passé du subjonctif** (Chapter 17), and **le plus-que-parfait du subjonctif** (Chapter 18). The past participle agrees in gender and number with a preceding direct object of verbs in all these compound tenses.

Using past participles: agreement with a preceding direct object

F. Agreement of past participle. In each of the sentences below, fill in the blank with *e*, *s*, *es*, or *X* (if nothing is needed).

1. —Qu'est-ce que tu as offert___ à ta mère pour son anniversaire?
   —J'ai offert___ de jolies fleurs (fém.) à ma mère.
   —Est-ce qu'elle les a aimé___?
   —Oui. Elle a adoré___ les fleurs.

2. —Lise a reçu___ une lettre hier.
   —La lettre que Lise a reçu___ est venu___ de son cousin.

3. —Quels films est-ce que vous avez vu___ l'été dernier?
   —J'ai vu___ beaucoup de films français. Je les ai beaucoup apprécié___!

Pronominal verbs: always conjugated with *être*

All pronominal verbs (see Chapter 3) are conjugated with **être** in the **passé composé** (and in the other compound tenses). The reflexive pronoun is usually a direct object, and the past participle agrees with it in gender and number.

se réveiller: to wake up

je me suis réveillé(e)	nous nous sommes réveillé(e)s
tu t'es réveillé/réveillé(e)	vous vous êtes réveillé(e)(s)
il s'est réveillé	ils se sont réveillés
elle s'est réveillée	elles se sont réveillées
on s'est réveillé	

s'amuser: to have fun; have a good time (literally: "to amuse oneself")

je me suis amusé(e)	nous nous sommes amusé(e)s
tu t'es amusé(e)	vous vous êtes amusé(e)(s)
il s'est amusé	ils se sont amusés
elle s'est amusée	elles se sont amusées
on s'est amusé	

How can you tell if the reflexive pronoun (**me, te, se, nous, vous**) is a direct object? Usually it is, but when there is another object, the reflexive pronoun is an *indirect* object, and there is no past participle agreement with an indirect object. In the following examples, the *direct objects* are italicized.

Elle *s'*est lavée.	agreement: The word **lavée** is feminine singular to agree with the preceding direct object, *s'* (=se).
Elle s'est lavé *les mains*.	no agreement: The direct object, ***les mains***, does not precede the verb. The word **se** is an indirect object (because there is also a direct object).
Ils *se* sont rencontrés au restaurant.	agreement: The word **rencontrer** has a direct object, and in this case, it's *se*, which comes before the verb.

Some verbs, like **parler (à)** and **téléphoner (à)**, have only an indirect object, which is generally introduced by the preposition à. With indirect objects, there is never any past participle agreement.

Ils se sont téléphoné.	no agreement: The verb **téléphoner** takes an indirect object, in this case **se**. There is never agreement with indirect objects, even when they precede the verb.

Using *passé composé*: pronominal verbs

Perspective personnelle

Vrai ou faux? Indicate whether each sentence is true (**vrai**) or false (**faux**) for you. Remember to read each sentence aloud to practice speaking.

_____   Je me suis réveillé(e) à 6h ce matin.

_____   Hier soir, je me suis couché(e) de bonne heure (early).

_____   Le weekend passé, moi et mes amis, nous nous sommes rencontrés dans un café.

_____   Je me suis douché(e) ce matin.

_____   Je ne me suis pas brossé les dents ce matin.

G. **What is the correct form?** Conjugate the verb in parentheses in the **passé composé**. Be sure to make the past participle agree when appropriate. When you finish, read the completed sentences aloud.

1. **Jeanne et Henri** _____ **(se marier) en juin.**

2. **Ma fille** _____ **(tomber) d'un arbre et** _____ **(se casser) le bras** (arm).

3. **Sylvie** _____ **(se réveiller) tôt ce matin.**

4. **Tu** _____ **(se lever) de bonne heure aujourd'hui?**

5. **Les enfants** _____ **(se laver) les mains avant le dîner.**

6. **Mon copain et moi, nous** _____ **(se disputer) hier.**

7. **Je** _____ **(s'endormir) en classe mardi. Le prof** _____ **(se fâcher)! Et mes amis** _____ **(se moquer) de moi.**

8. **Vous** _____ **(s'amuser) à la soirée?**

9. **Jérémie et Binta** _____ **(se parler) au téléphone hier soir.**

10. **Hier soir, comme d'habitude** (as usual), **Camille** _____ **(se deshabiller),** _____ **(se doucher) et** _____ **(se coucher).**

Review: Does the past participle agree?

With verbs in the **passé composé** and all other compound tenses, the past participle agrees as in these examples:

all verbs conjugated with *avoir*: The past participle agrees with a *direct object*, but only when it precedes the verb.	**Voilà la lettre *que* j'ai écrite.** **_Quels livres_ est-ce que tu as achetés?**
the verbs conjugated with *être*: The past participle agrees with the *subject*.	**Sabine est arrivée à l'heure.** **Olivier et moi, nous sommes revenus de la fac.**
all reflexive verbs: The past participle agrees with the reflexive pronoun when it is the *direct object*.	**Marie, est-ce que tu *t'*es levée de bonne heure?** **Nous *nous* sommes rencontrés à la librairie.**

Using and reviewing the *passé composé*

H. Way ahead! You and your siblings have already done everything your parents have asked you to do. When they ask if something is going to be done, say that the task has already been completed. Note that questions in the **vous** form are directed at you and your siblings together, so respond to those with the **nous** form. Insert **déjà** (already) just before the past participle. When you've completed each sentence, read it aloud!

EXAMPLES: Tu vas te réveiller?   Je me suis déjà réveillé(e).
            Ta sœur va nourrir le chat?   Elle a déjà nourri le chat.
            Vous allez faire la vaisselle?   Nous avons déjà fait la vaisselle.

1. **Ton frère va se lever?** _____

2. **Tu vas faire le lit?** _____

3. **Vous allez vous brosser les dents?** _____

4. **Tes sœurs vont s'habiller?** _____

5. **Tu vas mettre un pull chaud?** _____

6. **Vous allez prendre le petit déjeuner?** _____

7. **Ton frère va essuyer la table?** _____

8. **Tu vas te laver les mains?** _____

9. **Vous allez aller au magasin?** _____

10. **Tu vas passer l'aspirateur?** _____

11. **Tes frères vont sortir la poubelle?** _____

12. **Vous allez dire la vérité?** _____

13. **Ta sœur va finir ses devoirs?** _____

14. **Vous allez étudier pour votre examen?** _____

15. **Tes sœurs vont lire cet article?** _____

16. **Tu vas ouvrir la porte?** _____

17. **Ton frère va fermer la porte?** _____

18. **Tu vas écrire une lettre à ta tante?** _____

19. **Vous allez répondre à nos questions?** _____

20. **Tu vas aller à l'église?** _____

21. **Ta sœur va devenir une bonne étudiante?** _____

22. **Tes frères vont partir?** _____

I. Change each sentence from singular to plural.

Modèles: J'ai adoré le film! → Nous avons adoré le film!
Tu as fini les devoirs. → Vous avez fini les devoirs.
Elle a écrit le livre. → Elles ont écrit le livre.

1. **Elle a rougi quand il est entré.**

_____

2. **Je me suis réveillée tôt ce matin.**

_____

3. **Tu as bu du vin rouge?**

_____

4. **Je suis sortie avec Paul.**

_____

5. **Il est allé à la discothèque.**

_____

6. **Tu as suivi une inconnue dans la rue?**

_____

J. Change each sentence from plural to singular.

Modèles: Ils ont guéri les malades. → Il a guéri les malades.
Nous avons trouvé un bon médecin. → J'ai trouvé un bon médecin.
Vous avez vendu les livres? → Tu as vendu les livres?

1. **Elles sont passées par la boulangerie** (bakery).

_____

2. **Nous nous sommes reposées au café.**

_____

3. **Vous vous êtes vus dans le miroir?**

_____

4. **Ils ont reçu une médaille.**

_____

5. **Vous avez vendu la maison?**

_____

6. **Nous sommes revenus en avion.**

_____

K. Agreement? For each verb, decide if the past participle should show agreement. If so, add the necessary letter(s). If not, put an *X* in the blank.

1. **Il a chanté___ toute la nuit.**

2. **La mélodie qu'il a chanté___ a résonné___ longtemps dans mon oreille.**

3. **La grand-mère de Mme Poussin est mort___ la semaine dernière.**

4. **Nous nous sommes parlé___ pendant deux heures.**

5. **Élodie a préparé___ de la soupe pour sa mère.**

6. **La mère d'Élodie a beaucoup aimé___ la soupe qu'Élodie a préparé___.**

7. **Nous avons déjeuné___ au café.**

8. **Quelles émissions as-tu regardé___ à la télé hier soir?**

9. **Le train est parti___ à 11h25.**

10. **Les filles sont rentré___ tard vendredi soir.**

11. **Leurs parents se sont fâché___.**

12. **Est-ce que vous vous êtes déjà habillé___?**

13. **Thérèse est entré___ par l'autre porte.**

Les mots croisés 6

When a verb is provided, complete the clue with the **passé composé** of that verb.

Horizontal

4   Nous ___ (s'amuser) à la soirée vendredi.

5   Vous ___ (choisir)?

7   Tu ___ (lire) le journal ce matin?

9   Mes parents ___ (sortir) avec les Bourdonnay.

11   Richard ___ (devenir) professeur.

14   Je/j' ___ (se brosser) les dents.

17   Hervé ___ (finir) ses devoirs juste après l'école.

18   Vous ___ (pouvoir) joindre votre mère au téléphone?

19   Les garçons ___ (attendre) le train pendant deux heures.

21   Est-ce que tu ___ (monter) les valises au grenier?

22   Est-ce que ton voisin ___ (rendre) la tondeuse (lawnmower) **qu'il t'a empruntée?**

23   Marc ___ (se laver) les mains avant de préparer le dîner.

Vertical

1   Ta mère a aimé les fleurs que tu ___ (acheter)?

2   Denise ___ (aller) à Dakar.

3   Ma collègue ___ (mettre) le rapport sur mon bureau cet après-midi.

6   They (m.) went in: **Ils ___.**

7   Nous ___ (manger) des céréales pour le petit déjeuner.

8   Les nièces de Jacqueline ___ (naître) en Hongrie.

10   The girls laughed: **Les filles ___.**

12   She fell: **elle ___**

13   En quelle année est-ce que Proust ___ (écrire) *Du côté de chez Swann?*

15   Michelle et Henri ___ (se voir) dans la rue Montmartre.

16   Nous ___ (devoir) travailler tout le weekend pour satisfaire le patron.

20   I told the truth: **Je/j'___ la vérité.**

7
L'Imparfait

The **imparfait**, or imperfect tense, expresses past events and conditions that occurred for an indefinite or unspecified period of time. Verbs in the **imparfait** can tell what used to happen, describe how things were, and give background information. They can also describe what was going on, or what things were like, when another past action (expressed in the **passé composé**) took place.

Quand j'étais jeune, nous sortions au cinéma tous les samedis soirs.	When I was young, we would go out to the movies every Saturday night.
Je faisais mes devoirs quand le téléphone a sonné.	I was doing my homework when the phone rang.

How to form the *imparfait*

Every French verb has the same set of endings in the **imparfait**:

-ais	-ions
-ais	-iez
-ait	-aient

These endings are added to the **imparfait** stem, which you can find by dropping the **-ons** ending from the present-tense **nous** form of the verb.

habiter: present tense, *nous habitons*. The *imparfait* stem is *habit-*.

j'habitais	I lived, was living, used to live
tu habitais	you lived, were living, used to live
il/elle/on habitait	he/she/one lived, was living, used to live; we lived, were living, used to live*
nous habitions	we lived, were living, used to live
vous habitiez	you lived, were living, used to live
ils/elles habitaient	they lived, were living, used to live

*Remember that **on** is used in informal French for **nous: on habitait = nous habitions**.

There is only one exception to this rule for the **imparfait** stem: **ét-** for the verb **être**.

être

j'étais	**nous étions**
tu étais	**vous étiez**
il/elle/on était	**ils/elles étaient**

Some spelling changes

We saw that in the present tense, verbs that have stems ending in -**c** spell this as -**ç** before the ending -**ons**: **je commence**, but **nous commençons**. This shows that the verb stems are all pronounced in the same way. This spelling change with **ç (c cédille)** also happens before the **imparfait** endings that start with the letter **a**. So the **imparfait** of a verb like **commencer** looks like this:

commencer

je commençais	**nous commencions**
tu commençais	**vous commenciez**
il/elle/on commençait	**ils/elles commençaient**

Remember that the letter **ç** is *not* used (in fact, never used) before -**e** and -**i**: **commencer**, **nous commencions**, **vous commenciez**. Other verbs like **commencer** are:

   avancer: **j'avançais, tu avançais, il/elle/on avançait, . . . ils/elles avançaient**

   lancer: **je lançais, tu lançais, il/elle/on lançait, . . . ils/elles lançaient**

   placer: **je plaçais, tu plaçais, il/elle/on plaçait, . . . ils/elles plaçaient**

   remplacer: **je remplaçais, tu remplaçais, il/elle/on remplaçait, . . . ils/elles remplaçaient**

We also saw that in the **présent**, verbs that have stems ending in -**g** add the letter **e** before the ending -**ons**: **nous mangeons**. Again, this change shows that the verb stem is always pronounced in the same way. Like **ç**, this spelling change happens before the **imparfait** endings that start with the letter **a**. Here is the verb **manger** in the **imparfait**:

manger

je mangeais	**nous mangions**
tu mangeais	**vous mangiez**
il/elle/on mangeait	**ils/elles mangeaient**

Since the **g** sound is always soft before **e** or **i**, no letter **e** is added before the **nous** and **vous** endings: **nous mangions, vous mangiez**. Other verbs like **manger** are:

   changer: **je changeais, tu changeais, il/elle/on changeait, . . . ils/elles changeaient**

   nager: **je nageais, tu nageais, il/elle/on nageait, . . . ils/elles nageaient**

   ranger: **je rangeais, tu rangeais, il/elle/on rangeait, . . . ils/elles rangeaient**

   voyager: **je voyageais, tu voyageais, il/elle/on voyageait, . . . ils/elles voyageaient**

Using the *imparfait*

The **imparfait** is the past tense most used in French for description. It tells about events and conditions in the past without referring to a specific point in time or a specific length of time. Sentences in the **imparfait** correspond to different ways of expressing past events and conditions in English, as in these examples:

Quand *j'habitais* à New York, *nous faisions* souvent des promenades en ville. *Nous visitions* les musées et les magasins, et *nous mangions* dans tous les bons restaurants de la ville. L'été, *nous partions* au bord de la mer, mais *nous étions* toujours heureux de rentrer chez nous. *J'aimais* beaucoup New York!	When *I lived* in New York, *we often took walks (would take walks, used to take walks)* in the city. *We went (would go, used to go)* to the museums and stores, and *we ate (would eat, used to eat)* in all the city's good restaurants. In the summer, *we would go away (used to go away)* to the seashore, but *we were* always happy to come back home. *I* really *loved* New York!

Notice that this paragraph describes how things were in New York, but it doesn't point to a specific time or mention how long the speaker or writer lived there. For actions and events that took place at a specific time in the past, or for a specific length of time, French uses the **passé composé**. In the next chapter, we'll practice using these two tenses together.

Reviewing and using the *imparfait*

Perspective personnelle

Vrai ou faux? Indicate whether each sentence is true (**vrai**) or false (**faux**) for you. Remember to read each sentence aloud for practice.

_____ **Quand j'étais petit(e), j'étais mignon / mignonne.**

_____ **Quand j'avais 10 ans, je disais toujours la vérité.**

_____ **Autrefois, mes amis et moi, nous regardions la télé ensemble.**

_____ **Pendant mon enfance, mes parents me donnaient souvent de l'argent.**

_____ **Pendant ma jeunesse, ma famille et moi, nous dînions ensemble tous les soirs.**

A. Que faisait-on? Using the picture as a guide, describe what the following people were doing when Paul rang the doorbell. After writing your responses, read them aloud, pretending to explain to someone what was happening.

Modèle: Céline *parlait au téléphone.*

1. **Hervé** _____

2. **Alain** _____

3. **Claude** _____

4. **Marina et Christophe** _____

5. **Nicole** _____

6. **Cédric** _____

7. **Andrée** _____

8. **Chloë** _____

B. **What is the correct form?** Here is an excerpt from **Maigret à New York** by Georges Simenon, a well-known Belgian author of mystery novels. In this passage near the beginning of the novel, the author sets the scene (using the **imparfait**) for upcoming action. Conjugate each verb in parentheses in the **imparfait** to agree with the subject. You will not know all the words in the text, but you should be able to complete the task by focusing on the subject for each verb.

Maigret _____[1] **(fumer) sa pipe dans le crachin,** _____[2] **(regarder) un bateau gris, que les houles** _____[3] **(soulever) très haut et** _____[4] **(laisser) retomber [. . .]. Des officiers** _____[5] **(passer) [. . .] et** _____[6] **(disparaître) dans l'appartement du capitaine.**

On _____[7] **(ouvrir) les cales. Les cabestans** _____[8] **(fonctionner) déjà. Les passagers** _____[9] **(devenir) plus nombreux sur le pont et quelques-uns, [. . .],** _____[10] **(s'obstiner) à prendre des photographies. Il y en** _____[11] **(avoir) qui** _____[12] **(échanger) des adresses, qui** _____[13] **(se promettre) de se revoir, de s'écrire. D'autres encore, dans les salons,** _____[14] **(remplir) leurs déclarations de douane. (U.G.E. Poche Presses de la Cité, 1947, pp. 9–10)**

C. **Interview!** You have become famous. This means, of course, that people want to know everything about you. You have granted an interview to a reporter who wants to focus on your childhood, describing what your life was like at two different points. Write complete answers to the reporter's questions below. Then, after you finish, read your answers aloud for practice (and in case someone does interview you!).

Quand vous aviez cinq (5) ans . . .

1. **Quelle ville habitiez-vous?**

2. **Avec qui habitiez-vous?**

3. **Aviez-vous des animaux?**

4. **Quelles activités aimiez-vous?**

5. **Quels sports faisiez-vous?**

6. **Jouiez-vous de la musique?**

7. **Qu'est-ce que vous aimiez manger?**

8. **Qu'est-ce que vous ne mangiez pas?**

9. **Étiez-vous sage (well-behaved)?**

10. **Étiez-vous content(e)?**

Quand vous aviez quinze (15) ans . . .

11. **Quelle ville habitiez-vous?**

12. **Avec qui habitiez-vous?**

13. **Sortiez-vous souvent avec des amis?**

14. **Quelles activités aimiez-vous?**

15. **Quels sports faisiez-vous?**

16. **Jouiez-vous de la musique?**

17. **Aviez-vous un copain / une copine (boyfriend/girlfriend)?**

18. **Étudiiez-vous beaucoup?**

19. **Parliez-vous une langue étrangère (foreign language)?**

20. **Étiez-vous content(e)?**

D. Which verb? Complete each paragraph with verbs from the list above it. For each blank, choose the verb that makes the best sense, and conjugate it to agree with the subject. When you've completed each paragraph, read it aloud!

aller	lire	vouloir	être
travailler	arriver	habiter	dire
étudier	avoir	écrire	faire

Autrefois, la famille Perbal _____ [1] Paris. Pendant la semaine, tout le monde _____ [2] très occupé. M. et Mme Perbal _____ [3] tous les jours. Le soir, Mme Perbal _____ [4] des magazines et _____ [5] des courriels. M. Perbal _____ [6] à la maison si fatigué qu'il ne _____ [7] même pas regarder la télévision. Les enfants _____ [8] à l'école pendant la journée et _____ [9] beaucoup le soir.

aller	se souvenir	s'amuser
aimer	être	prendre
se promener	voir	croire

Le samedi, les Perbal _____ [10] passer du temps ensemble. Ils _____ [11] souvent aux musées où ils _____ [12] beaucoup d'expositions intéressantes. Ils _____ [13] dans Paris et _____ [14] dans les jardins publiques. De temps en temps, ils _____ [15] le train pour aller à Versailles.

venir	faire	boire	aller	aimer
préparer	avoir	manger	commencer	se détendre
emmener (to bring a person)	acheter	prendre	s'endormir	apporter

Le dimanche, M. Perbal _____ [16] au marché, _____ [17] beaucoup de nourriture, et _____ [18] un grand dîner. Les oncles et les tantes _____ [19] le voyage de la banlieue (suburbs) pour le dîner du dimanche. Ils _____ [20] tous les petits cousins. La vieille grand-mère _____ [21] aussi et _____ [22] toujours une belle tarte tatin (apple pie). Toute la famille _____ [23] bien et _____ [24] un peu de vin. Après le dîner, Papy _____ [25] à raconter des histoires. Les enfants _____ [26] beaucoup écouter, mais il y _____ [27] toujours quelqu'un qui _____ [28] avant la fin.

E. Change each sentence from singular to plural.

EXAMPLES:
J'étais adorable!	→	Nous étions adorables!
Tu parlais français.	→	Vous parliez français.
Elle se préparait.	→	Elles se préparaient.

1. Tu avais les cheveux courts quand tu étais jeune?

   _____

2. Je me couchais à 8h tous les soirs.

   _____

3. Il s'ennuyait en classe.

   _____

4. Je faisais de la gymnastique.

_____

5. Elle comprenait tout de suite.

_____

6. Tu voulais être médecin?

_____

F. Change each sentence from plural to singular.

EXAMPLES: Ils guérissaient les malades.   →   Il guérissait les malades.
             Nous cherchions un bon médecin.   →   Je cherchais un bon médecin.
             Vous vendiez les livres?   →   Tu vendais les livres?

1. Elles se trompaient régulièrement.

_____

2. Nous savions nager quand nous avions seulement trois ans.

_____

3. Vous exagériez beaucoup autrefois.

_____

4. Ils vouvoyaient le professeur.

_____

5. Vous balayiez la cuisine tous les jours.

_____

6. Nous voyagions souvent à l'étranger.

_____

Les mots croisés 7

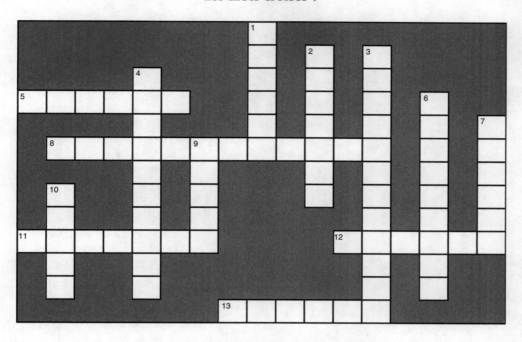

When a verb is given, complete the clue with the **imparfait** of that verb.

Horizontal

5   **Vous ___ (jeter) des pierres dans la rivière pour vous amuser?**

8   I used to disobey my parents: **Je/j' ___ à mes parents.**

11 We had to (it was necessary to) speak Japanese in class: **Il ___ parler japonais en classe.**

12 **Fiona___ (vivre) avec son vieux grand-père quand elle était jeune.**

13 **Je/J'___ (aller) au cinéma chaque vendredi.**

Vertical

1   **Nous ___ (être) si insouciants (carefree)!**

2   **Est-ce que tu ___ (nager) quand tu avais trois ans?**

3   **Nous ___ (choisir) toujours d'aller en voiture si possible.**

4   **À l'âge de 8 ans, je/j' ___ (se coucher) à 8h.**

6   I always preferred chocolate: **Je/J' ___ toujours le chocolat.**

7   **On ___ (boire) toujours un bon verre de vin au dîner.**

9   **Mon mari ___ (être) beau et extraverti quand je l'ai rencontré.**

10 She was 20 years old: **Elle ___ vingt ans.**

8
Using the *Passé Composé* and the *Imparfait*

As you have seen, French has two tenses that relate events and conditions that occurred in the past. Generally speaking, the **passé composé** *tells what happened*, and the **imparfait** *describes the background*, or *how things were*.

Verbs in the **passé composé** relate what happened in the past, always at a specific moment or for a specified duration of time. The moment or duration of time may be stated, or it may be implied by the context.

Hier, *j'ai téléphoné* à mes parents.	I called my parents yesterday.
Pardon, qu'est-ce que *tu as dit*?	I'm sorry, what did you say? (implied moment; just now)
***Je n'ai* jamais *visité* le Canada.**	I've never been to Canada. (implied duration; in my entire life)

Verbs in the **imparfait**, on the other hand, describe how things were in the past. They also relate habitual or repeated actions, but without referring to a specific moment or duration of time.

***Je téléphonais* tous les jours à mes parents.**	I called my parents every day. (for an unspecified duration of time)
***Mon père disait* . . .**	My father used to say . . . (habitually; duration of time not specified)
***Nous visitions* les musées de New York.**	We would go to the New York museums. (when I lived there; duration of time not specified)

Often, a verb in the *imparfait* describes what was going on when a **passé composé** event took place.

Nous *prenions* le dîner quand le téléphone a sonné.	We were having dinner when the phone rang.
Quand je suis sorti, il *pleuvait*.	It was raining when I went out.

Weather expressions, since they describe conditions, are usually in the *imparfait*. If they describe how the weather was for a certain period of time, though, they are in the **passé composé**.

Quel temps *faisait-il* à Paris? *Il faisait* très beau.	How was the weather in Paris? It was very nice.
but:	
Il a plu toute la journée hier!	It rained all day yesterday! (specified period; the entire day)

Some verbs can have different meanings when they are used in the **imparfait** and the **passé composé**. Since the **passé composé** tells what happened at a specific moment, in these cases it tells what changed.

Quand nous sommes arrivés au restaurant, j'avais faim.	When we got to the restaurant, I was hungry. (description)
but:	
Quand j'ai vu le menu, j'ai eu faim.	When I saw the menu, I got hungry. (change)
Quand Joëlle a vu le chien, elle a eu peur.	When Joëlle saw the dog, she got scared. (change)
Hier, Marc a eu 18 ans.	Yesterday, Marc turned 18. (change)

Using the past tenses in narration

The **passé composé** and the *imparfait* are often used together in narrating the past. Remember that the **passé composé** tells what happened. Sentences in the **passé composé** may answer the question: **Qu'est-ce qui s'est passé ensuite?** ("What happened next?"). Note that the **passé composé** is, of course, used in this question! You could say that "next" is the specific moment in time for these verbs in the **passé composé**. The *imparfait*, on the other hand, describes how things were. It paints a picture of the background, without referring to a specific moment or length of time.

The following excerpt is from the famous novel *L'étranger* by Albert Camus. In this passage from the beginning of the novel, the narrator, Meursault, has just learned that his mother has died, and he is going to the home where she had been living to make the funeral arrangements. Notice how the verbs in the **passé composé** tell "what happened next," while the verbs in the *imparfait*, printed in *italics*, describe the background: the weather, how people thought or felt, and what they were doing when specific (**passé composé**) events took place.

J'ai pris l'autobus à deux heures. *Il faisait* très chaud. J'ai mangé au restaurant, chez Céleste, comme d'habitude. *Ils avaient tous beaucoup de peine pour moi* et Céleste m'a dit : «On n'a qu'une mère.» Quand je suis parti, ils m'ont accompagné à la porte. *J'étais* un peu étourdi parce qu'il a fallu que je monte chez Emmanuel pour lui emprunter une cravate noire et un brassard. Il a perdu son oncle, il y a quelques mois.

J'ai couru pour ne pas manquer le départ. [. . .] J'ai dormi presque tout le trajet. Et quand je me suis réveillé, *j'étais* tassé contre un militaire qui m'a souri et qui m'a demandé si *je venais* de loin. J'ai dit «oui» pour n'avoir plus à parler.

Albert Camus, *L'étranger*. Paris: Gallimard, 1942.

I took the bus: what happened—and at a specific time, 2:00. *It was hot*: description. I ate: next event. *They were all worried*: description, how they felt. Celeste said to me: next event. When I left, they walked me to the door: next events. *I was a little distracted*: description, how I felt. I had to go up: next event. He lost his uncle: what happened to him a few months ago.

I ran: next event. I slept: next event—and for a specific length of time (almost the entire trip). When I woke up: next event. *I was leaning*: description. Who smiled and asked: next events. *If I came from far away*: description. I said: next event.

Look again at Exercise B from Chapter 7. In this entire scene from Simenon's novel, nothing has happened yet. It's all description, and all the verbs are in the **imparfait**. At some point, there will be a verb in the **passé composé**. That's when the action of the scene begins.

Using the *passé composé* and the *imparfait*

Perspective personnelle

Vrai ou faux? Indicate whether each sentence is true (**vrai**) or false (**faux**) for you. Remember to read each sentence aloud for practice.

_____ Quand je me suis réveillé(e) ce matin, mon époux/épouse préparait le petit déjeuner.

_____ Mes amis et moi avons fait du camping le weekend dernier.

_____ Quand j'étais petit(e), ma famille mangeait rarement au restaurant.

_____ J'ai quitté mon dernier travail parce que mon patron était méchant.

_____ La dernière fois que j'ai joué au Monopoly, j'avais moins de (less than) dix ans.

A. **Passé composé ou imparfait?** Based on the context of the sentence, decide which tense is appropriate. Then choose the correct form.

Modèles: Michèle (a pris / prenait) son sac et (est allée / allait) au centre commercial.
Yannick (s'est baigné / *se baignait*) quand son frère est rentré.

1. **Philippe (a téléphoné / téléphonait) à Thérèse parce qu'il (a voulu / voulait) l'inviter à dîner.**

2. **Quand nous (avons été / étions) jeunes, nous (avons lu / lisions) des bandes dessinées** (comic books).

3. **Vous (avez eu / aviez) quel âge en 1998?**

4. **Martine (est née / naissait) à Dakar en 1986.**

5. Je/j' (ai vu / voyais) un film très intéressant hier. Ça/c' (a été / était) un documentaire sur le fast food.

6. Il (a été / était) 16h quand l'agent de police (est arrivé / arrivait) chez Hugo.

7. J'(ai été / étais) au café quand il (a commencé / commençait) à pleuvoir.

8. Quand nous (sommes rentrés / rentrions) hier, nous (avons ouvert / ouvrions) le réfrigérateur tout de suite. Nous (n'avons rien trouvé / ne trouvions rien), alors, nous (sommes partis / partions) au restaurant.

9. Nous (sommes allés / allions) au restaurant parce qu'il n'y (a rien eu / avait rien) dans le frigo.

10. Est-ce que tu (t'es moqué / te moquais) de tes professeurs quand tu (as été / étais) au lycée?

11. Quand j'(ai eu / avais) cinq ans, je ne (me suis pas brossé / me brossais pas) souvent les dents.

B. **Passé composé ou imparfait?** Read through this story about a mother goat and her kids. Then, for each blank, decide whether to use the **passé composé** or the **imparfait**, and conjugate the verb appropriately. Remember to choose the right auxiliary verb (**être** or **avoir**) for verbs in the **passé composé** and to pay attention to the agreement of past participles. When you are finished, read the story aloud.

Il était une fois (Once upon a time there was) une mère chèvre (goat) qui _____[1] (avoir) sept petits chevreaux (kids). Ils _____[2] (habiter) dans une petite maison près d'une grande forêt. Et dans cette forêt _____[3] (vivre) un loup méchant (wicked wolf). Un jour, la mère _____[4] (devoir) faire des courses. Elle _____[5] (réunir [gather]) tous ses enfants et leur _____[6] (dire): «N'ouvrez pas la porte pendant que (while) je suis absente parce que ça pourrait être le loup qui voudrait vous manger!» Les sept chevreaux _____[7] (promettre) de ne pas ouvrir la porte, et la mère _____[8] (partir). Bientôt après, les chevreaux _____[9] (entendre) frapper (knocking) à la porte. Une voix (voice) _____[10] (dire): «Laissez-moi entrer, chers enfants. C'est votre mère!» Les chevreaux _____[11] (aller) ouvrir la porte quand ils _____[12] (voir) une patte noire (black paw) sur la fenêtre. «Vous n'êtes pas notre mère! Notre mère a des pattes blanches.» Alors, le loup _____[13] (partir). Il _____[14] (mettre) de la farine (flour) sur les pattes, et il _____[15] (revenir) à la petite maison. Cette fois-ci, les chevreaux _____[16] (voir) une patte blanche et _____[17] (ouvrir) la porte. Le loup _____[18] (entrer) en bondissant (bounded in). Les chevreaux _____[19] (avoir) peur et _____[20] (se cacher [to hide]). Mais le loup les _____[21] (trouver) et les _____[22] (mettre) dans un grand sac—tous sauf le plus petit qui _____[23] (être) caché sous le lit. Puis le loup _____[24] (partir) avec son sac. Mais le sac _____[25] (être) si lourd que le loup _____[26] (devenir) très fatigué et _____[27] (s'arrêter [to stop]) pour se reposer. Quand la mère chèvre _____[28] (rentrer) chez elle, tout _____[29] (être) en désordre (a mess). Elle _____[30] (être) choquée de trouver que ses petits _____[31] (ne pas être) là! Tout à coup (all of a sudden) elle _____[32] (entendre) un petit bruit dans la chambre et le plus petit chevreau _____[33] (sortir) de sa cachette (hiding place). Il _____[34] (raconter) à sa mère ce qui s'était passé (what had happened). Alors, la mère chèvre _____[35] (partir) à la recherche du (in search of) loup. Elle le/l'_____[36] (trouver) sous un arbre. Il _____[37] (dormir) à côté d'un grand sac. Et quelque chose dans le sac _____[38] (bouger [to move])! Pendant que le loup _____[39] (rêver [to dream]), elle _____[40] (ouvrir) le sac et les chevreaux en _____[41] (sortir). Puis elle _____ [42] (remplir [to fill]) le sac de grosses pierres (big rocks) et le/l'_____ [43] (refermer [to close back up]). Peu de temps après (Shortly after), le loup _____ [44] (se réveiller). Il _____ [45] (prendre) son sac et _____ [46] (rentrer) chez lui. Pendant qu'il _____ [47] (marcher), il _____ [48] (penser) aux chevreaux dans son sac et _____ [49] (imaginer) le dîner splendide qu'il _____ [50] (aller) préparer. Quand il_____ [51] (arriver) chez lui, le loup _____ [52] (avoir) très faim, et il _____ [53] (ouvrir) le sac tout de suite. «Quoi! Des pierres!?!» Le loup _____ [54] (être) très fâché et déçu (disappointed). Il _____ [55] (commencer) à pleurer et il _____ [56] (rentrer) chez sa maman et _____ [57] (ne jamais revenir) dans la forêt.

C. **Comment dit-on?** Complete the following sentences by translating the missing portions into French.

1. Max left his girlfriend because she wasn't nice.

   Max _____ (quitter) sa copine parce qu'elle _____ (ne pas être) gentille.

2. Alex got mad because his friend stole his car.

   Alex _____ (se fâcher) parce que son amie _____ (voler) sa voiture.

3. In her youth, Irene spoke French, English, and Japanese. She was interested in German, too.

   Pendant sa jeunesse, Irène _____ (parler) français, anglais, et japonais. Elle _____ (s'intéresser à) l'allemand aussi.

4. Yesterday it was snowing. So I bought new skis. This morning, it started to rain!

   Hier, il _____ (neiger) . Alors, je/j' _____ (acheter) de nouveaux skis. Ce matin, il _____ (commencer) à pleuvoir!

5. Monday, Alain was very busy. He worked ten hours at the office. Then he did the shopping and prepared a big dinner for his wife's birthday. He fell asleep immediately after dessert. He missed coffee.

   Lundi, Alain _____ (être) très occupé. Il _____ (travailler) dix heures au bureau puis il _____ (faire) les courses et _____ (préparer) un grand dîner pour l'anniversaire de sa femme. Il _____ (s'endormir) tout de suite après le dessert. Le pauvre! Il _____ (manquer) le café.

6. On Saturdays, we would often take a walk in the country. We would usually have a picnic. Then we would come home tired but happy.

   Le samedi, nous _____ (se promener) souvent à la campagne. D'habitude nous _____ (faire) un pique-nique. Puis nous _____ (rentrer) chez nous fatigués mais contents.

7. When you were eight, did you listen to classical music? Did you always obey your parents?

   Quand vous _____ (avoir) huit ans, est-ce que vous _____ (écouter) la musique classique? Est-ce que vous _____ (obéir) toujours à vos parents?

8. Yesterday morning, Elise entered her office and answered the phone that was ringing.

   Hier matin, Elise _____ (entrer) dans son bureau et _____ (répondre) au téléphone qui _____ (sonner).

D. Du présent au passé. Change each of the following sentences from the present to the past, using the **passé composé** and/or the **imparfait**. Change **aujourd'hui** to **hier**. Be sure to change all conjugated verbs!

1. D'habitude, je finis mes devoirs après le dîner, et ensuite j'écris des courriels.

   _____

2. Aujourd'hui, Bertrande vient chez Louis. Ils sortent ensemble, mais ils se disputent. Louis se met à pleurer, et Bertrande commence à crier. Puis, ils se regardent et rient.

   Hier, _____

   _____

3. Il fait beau. Alors, Lilianne appelle son amie Évelyne et elles montent dans la décapotable (convertible) d'Évelyne et vont à la plage où elles prennent un bain de soleil.

   _____

   _____

4. Le dimanche (On Sundays), Mme Goudron va toujours au match de foot de son fils Julien. Julien n'aime pas ça et il dit à sa mère de ne pas venir. Mme Goudron ne veut pas manquer les matchs. Alors après, elle se déguise chaque semaine et Julien ne sait pas qu'elle est là!

   _____

   _____

   _____

9
Le Plus-que-parfait

The **plus-que-parfait**, or pluperfect tense, expresses events that happened in the past before another past event or state. This tense often states what had (already) happened when another event took place.

Quand je suis arrivé, le professeur *avait commencé* **la leçon.**	When I arrived, the teacher had started the lesson.
Je ne savais pas que tu *étais* **déjà** *rentrée.*	I didn't know that you had already come back.
Robert nous a dit qu'il *avait acheté* **une nouvelle voiture.**	Robert told us that he had bought a new car.

As these examples show, the verb in the **plus-que-parfait** expresses something that had happened before the main event or state (also in the past): The teacher had started the lesson (before I arrived); you had already come back (before I knew about it); Robert had bought a new car (before he told us about it). Verbs in the **plus-que-parfait** are conjugated in English with the auxiliary verb **had: had started, had come back, had bought**.

How to form the *plus-que-parfait*

The **plus-que-parfait** is a compound past tense that, like the **passé composé**, is formed with an auxiliary verb and the past participle. The auxiliary verb, **avoir** or **être**, is in the **imparfait**.

an **avoir** verb: **parler**

j'avais parlé	I had spoken
tu avais parlé	you had spoken
il/elle/on avait parlé	he/she/one had spoken; we had spoken
nous avions parlé	we had spoken
vous aviez parlé	you had spoken
ils/elles avaient parlé	they had spoken

an **être** verb: **partir**

j'étais parti/partie	I had left
tu étais parti/partie	you had left
il était parti	he had left
elle était partie	she had left
on était parti	one had left; we had left
nous étions partis/parties	we had left
vous étiez parti/partie/partis/parties	you had left
ils étaient partis	they had left
elles étaient parties	they had left

a pronominal verb: **se lever**

je m'étais levé(e)	I had gotten up
tu t'étais levé(e)	you had gotten up
il s'était levé	he had gotten up
elle s'était levée	she had gotten up
on s'était levé	one had gotten up
nous nous étions levé(e)s	we had gotten up
vous vous étiez levé(e)(s)	you had gotten up
ils s'étaient levés	they had gotten up
elles s'étaient levées	they had gotten up

As in all compound tenses, the past participle in the **plus-que-parfait** agrees in gender and in number:

- with the subject of a verb conjugated with **être**

- with a preceding direct object of verbs conjugated with **avoir**

- with the reflexive pronoun (a preceding direct object) of pronominal verbs

Using the *plus-que-parfait*

Perspective personnelle

Vrai ou faux? Indicate whether each sentence is true (**vrai**) or false (**faux**) for you. Remember to read each sentence aloud for practice.

_____ **Avant de me lever du lit ce matin, j'avais déjà allumé** (to turn on) **la télé.**

_____ **Avant de quitter la maison ce matin, mon époux/épouse (mon père/ma mère) n'avait pas encore pris le petit déjeuner.**

_____ **Avant de dîner hier soir, j'étais allé(e) au restaurant.**

_____ **Avant d'aller au cinéma la dernière fois, mes amis et moi avions lu les critiques des films.**

_____ **Avant d'étudier le français aujourd'hui, j'avais travaillé au bureau.**

A. En quel ordre? For each item, indicate which action happened first.

Modèle:

Marc est arrivé chez sa copine Sabine. Elle l'attendait parce qu'il avait téléphoné avant de venir.

arriver | téléphoner |

1. **As-tu lu la lettre qu'elle t'avait envoyée?**

   lire   envoyer

2. **Je me suis réveillé ce matin. Je n'étais plus fatigué parce que j'avais dormi dix heures!**

   se réveiller   dormir

3. **Il s'était bien préparé pour le match, mais il n'a pas bien joué.**

   se préparer   ne pas bien jouer

4. **J'ai bien apprécié le livre que tu m'avais recommandé.**
   apprécier   recommander

5. **Ils s'etaient beaucoup disputés au début, mais ils se sont mariés à la fin.**
   se disputer   se marier

6. **Les enfants ont mangé les biscuits que leur mère avait préparés.**
   manger   préparer

7. **Je suis allé rendre visite** (visit) **à ma vieille tante, mais elle était partie en vacances.**
   rendre visite   partir

8. **La famille est retournée à la même plage où tout le monde s'était tellement amusé l'année précédente.**
   retourner   s'amuser

B. **Au travail.** In an office, the boss, Madame Crenn, is always telling people to do things that they've already done. Below is a list of some of the boss's requests yesterday. State that the people in question had already completed the tasks (by the time she asked) by using the **plus-que-parfait**. Remember to consider if the past participle should show agreement!

Modèle: Mme Crenn a demandé à Mme Bourdonnay de taper (type) ses lettres.
            Mme Bourdonnay avait déjà tapé ses lettres.

1. **Mme Crenn a demandé à M. Thomas d'aller à l'imprimerie** (printer).
   _____

2. **Mme Crenn a demandé à Mlle Grégoire et M. Bonacieux de finir leur projet.**
   _____

3. **Mme Crenn a demandé à Mme Robert et Mme Huchet de s'occuper du budget.**
   _____

4. **Mme Crenn a demandé à Mme Bernier d'apprendre le nouveau logiciel** (software).
   _____

5. **Mme Crenn a demandé à M. Nicolas de payer les factures** (bills).
   _____

6. **Mme Crenn a demandé à Mlle Julien d'écrire une lettre au président de la société.**
   _____

7. **Mme Crenn a demandé à M. Troude et M. Quinot de réfléchir aux objectifs.**
   _____

8. **Mme Crenn a demandé à Mme Polnichet de vendre des actions** (shares of stock).
   _____

9. **Mme Crenn a demandé à M. David de nourrir son poisson** (feed her fish).
   _____

C. En retard. Paul was on his way to Marie's birthday party when he had a minor car accident. Since he had promised to come, he continued on to the party, but he arrived *very* late. What had already happened when Paul arrived?

Modèle: **Marie et Isabel: lamenter l'absence de Paul**
            Marie et Isabel avaient lamenté l'absence de Paul.

1. **tu: offrir l'apéritif**

   _____

2. **les invités: se mettre à table**

   _____

3. **Julie: servir l'entrée**

   _____

4. **nous: prendre le plat principal**

   _____

5. **Jacques: couper le gâteau**

   _____

6. **les adultes: boire du champagne**

   _____

7. **Marie: ouvrir des cadeaux**

   _____

8. **Thomas: lire un poème qu'il avait écrit pour Marie**

   _____

9. **Rachel: rire des plaisanteries (jokes) de M. Jacob**

   _____

10. **les enfants: se coucher**

   _____

11. **vous: faire la vaisselle**

   _____

12. **tout le monde: partir**

   _____

D. Histoire de rupture. Complete the paragraph below by choosing appropriate verbs from the list and conjugating them in the **plus-que-parfait**. Remember to think about agreement of past participles!

acheter	sortir	rencontrer
offrir	se connaître (to meet)	suivre
mettre	vivre	faire

Luc et Bénédicte se sont mariés en 1996. Ils _____¹ à l'université et _____² des cours (courses) ensemble. Ils _____³ ensemble pendant trois ans avant de se fiancer. Mais le 26 décembre 2001, Luc a expliqué à Bénédicte qu'il _____⁴ une autre femme et qu'il quittait la maison. Bénédicte a pleuré pendant quelques minutes. Puis, elle a pris la bague (ring) que Luc lui _____⁵ , et elle l'a jetée par la fenêtre. Puis elle a vendu la voiture qu'ils _____⁶ ensemble. Et finalement, elle a pris tout l'argent qu'ils _____⁷ dans leur compte en banque (bank account), et elle est partie à Tahiti (où elle _____⁸ avant d'aller à l'université).

E. Un matin occupé? What had you done this morning by 11:00? Make a list of sentences that include the **plus-que-parfait** and the verbs in the list below.

aller   apprendre   faire
se réveiller   s'habiller   lire
nettoyer   finir   travailler

Modèle: J'avais pris le petit déjeuner.

1. _____
2. _____
3. _____
4. _____
5. _____
6. _____
7. _____
8. _____
9. _____

Les mots croisés 9

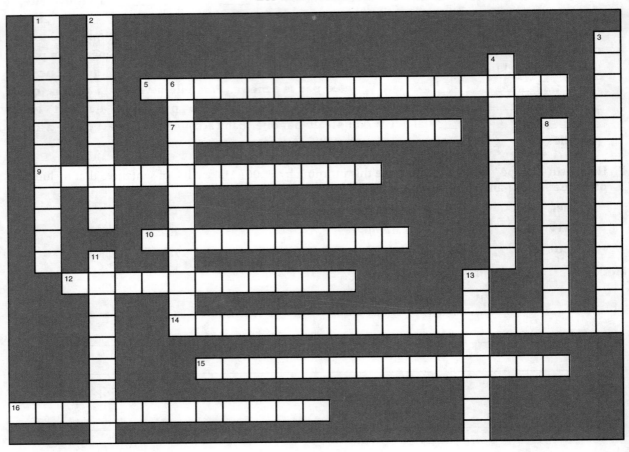

When a verb is given, complete the clue with the **plus-que-parfait** of that verb.

Horizontal

5	**Les fleurs ___ (s'ouvrir).**
7	**La bonne dame ___ (essuyer) la table.**
9	**Tu ___ (embrasser) ta mère.**
10	**Vous ___ (perdre) votre voiture?**
12	**Nous ___ (épeler) le mot correctement.**
14	**Les filles ___ (s'habiller).**
15	**Marianne ___ (descendre) en ville.**
16	**Le film ___ (effrayer) les petits.**

Vertical

1	They had gone to work: **Ils ___ au travail.**
2	We had made the bed: **Nous ___ le lit.**
3	The kids had surprised their parents: **Les enfants ___ leurs parents.**
4	**Thomas ___ (monter) dans le train.**
6	The critics had come to see the movie: **Les critiques ___ voir le film.**
8	I had danced: **Je/j'___.**
11	**Je/j'___ (prendre) mon petit déjeuner.**
13	**Nous ___ (boire) notre café.**

10

The Literary Past Tenses:
le Passé Simple,
le Passé Antérieur

French has two past tenses that are used in formal literary style. They are the **passé simple** (corresponding to the **passé composé**) and the **passé antérieur** (corresponding to the **plus-que-parfait**).

The *passé simple*

The **passé simple** may (optionally) be used in some written contexts in place of the **passé composé**. This past tense is used in literature, including children's stories and fairy tales, and in historical documents of an official or formal nature. These texts can be seen as archival, set aside from the present moment by style, intent, status, or history.

The **passé simple** is not used, even in official and formal contexts, for recent events that are related to the present moment. This tense is not usually used in journalism because news writing does not report on archives but on things that have just happened and have a connection to the present. For this reason, the **passé simple** is not used in writing letters—or e-mail! And it is never used in conversation.

How to recognize the *passé simple*

The **passé simple** stem of most verbs comes from the infinitive.

infinitive	passé simple stem
gagner	gagn-
finir	fin-
rendre	rend-

The **passé simple** endings for all **-er** verbs are the same.

gagner: stem gagn(er) = gagn-

je gagnai	nous gagnâmes
tu gagnas	vous gagnâtes
il/elle/on gagna	ils/elles gagnèrent

se lever: stem **lev(er) = lev-**

je me levai	nous nous levâmes
tu te levas	vous vous levâtes
il/elle/on se leva	ils/elles se levèrent

aller: stem **all(er) = all-**

j'allai	nous allâmes
tu allas	vous allâtes
il/elle/on alla	ils/elles allèrent

Regular **-ir** and **-re** verbs have a second set of endings. Note that the stem does not change.

finir: stem **fin(ir) = fin-**

je finis*	nous finîmes
tu finis*	vous finîtes
il/elle/on finit*	ils/elles finirent

*These **passé simple** forms look just like the present tense. The context helps you to recognize, though, when they are **passé simple** verbs.

rendre: stem **rend(re) = rend-**

je rendis	nous rendîmes
tu rendis	vous rendîtes
il/elle/on rendit	ils/elles rendirent

For many verbs, the **passé simple** stems, and sometimes the endings, are irregular.

avoir: stem **e-**

j'eus	nous eûmes
tu eus	vous eûtes
il/elle eut	ils/elles eurent

être: stem **f-**

je fus	nous fûmes
tu fus	vous fûtes
il/elle fut	ils/elles furent

tenir: stem **tin-**

je tins	nous tînmes
tu tins	vous tîntes
il/elle tint	ils/elles tinrent

venir: stem **vin-**

je vins	nous vînmes
tu vins	vous vîntes
il/elle vint	ils/elles vinrent

A helpful pattern: Several verbs have **passé simple** stems in **-u-** that match their past participles.

infinitive	past participle	passé simple
connaître	connu	il/elle connut, ils/elles connurent
courir	couru	il/elle courut, ils/elles coururent
croire	cru	il/elle crut, ils/elles crurent
devoir	dû	il/elle dut, ils/elles durent
lire	lu	il/elle lut, ils/elles lurent
pouvoir	pu	il/elle put, ils/elles purent

Note the **passé simple** of **naître** and **mourir**. You will see these verbs often in historical and biographical texts.

naître	(né)	il/elle naquit, ils/elles naquirent
mourir	(mort)	il/elle mourut, ils/elles moururent

For these last verbs, we list just the third-person forms, singular and plural. These are the **passé simple** forms that you will see most often. Remember that the **passé simple** expresses past events in texts that are set off from the present and are archival in nature. These events are most often narrated in the third person.

The *passé simple* in narration

Like the **passé composé**, the **passé simple** is used with other tenses in narration. In the following text, verbs in the **passé simple** relate what happened (just like the **passé composé**), and verbs in the **imparfait** describe the characters and the background. See if you can read this story. We're sure you will recognize it.

BOUCLE D'OR ET LES TROIS OURS

Tout près de la forêt habitait une petite fille qui avait les cheveux si blonds et si bouclés qu'on l'appelait "Boucle d'Or".

Dans la forêt, près de la maison de Boucle d'Or, vivait une famille ours.

Il y avait le grand ours, le moyen ours et le petit ours.

Comme il faisait très beau ce jour là et parce que la soupe était bien trop chaude pour être mangée tout de suite, les trois ours décidèrent de faire une petite promenade en attendant que le déjeuner refroidisse un peu.

Ils sortirent donc tous les trois laissant derrière eux la porte de la maison entrouverte; ils ne craignaient pas les voleurs.

Boucle d'Or ce jour là avait aussi eu l'envie de se promener dans la forêt et, chemin faisant, elle arriva près de la maison des trois ours.

Elle frappa à la porte mais n'entendit aucune réponse.

Alors comme elle était bien curieuse de savoir qui pouvait vivre ici elle entra.

En arrivant dans la salle à manger elle remarqua sur la table trois bols de soupe.

Elle s'approcha du grand bol, celui du grand ours, goûta la soupe et la trouva bien trop chaude.

Elle s'approcha alors du moyen bol, celui du moyen ours, goûta la soupe et la trouva bien trop salée.

Elle s'approcha enfin du petit bol, celui du petit ours, goûta la soupe et la trouva tellement à son goût qu'elle la mangea jusqu'à la dernière goutte.

Ensuite elle voulut s'asseoir.

Elle s'assit sur la grande chaise, celle du grand ours, mais la trouva bien trop haute.

Elle s'assit sur la moyenne chaise, celle du moyen ours, mais la trouva trop bancale.

Elle s'assit alors sur la petite chaise, mais comme Boucle d'Or était trop lourde, elle la cassa.

"Ce n'est pas grave, se dit-elle, continuons la visite".

Elle vit alors un escalier au bout de la pièce et entreprit de le monter.

Arrivée en haut elle vit une grande chambre à coucher dans laquelle se trouvaient trois lits: un grand, un moyen et un petit.

Elle se coucha sur le grand lit, celui du grand ours évidemment, mais elle le trouva trop dur, alors elle se coucha sur le moyen lit, celui du moyen ours bien entendu, mais elle le trouva trop mou.

Enfin elle se coucha sur le petit lit, celui du petit ours, cela va de soi, et elle le trouva tout à fait comme il faut alors elle s'y endormit.

Les trois ours, comme ils avaient terminé leur petite promenade, rentrèrent à la maison.

Le grand ours
voyant son bol s'écria:
"quelqu'un a touché à ma soupe!!"

Le moyen ours
voyant son bol s'exclama:
"quelqu'un a touché à ma soupe!!"

Le petit ours
regardant son bol dit:
"quelqu'un a mangé toute ma soupe!!"

Le grand ours
avança dans la pièce et vit sa chaise:
"quelqu'un s'est assis sur ma chaise!!"

Le moyen ours,
s'avançant alors vers sa chaise affirma:
"quelqu'un s'est aussi assis sur ma chaise!!"

Et le petit ours,
comme il se doit, s'approchant à son tour pleurnicha:
"quelqu'un a cassé ma chaise!!"

D'un pas décidé le grand ours se dirigea vers l'escalier qu'il grimpa quatre à quatre suivi par le moyen ours et par le petit ours qui séchait ses larmes.

Le grand ours
une fois dans la chambre avança vers son lit:
"quelqu'un s'est couché sur mon lit!!"

Le moyen ours
s'approchant aussi dit :
"quelqu'un s'est couché également sur mon lit!!"

Et le petit ours
alors s'étonna:
"Il y a quelqu'un sur mon lit!!"

Boucle d'Or, réveillée par la voix des ours, ouvrit les yeux et vit les trois ours penchés au-dessus d'elle.

Elle eut très peur et, voyant la fenêtre ouverte, elle s'y précipita et sauta par dessus pour courir vite jusque chez elle!

Boucle d'Or et les trois ours comes from a collection of stories at www.momes.net and is reproduced here with the kind permission of www.Doctissimo.fr.

Practice with the *passé simple*

A. **Now that** you've read **Boucle d'Or et les trois ours,** underline in the text all the verbs you can find in the **passé simple.** Hint: We saw 53 verbs in the **passé simple.**

B. **Next, re-write** all of the sentences you found in the **passé simple,** using the **passé composé.** We've done the first three for you.

1. **Les trois ours <u>décidèrent</u> de faire une petite promenade.**

   Les trois ours <u>ont décidé</u> de faire une petite promenade.

2. **Ils <u>sortirent</u> donc tous les trois.**

   Ils <u>sont sortis</u> donc tous les trois.

3. **Elle <u>arriva</u> près de la maison des trois ours.**

   Elle <u>est arrivée</u> près de la maison des trois ours.

4. (Find the other verbs . . .)

C. **Passé composé au passé simple.** Rewrite the following sentences, changing the verbs in the **passé composé** to the **passé simple.**

Modèle: **Elle est allée au musée.**   *Elle alla au musée.*

1. **Les enfants ont eu peur.**

2. **Le messager est venu chez le roi.**

3. **Valmont et la Marquise de Merteuil ont lu beaucoup de lettres. Ils en ont beaucoup écrit aussi.**

4. **Albert Camus est né en 1913 et est mort en 1960.**

5. **La porte s'est ouverte et d'Artagnan et Porthos sont entrés.**

6. **Swann est tombé amoureux d'Odette.**

The *passé antérieur*

The **passé antérieur** is a literary tense that relates events that took place in the past before another past event. Its use is parallel to that of the **plus-que-parfait:**

Lorsque j'eus parcouru la note [. . .], je relus de bout en bout [. . .] les instructions du Conseil. (Julien Gracq, *Le rivage des Syrtes*)	When I had looked over the bill, I re-read the Council's instructions from top to bottom.
Après que Jacques fut reparti, je me suis agenouillé près d'Amélie. (André Gide, *La Symphonie Pastorale*)	After Jacques had departed, I knelt down next to Amélie.

The **passé antérieur** is a compound past tense that, like the **passé composé,** is formed with an auxiliary verb (**avoir** or **être**) and the past participle. The auxiliary verb is in the **passé simple.**

terminer (passé composé: j'ai terminé, etc.)

quand j'eus terminé	when I had finished
quand tu eus terminé	when you had finished
quand il/elle/on eut terminé	when he/she/one had finished; when we had finished
quand nous eûmes terminé	when we had finished
quand vous eûtes terminé	when you had finished
quand ils/elles eurent terminé	when they had finished

arriver (passé composé: je suis arrivé/arrivée, etc.)

quand je fus arrivé(e)	when I had arrived
quand tu fus arrivé(é)	when you had arrived
quand il/on fut arrivé	when he had arrived; when we had arrived
quand elle fut arrivée	when she had arrived
quand nous fûmes arrivé(e)s	when we had arrived
quand vous fûtes arrivé(e)(s)	when you had arrived
quand ils furent arrivés	when they had arrived
quand elles furent arrivées	when they had arrived

As in all compound tenses, the past participle in the **passé antérieur** agrees in gender and in number:

- with the subject of a verb conjugated with **être**
- with a preceding direct object of verbs conjugated with **avoir**
- with the reflexive pronoun (a preceding direct object) of pronominal verbs

Like the **passé simple**, the **passé antérieur** is used in archival writing: literature, children's stories and fairy tales, and historical documents of an official or formal nature. It is not used in journalism, in informal writing, or in conversation.

   The **passé antérieur** is often used in clauses beginning with **quand** (when), **lorsque** (when), **dès que** (as soon as), and **aussitôt que** (as soon as) to express an action that took place before another past action. Like the **passé simple**, it is usually found only in the third person. Here are some examples.

Quand les invités furent partis, Emma alla se coucher.	When the guests had left, Emma went to bed.
Lorsqu'elle eut lu la lettre, elle la déchira.	When she had read the letter, she tore it up.
Dès que Charles l'eut quittée, elle se mit à pleurer.	As soon as Charles had left her, she started to cry.
Aussitôt qu'il fut rentré, il se rendit compte de son erreur.	As soon as he had arrived home, he realized his mistake.

Practice with the *passé simple* and the *passé antérieur*

D. **Les Trois Mousquetaires.** Choose the correct verb forms to complete these sentences taken from **Les Trois Mousquetaires** by Alexandre Dumas (1802–1870). Translations are provided to help you.

1. **Les voisins [. . .] (refermèrent / eurent refermé) [les fenêtres] dès qu'ils (virent / eurent vu) s'enfuir les quatre hommes . . .** (p. 128)

   The neighbors closed their windows again as soon as they had seen the four men run away.

2. **D'Artagnan (offrit / eut offert) son bras à Mme Bonacieux, qui (s'y suspendit / s'y fut suspendue), moitié rieuse, moitié tremblante, et tous deux (gagnèrent / eurent gagné) le haut de la rue de La Harpe.** (p. 144)

   D'Artagnan offered his arm to Mme Bonacieux, who suspended herself from it, half laughing, half trembling, and the two of them reached the top of La Harpe Street.

3. **M. de Tréville (écouta / eut écouté) le récit du jeune homme avec une gravité qui prouvait qu'il voyait autre chose, dans toute cette aventure, qu'une intrigue d'amour; puis, quand d'Artagnan (acheva / eut achevé): «Hum!»** (p. 284)

   M. de Tréville listened to the young man's story with a gravity proving that he saw something in all this adventure other than a love affair; then, when d'Artagnan had finished: «Hum!»

4. **D'Artagnan (descendit / fut descendu) le premier . . .** (p. 289)

   D'Artagnan got down first . . .

5. **A peine Ketty (sortit-elle / fut-elle sortie), que d'Artagnan (se dirigea / se fut dirigé) vers la rue Férou.** (p. 398)

   Scarcely had Ketty left than d'Artagnan directed himself toward Férou Street.

6. **D'Artagnan (se leva / se fut levé) et (prit / eut pris) son chapeau; Milady lui (donna / eut donné) sa main à baiser.** (p. 407)

   D'Artagnan got up and took his hat; Milady gave him her hand to kiss.

7. **Athos (l'examina / l'eut examinée) et (devint / fut devenu) très pâle, puis il (l'essaya /l'eut essayée) à l'annulaire de sa main gauche . . .** (p. 411)

   Athos examined it and became very pale; then he tried it on the ring finger of his left hand . . .

8. **Milady lui (tendit / eut tendu) une main qu'il (baisa / eut baisé) tendrement.** (p. 422)

   Milady held out a hand to him, which he kissed tenderly.

9. **Il (traversa / eut traversé) la cour, (monta / eut monté) les deux étages d'Athos et (frappa / eut frappé) à la porte à tout rompre.** (p. 430)

   He crossed the courtyard, went up Athos's two flights of stairs, and knocked at the door as if to break it down.

[All citations from **Éditions Gallimard, Collections Folio Classique,** 1962.]

Part Three
The Future and Conditional Tenses

The Future and the Conditional: an Overview

What is the future tense?

In English, the future tense is expressed with the verb *will* in order to indicate something that will take place in time to come. In French, **le futur** is conjugated with endings added to the stem.

Demain, je téléphonerai à Marie.	Tomorrow, I will phone Mary.
Nous irons au Maroc dans deux ans.	We're going to Morocco in two years.

There is also a ***future perfect tense*** in both English and French (French: **le futur antérieur**) that is used to express something in the past, but from the point of view of some time in the future.

La semaine prochaine, ils seront déjà partis.	Next week, they will have already left.
Quand tu auras fini de manger, on ira au cinéma.	When you've finished eating, we'll go to the movies.

The **futur antérieur** is a compound tense made up of an auxiliary verb in the **futur** and the past participle of the verb.

What is the conditional?

In English, the conditional is expressed by the verb *would* in order to indicate something that would happen—under certain conditions. In French, **le conditionnel** is conjugated with endings added to the stem.

Je téléphonerais à Marie, mais je ne peux pas retrouver mon portable.	I would phone Mary, but I can't find my cell phone.
Nous irions volontiers au Maroc, mais nous n'avons pas d'argent.	We would gladly go to Morocco, but we don't have any money.

There is also a *past conditional tense* in English and French that is used to express something that would have happened in the past—under certain conditions.

J'aurais téléphoné à Marie, mais je ne pouvais pas retrouver mon portable.	I would have phoned Mary, but I couldn't find my cell phone.
Nous serions allés au Maroc, mais nous n'avions pas d'argent.	We would have gone to Morocco, but we didn't have any money.

This tense, **le conditionnel passé**, is also a compound tense made up of an auxiliary verb, this time in the **conditionnel**, and the past participle of the verb.

11
Le Futur

You can use the **futur** (the future tense) to express what you and others will do or what will happen.

Nous voyagerons en France pour apprendre le français.	We will travel to France in order to learn French.
Le Président parlera à la télé ce soir.	The president will speak on TV tonight.
La météo dit qu'il fera chaud demain.	The weather report says that it will be hot tomorrow.

To form the **futur**, add these endings to the **futur** stem of the verb:

-ai   -ons
-as   -ez
-a   -ont

The **futur** endings are always the same for all verbs. The **futur** stem of most verbs is identical to the infinitive. For **-re** verbs, drop the final **e** from the infinitive.

voyager	partir	dire [*futur* stem: dir-]
je voyagerai	**je partirai**	**je dirai**
tu voyageras	**tu partiras**	**tu diras**
il/elle/on voyagera	**il/elle partira**	**il/elle/on dira**
nous voyagerons	**nous partirons**	**nous dirons**
vous voyagerez	**vous partirez**	**vous direz**
ils/elles voyageront	**ils/elles partiront**	**ils/elles diront**

Regular **-er** verbs that have two stems in the present tense reflect these stem changes in the **futur**, as well. Note how in these verbs, the **futur** stem no longer looks like the infinitive, but like the changed stem—with a doubled consonant, **è** instead of **e**, or **i** instead of **y**.

acheter: *présent*	acheter: *futur*
j'achète	**j'achèterai**
tu achètes	**tu achèteras**
il/elle/on achète	**il/elle/on achètera**
nous achetons	**nous achèterons**
vous achetez	**vous achèterez**
ils/elles achètent	**ils/elles achèteront**

présent: changed stem with *je, tu,* *il/elle/on, ils/elles*	*futur:* always the same stem (the changed one)
appeler: j'appelle (doubled stem consonant)	**j'appellerai, nous appellerons**
jeter: je jette (doubled stem consonant)	**je jetterai, nous jetterons**
acheter: j'achète (stem vowel **e** becomes **è**)	**j'achèterai, nous achèterons**
se lever: je me lève (stem vowel **e** becomes **è**)	**je me lèverai, nous nous lèverons**
essayer: j'essaie (stem consonant **y** becomes **i**)	**j'essaierai, nous essaierons**
payer: je paie (stem consonant **y** becomes **i**)	**je paierai, nous paierons**

There is an exception to this pattern. Verbs with present stem vowels that change from **é** to **è** do *not* have this change in the **futur** stem. This is true for all verbs with present stem vowel **é**.

présent: changed stem with *je, tu,* *il/elle/on, ils/elles*	*futur:* the stem still looks like the infinitive (The stem vowel is always **é**.)
préférer: je préfère (stem vowel **é** becomes **è**)	**je préférerai, nous préférerons**
répéter: je répète (stem vowel **é** becomes **è**)	**je répéterai, nous répéterons**

Many verbs in French have **futur** stems that are irregular. Although irregular, many **futur** stems follow similar patterns, and all **futur** stems end in **r**—sometimes **rr**. Here are some irregular **futur** stems (most shown in the **je** form) that have similar patterns in their formation.

tenir	je tiendrai	pouvoir	je pourrai
venir	je viendrai	courir	je courrai
		mourir	je mourrai
voir	je verrai		
envoyer	j'enverrai	être	je serai
		faire	je ferai
avoir	j'aurai		
savoir	je saurai	aller	j'irai
devoir	je devrai	vouloir	je voudrai
recevoir	je recevrai	falloir	il faudra*
		valoir	il vaudra*

*Remember that **falloir** is always used in the third person: **il faut, il fallait, il faudra**. **Valoir** is usually used in the third person as well: **il vaut mieux, il valait mieux, il vaudra mieux**.

Expressing future events

Although the **futur** (the future tense) expresses what you and others will do and what will happen, remember that you can also use the **futur proche** to talk about things that are going to happen in the near or foreseeable future. The **futur proche** is formed with the present tense of the verb **avoir** and the infinitive. This tense is most often used in informal everyday conversation.

Nous allons voyager en France pour apprendre le français.	We're going to travel to France to learn French.
Le Président va parler à la télé ce soir.	The president is going to speak on TV tonight.
La météo dit qu'il va faire chaud demain.	The weather report says that it's going to be hot tomorrow.

You can also use just the **présent** to talk about something that is expected to happen fairly soon or in the foreseeable future. In this case, the future may be shown with an expression of time: **tout de suite**, **dans quelques minutes**, **demain**, **cet été**, etc. Sometimes, the context of the sentence hints at the future.

Attends; j'arrive!	Wait; I'll be right there!
Elle revient demain matin.	She'll be back tomorrow morning.
On va en Europe cet été.	We're going to Europe this summer.

In clauses beginning with **quand** or **lorsque** (when) and **aussitôt que** or **dès que** (as soon as), the **futur** is used in French when the sentence expresses a future action or idea. This construction is more specific than in English, in which the *present* tense is used, even for actions in the *future*, in clauses with *when* and *as soon as*.

Quand tu *arriveras* [futur] à la maison, donne-moi un coup de fil sur mon portable.	When you *get* home [present], give me a call on my cell phone.
Je paierai cette facture dès que je le *pourrai* [futur].	I'll pay this bill as soon as I *can* [present].

The **futur** may be used instead of the **impératif** (see Chapter 19) to give an instruction or an order.

Pour demain, vous lirez les pages 10 à 25.	For tomorrow, you will read pages 10 to 25.
Tu ne tueras point.	Thou shalt not kill.

Using the *futur*

Perspective personnelle

Vrai ou faux? Indicate whether each sentence is true (**vrai**) or false (**faux**) for you. Remember to read each sentence aloud for practice.

______ **J'irai à Paris la semaine prochaine.**
______ **Dans dix ans, j'aurai des enfants.**
______ **Ce soir, mon ami et moi, nous irons au théâtre.**
______ **Quand j'aurai 70 ans, je ne travaillerai plus.**
______ **Je monterai la Tour Eiffel un jour.**

A. Un nouveau travail. Marc is starting a new job today. Using the expressions below and the **futur**, write a paragraph describing what he will do on this first day of work.

se réveiller de bonne heure   se doucher

se brosser les dents   mettre un nouveau costume

prendre un bon petit déjeuner   boire un café

acheter le journal   lire le journal

attendre le bus   arriver au bureau

être un peu nerveux   saluer son patron

sourire à ses collègues   commencer à travailler

Marc se réveillera de bonne heure. Il _____

_____

_____

_____

_____

_____

B. Votre futur. An old friend of the family is concerned about your future. Write complete answers to his questions below. Then, after you finish, read your answers aloud for practice speaking.

Dans 20 ans . . .

1. **Où vivras-tu?**

   _____

2. **Seras-tu marié(e)?**

   _____

3. **Auras-tu des animaux familiers ou des enfants?**

   _____

4. **Feras-tu la cuisine, or mangerez-vous au restaurant?**

   _____

5. **Quel sera ton travail?**

   _____

6. **Qu'est-ce que tu feras le weekend?**

   _____

C. La voyante. You and your friends visit a fortune teller (**une voyante**) for fun. While you are waiting, you hear what she says to the people ahead of you. Write what you hear. (Remember! She'll always use the **vous** form of the **futur**.) After writing, practice speaking by reading the predictions aloud with an ominous tone!

Modèle: recevoir le Prix Nobel   **Vous recevrez le Prix Nobel.**

1. **vivre à Tahiti** _____

2. **devenir astronaute** _____

3. avoir 100 chats _____

4. découvrir un remède pour le SIDA (AIDS) _____

5. aller en prison _____

6. se marier 5 fois _____

7. être millionnaire _____

8. tomber amoureux/euse d'un pingouin _____

9. mourir à l'âge de 120 ans _____

10. s'intéresser à la religion des éléphants _____

11. posséder un avion (plane) _____

12. essayer de monter le mont Everest _____

13. vendre des vidéos illégales _____

14. étudier la philosophie chinoise _____

15. détenir le record du saut en longueur (hold the record for the long jump) _____

D. Quelles vacances? You are trying to choose between two organized trips. Complete each paragraph with verbs from the list above it (in the **futur**). For each blank, choose the verb that makes the most sense, and conjugate it to agree with the subject. When you've completed each paragraph, read it aloud! Then decide which trip you will choose and why!

aller	dormir	être	faire
voir	partir	falloir	détester
recevoir	découvrir	boire	devoir

Ce voyage _____[1] de Los Angeles le 10 juin. Nous _____[2] en Afrique où nous _____[3] un safari. Nous _____[4] beaucoup d'animaux sauvages. Nous _____[5] sous la belle étoile (outdoors) et nous _____[6] le Sahara. Il _____[7] apporter des vêtements très légers et on ne _____[8] pas oublier son chapeau.

passer	faire	vouloir	souffler
neiger	prendre	quitter	pouvoir
danser	avoir	manger	tomber
briller	nager	se détendre	partir

Pour ce voyage, nous _____[9] en croisière. Le bateau _____[10] le port de New York le 23 janvier. Il _____[11] peut-être à New York ce jour-là, mais il _____[12] un temps splendide aux îles Caraïbes. Le soleil _____[13] et un vent léger _____[14]. Les voyageurs _____[15] leur temps à bord comme ils _____[16] : ils _____[17] dans les trois piscines, ils _____[18] des bains de soleil, ils _____[19] des fruits frais, ou ils _____[20] à la discothèque. Aux escales (ports of call), les touristes _____[21] explorer et faire des achats. Il y _____[22] un spectacle chaque soir après le dîner.

23. **Quel voyage choisirez-vous? Pourquoi?**

_____

_____

E. Change each sentence from présent to futur.

Modèle: Je vais en France.   →   J'irai en France.

1. **Il y a un bon film au cinéma.**

_____

2. **Tu sais toutes les réponses.**

_____

3. **Nous venons d'Europe.**

_____

4. **Préférez-vous habiter à Madrid ou à Paris?**

_____

5. **Bernard nettoie la maison pour ses parents.**

_____

6. **En mangeant trop de chocolat, tu grossis.**

_____

7. **Je suis têtue.**

_____

8. **Vous adorez la maison des Caillebotte.**

_____

F. **Des commandes.** Change each command to a more polite request using the **futur**. Remember that, with the **futur**, you will use a subject pronoun (**tu** or **vous**).

Modèle: Mets le rôti au four à 4h30.   →   Tu mettras le rôti au four à 4h30.

1. **Ne porte pas cette veste démodée.**

_____

2. **Faites votre lit avant de partir.**

_____

3. **Mangez vos petits pois.**

_____

4. **Sois sage!**

_____

5. **N'ouvre la porte pour personne.**

_____

6. **Ne vous disputez pas.**

_____

G. **Vos projets.** Tell about your plans for the future by completing the following sentences. Remember that (unlike in English), the **futur** is used after the expressions **quand**, **lorsque**, **dès que**, and **aussitôt que**. Choose from the verbs listed below.

trouver	être	avoir
se marier	voyager	travailler
aller	lire	acheter
se coucher	préparer	prendre

Modèle: **Quand je terminerai mes études à l'université, je trouverai un travail à Paris.**

1. **Lorsque je comprendrai bien le français,** _____

2. **Aussitôt que je gagnerai à la loterie,** _____

3. **Quand j'arriverai chez moi ce soir,** _____

4. **Dès que je pourrai,** _____

5. **Quand j'aurai 50 ans,** _____

Les mots croisés 11

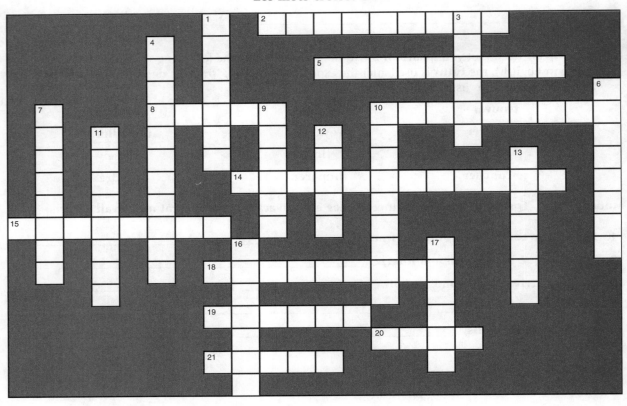

Complete the crossword puzzle with the **futur**.

Horizontal

2	You will buy: **Tu** ___
5	They will sleep: **Elles** ___
8	**faire: tu**
10	I will sing: **Je/J'**___
14	You will work: **Vous** ___
15	**mourir: nous**
18	**se moquer: elle**
19	**voir: je**
20	**être: on**
21	**aller: nous**

Vertical

1	**vouloir: je**
3	We will have: **Nous** ___
4	**préférer: ils**
6	**venir: vous**
7	We will finish: **Nous** ___
9	**savoir: tu**
10	You will choose: **Vous** ___
11	**pouvoir: elles**
12	**devoir: on**
13	**s'en aller: je**
16	**recevoir: elle**
17	It will be necessary: **Il** ___

12
Le Futur Antérieur

The **futur antérieur**, or future perfect tense, expresses, as in English, what will have (already) happened at some point in the future or when another future action or event takes place.

J'aurai terminé ma rédaction avant la fin de la semaine.	I will have finished my composition before the end of the week.
Quand tu arriveras, nous serons déjà partis en vacances.	When you arrive, we will have already left for vacation.

A verb in the **futur antérieur** expresses something that will have happened before the main event or state (also in the future): I will have finished my composition before the end of the week; we will already have left for vacation when you arrive. Verbs in the **futur antérieur** are expressed in English with the auxiliary verb *will have: will have finished, will have left.*

How to form the *futur antérieur*

The **futur antérieur** is a compound tense (like the **passé composé**). The auxiliary verb is stated in the **futur** tense.

an **avoir** verb: **parler**

j'aurai parlé	I will have spoken
tu auras parlé	you will have spoken
il/elle/on aura parlé	he/she/one will have spoken; we will have spoken
nous aurons parlé	we will have spoken
vous aurez parlé	you will have spoken
ils/elles auront parlé	they will have spoken

an **être** verb: **partir**

je serai parti/partie	I will have left
tu seras parti/partie	you will have left
il sera parti	he will have left
elle sera partie	she will have left
on sera parti	one will have left; we will have left
nous serons partis/parties	we will have left
vous serez parti/partie/partis/parties	you will have left
ils seront partis	they will have left
elles seront parties	they will have left

a pronominal verb: **se lever**

je me serai levé(e)	I will have gotten up
tu te seras levé(e)	you will have gotten up
il se sera levé	he will have gotten up
elle se sera levée	she will have gotten up
on se sera levé	one will have gotten up
nous nous serons levé(e)s	we will have gotten up
vous vous serez levé(e)(s)	you will have gotten up
ils se seront levés	they will have gotten up
elles se seront levées	they will have gotten up

As in all compound tenses, the past participle in the **futur antérieur** agrees in gender and in number:

- with the subject of a verb conjugated with **être**

- with a preceding direct object of verbs conjugated with **avoir**

- with the reflexive pronoun (a preceding direct object) of pronominal verbs.

More contexts for the *futur antérieur*

As we saw in Chapter 11, in clauses beginning with **quand** or **lorsque** (when) and **aussitôt que** or **dès que** (as soon as), the **futur** is used in French when the sentence expresses a future action or idea. Remember that the present tense is used in English in this context. This rule applies, as well, to the **futur antérieur**, which we use with **quand** or **lorsque** and **aussitôt que** or **dès que** for events that will have taken place before the main future action of the sentence. As you see in the examples below, the present perfect tense is used in English in clauses with *when* and *as soon as*.

Dès que tu auras fini tes devoirs, allons prendre un café.	As soon as you've finished your homework, let's go out for coffee.
Lorsque Paul se sera rendu compte de son erreur, il fera tout ce qu'il pourra pour la corriger.	When Paul has realized his mistake, he will do everything he can to correct it.

Occasionally, the **futur antérieur** can express that something probably happened *in the past*! The context will make this clear. Be sure not to translate with the future perfect.

—**Jean n'a pas payé l'électricité.**	Jean hasn't paid the electric bill.
Ah, il aura oublié.	Oh, he probably forgot.

Remember that the usual way to say that something probably happened is to use the **passé composé** of **devoir**:

—**Ah, il a dû oublier.**	Oh, he must have forgotten.

Using the *futur antérieur*

Perspective personnelle

Vrai ou faux? Indicate whether each sentence is true (**vrai**) or false (**faux**) for you. Remember to read each sentence aloud for practice.

Quand j'aurai 80 ans . . .

_____ j'aurai voyagé en Asie.

_____ j'aurai mangé des escargots (snails).

_____ je serai marié(e) trois fois.

_____ je serai monté(e) dans un hélicoptère.

_____ j'aurai fêté mon anniversaire avec une personne célèbre.

_____ je serai allé(e) en haut de (to the top of) la Tour Eiffel.

A. **Avant la soirée.** You are a guest in the home of a French-speaking family. Tonight, they are hosting a party in your honor. Using the verbs given and the **futur antérieur**, describe what the people below *will have done* before the guests arrive.

Modèle: M. et Mme Martin: inviter des amis
                 M. et Mme Martin auront invité des amis.

1. Mme Martin: lire la recette pour le plat principal

   _____

2. Mme Martin et Paul: aller au marché

   _____

3. M. Martin: choisir le vin

   _____

4. Paul: acheter un gâteau

   _____

5. on: nettoyer la maison

   _____

6. les enfants: ranger leurs jouets

   _____

7. Nadine: mettre la table

   _____

8. moi: se doucher

   _____

9. les Martin et moi: s'habiller élégamment

   _____

10. Mme Martin: se maquiller

    _____

B. **Now, write sentences of your own!** The party (from Exercise A) is now in full swing. Using the verbs given and the **futur antérieur**, describe what some people *will have done* before the end of the party. For each box, create two sentences by choosing one expression from each column and conjugating the verb accordingly. Read your sentences aloud for practice.

le chien **Mme Martin** **nous**	**répondre à la sonnette** (doorbell) **aboyer aux invités** **recevoir des fleurs** (flowers)

1. _____

   _____

vous **les invités** **tu**	**arriver** **prendre l'apéritif** **manger**

2. _____

   _____

nous **je** **on**	**boire du vin** **rire** **s'amuser**

3. _____

   _____

les enfants **je** **Élise**	**danser** **s'ennuyer** **raconter des histoires**

4. _____

   _____

Patrick **mes amis** **Nadine**	**dire au revoir** **partir avec une nouvelle amie** **faire une gaffe** (to make a faux pas)

5. _____

   _____

C. Avant les vacances. The Maigret family (from Québec) is going on vacation in Spain next month. There are many things still left to do, but they will all be done before the family leaves. Complete the paragraphs using appropriate verbs from the list conjugated in the **futur antérieur**.

réserver	trouver	feuilleter
apprendre	obtenir	faire
acheter	dire	aller

Tout le monde _____¹ beaucoup d'effort pour préparer le voyage. M. Maigret _____² à l'agence de voyage et _____³ les billets d'avion. Jean-Philippe et Marina _____⁴ les sites à visiter en recherchant sur l'Internet. Mme Maigret _____⁵ un hôtel. Comme Gisèle, la plus jeune, n'a jamais voyagé à l'étranger (abroad), sa mère _____⁶ un passeport pour elle. Les enfants et les parents _____⁷ quelques mots d'espagnol et _____⁸ des livres sur l'Espagne à la librairie.

avoir du mal (to have a hard time)	partir	sortir
être	faire	prendre

Avant de se coucher la veille (the day before) de leur départ, les parents _____⁹ les valises et les enfants _____¹⁰ du mal à se calmer. Marina _____¹¹ avec son copain une dernière fois pour dire au revoir.

appeler	boire	se coucher	se réveiller
partir	prendre	dire	entrer

Le jour du voyage, avant d'arriver à l'aéroport, les filles _____¹² très tôt. Toute la famille _____¹³ le petit déjeuner et Jean-Philippe _____¹⁴ au revoir au chien. Ils _____¹⁵ un taxi et ils _____¹⁶.

D. Avant de dormir demain. Using at least five verbs from this list, explain what you will have done before going to sleep tomorrow night. Remember to use the **futur antérieur**. You may need to add words following the verb to complete your sentences.

Modèle: *J'aurai regardé la télé.*

regarder	s'amuser	lire	manger
aller	acheter	se brosser les dents	finir
se doucher	prendre	écrire	sortir
recevoir	faire		

1. _____

2. _____

3. _____

4. _____

5. _____

E. Un gâteau spécial. Jeannine wants to prepare a cake for her husband's birthday. She looks on the internet (www.baycriscuisine.com) and finds the recipe below. Complete the paragraphs below the recipe to describe how she will make the cake. Refer to the recipe to find the appropriate verbs. You will need to use both the **futur** *and* the **futur antérieur**. We have filled in the first few blanks for you.

Gâteau coeur (heart-shaped cake) :

3 oeufs (eggs)
150 g de farine (flour)
150 g de beurre (butter)
150 g de sucre en poudre (granulated sugar)
le zeste râpé d'un citron (grated lemon zest)
2 sachets (packets) **de sucre vanillé** (vanilla sugar)
40 g de sucre glace (confectioners' sugar)
30 cl de crème fraîche liquide (fresh cream)

pour le décor:
300 g de fraises (strawberries)
2 cuillères à soupe (tablespoons) **de noix de coco en poudre** (powdered coconut)
Petits décors en sucre (au rayon des produits pour la pâtisserie des magasins d'alimentation)
Recettes Gâteau coeur :

* **Faites fondre le beurre dans une petite casserole** (saucepan).
Préchauffez le four thermostat 6 (180°C).
Cassez les oeufs.
Séparez les jaunes des blancs.
Mélangez les jaunes avec le sucre en poudre.
Ajoutez à cette préparation le zeste d'un citron très finement râpé, puis, tout en mélangeant, le beurre fondu et refroidi pour obtenir une préparation onctueuse et lisse.
Tamisez (sift) **la farine et incorporez-la à ce mélange.**

* **Battez** (beat) **les blancs d'oeufs en neige très ferme et incorporez-les délicatement à la pâte** (batter).
Versez (pour) **cette préparation dans le moule** (mold) **et enfournez** (put in oven) **pendant 45 minutes.**
Eteignez (turn off) **et laissez le gâteau reposer 5 minutes dans le four avant de le démouler** (take out of mold).

* **Pendant la cuisson, préparez un chantilly bien ferme en fouettant** (whipping) **la crème fraîche avec le sucre vanillé.**
Ajoutez, en cours de préparation, le sucre glace.
Décorez le gâteau de coco en poudre et placez dessus les petits sujets en sucre.
Posez (put) **le gâteau sur un plat et disposez autour les fraises découpées en tranches** (sliced).
Servez, en accompagnement, la crème chantilly.

The recipe for *Gateau coeur* is reproduced with the kind permission of BaycrisCuisine (www. baycriscuisine.com).

Jeannine *fera* fondre[1] le beurre.

Quand elle *aura fondu* le beurre, elle *préchauffera* le four.

---

[1] See Chapter 20 for an explanation of the **faire causatif** construction.

Aussitôt qu'elle *aura préchauffé* le four, elle *cassera* les œufs.

1. Dès qu'elle _____ les œufs, elle _____ les jaunes des blancs.

2. Lorsqu'elle _____ les jaunes des blancs, elle _____ les jaunes avec le sucre en poudre.

3. Quand elle _____ les jaunes avec le sucre en poudre, elle _____ le zeste du citron et le beurre fondu.

4. Aussitôt qu'elle _____ ces ingrédients, elle _____ la farine.

5. Lorsqu'elle _____ la farine, elle l'_____ au mélange.

6. Jeannine _____ les blancs d'œufs en neige.

7. Dès qu'elle _____ les œufs, elle les _____ à la pâte.

8. Quand elle _____ les œufs, elle _____ cette préparation dans le moule.

9. Aussitôt qu'elle _____ la préparation dans le moule, elle l'_____ .

10. Elle _____ le four après 45 minutes et elle _____ reposer le gâteau dans le four pendant 5 minutes.

11. Quand le gâteau sera reposé, elle le _____ .

12. Pendant la cuisson, Jeannine _____ un chantilly.

13. Après la cuisson, Jeannine _____ le gâteau de coco en poudre.

14. Quand elle l'_____ de coco en poudre, elle _____ dessus les petits sujets en sucre.

15. Dès qu'elle _____ les petits sujets en sucre, elle _____ le gâteau sur un plat.

16. Lorsqu'elle _____ le gâteau sur un plat, elle _____ autour les fraises découpées en tranches.

17. Quand elle _____ les fraises, elle _____ le gâteau! Bon appétit!

Les mots croisés 12

Use the **futur antérieur** of the verbs in parentheses to complete the crossword puzzle.

Horizontal

1   En 2012, vous ___ (passer) huit ans à étudier le français.

4   Aussitôt que Maman ___ (s'endormir), moi et mon frère nous relèverons pour regarder la télé.

6   Si vous continuez avec ce régime, vous ___ (perdre) 10 kilos avant Noël.

9   Si nous ne nous dépêchons pas, le train ___ (partir) quand nous arriverons à la gare.

10   Le médecin dit que la vieille dame ___ (mourir) avant la fin du mois.

11   Ils ___ (commencer) la réunion quand j'arriverai.

12   Je prédis (predict) qu'Odette et Adam ___ (se marier) avant la fin de l'année.

Vertical

2   Quand tu rentreras, je/j'___ (finir) de dîner.

3   Lorsque vous reviendrez pour acheter cette chemise, on l'___ déjà ___ (vendre).

4   Quand Marie et Bertrande ___ (revenir) du supermarché, elles prépareront le dîner.

5   Dès que tu ___ (faire) la vaisselle, nous pourrons sortir.

7   Au mois de mai, je/j'___ (terminer) mes études.

8   Avant le mois de novembre, il ___ (y avoir) plusieurs ouragans dans l'Atlantique.

13
Le Conditionnel

The **conditionnel**, or more precisely **le conditionnel présent** (the present conditional), expresses what would happen under certain conditions or if specific events occurred. The **conditionnel** is also used to report what people said or thought would happen, as well as to express wishes and requests.

Gagner à la loterie? Ce serait super!	Winning the lottery? That would be great!
Si tu étais riche, qu'est-ce que tu ferais?	If you were rich, what would you do?
La prof a dit qu'elle arriverait en retard.	The teacher said she would arrive late.
Je voudrais un Perrier, s'il vous plaît.	I would like a Perrier, please.

Verbs in the **conditionnel** always have the same stem as verbs in the **futur**. The verb is conjugated with the **conditionnel** endings:

-ais	-ions
-ais	-iez
-ait	-aient

The **conditionnel** endings are the same as the **imparfait** endings, and they are always the same for all verbs—but be sure to attach them to the **futur** stem. As we saw in the previous chapter, the **futur** stem of most verbs, as well as the **conditionnel** stem, is identical to the infinitive. For -**re** verbs, drop the final **e** from the infinitive.

voyager	partir	dire [*conditionnel* stem: dir-]
je voyagerais	je partirais	je dirais
tu voyagerais	tu partirais	tu dirais
il/elle/on voyagerait	il/elle partirait	il/elle/on dirait
nous voyagerions	nous partirions	nous dirions
vous voyageriez	vous partiriez	vous diriez
ils/elles voyageraient	ils/elles partiraient	ils/elles diraient

Regular -**er** verbs that have two stems in the present tense reflect these stem changes in the **conditionnel**, also. As we saw with the **futur**, the **conditionnel** stem no longer looks like the infinitive, but like the changed stem—with a doubled consonant, **è** instead of **e**, or **i** instead of **y**.

acheter: présent	acheter: conditionnel
j'achète	j'achèterais
tu achètes	tu achèterais
il/elle/on achète	il/elle/on achèterait
nous achetons	nous achèterions
vous achetez	vous achèteriez
ils/elles achètent	ils/elles achèteraient

present tense: changed stem with *je, tu, il/elle/on, ils/elles*	conditionnel: always the same stem (the changed one)
appeler: j'appelle (doubled stem consonant)	**j'appellerais, nous appellerions**
jeter: je jette (doubled stem consonant)	**je jetterais, nous jetterions**
acheter: j'achète (stem vowel e becomes è)	**j'achèterais, nous achèterions**
se lever: je me lève (stem vowel e becomes è)	**je me lèverais, nous nous lèverions**
essayer: j'essaie (stem consonant y becomes i)	**j'essaierais, nous essaierions**
payer: je paie (stem consonant y becomes i)	**je paierais, nous paierions**

As in the **futur**, there is an exception to this pattern. Verbs with present stem vowels that change from **é** to **è** do not make this change in the **conditionnel** stem. This is true for all verbs with present stem vowel **é**.

présent: changed stem with *je, tu, il/elle/on, ils/elles*	conditionnel: **The stem still looks like the infinitive (the stem vowel is always é).**
préférer: je préfère (stem vowel é becomes è)	**je préférerais, nous préférerions**
répéter: je répète (stem vowel é becomes è)	**je répéterais, nous répéterions**

The irregular **futur** stems now reappear as the same irregular **conditionnel** stems. Here they are again in the **je** forms of the verbs, grouped together to show some similar patterns in their formation.

tenir	je tiendrais	pouvoir	je pourrais
venir	je viendrais	courir	je courrais
		mourir	je mourrais
voir	je verrais		
envoyer	j'enverrais	être	je serais
		faire	je ferais
avoir	j'aurais		
savoir	je saurais	aller	j'irais
devoir	je devrais	vouloir	je voudrais
recevoir	je recevrais	falloir	il faudrait*
		valoir	il vaudrait*

*Remember that **falloir** is always used in the third person: **il faut, il fallait, il faudra, il faudrait**. **Valoir** is usually used in the third person, as well: **il vaut mieux, il valait mieux, il vaudra mieux, il vaudrait mieux**.

Using the *conditionnel*

Perspective personnelle

Vrai ou faux? Indicate whether each sentence is true (**vrai**) or false (**faux**) for you. Remember to read each sentence aloud for practice.

_____ Si j'avais le temps, j'apprendrais à jouer du violon.

_____ Si j'avais plus d'argent, j'enverrais de l'argent aux victimes des catastrophes.

_____ Ma mère m'a dit qu'elle m'aimerait toujours.

_____ Mes amis et moi, nous serions de bons diplomates.

_____ Je voudrais une bière.

A. **What is the correct form?** Conjugate the verb in parentheses in the **conditionnel** so that it agrees with the subject. Then read the completed sentence aloud.

1. Ma mère _____ (voyager) en Égypte si elle pouvait.

2. Si j'avais six ans, je _____ (essayer) d'apprendre une langue étrangère.

3. Guillaume a dit qu'il _____ (travailler) en Pologne l'année suivante.

4. Nous _____ (aimer) avoir un pied-à-terre à Paris.

5. Qu'est-ce que vous _____ (vouloir) boire?

6. Si tu avais ton propre avion, où _____ (aller)-tu?

Expressing events in the *conditionnel*

There are three common ways in which the **conditionnel** is used. The first is to express things that would happen under certain conditions. The conditions may be implied in the context, but are often expressed with a **si** clause with its verb in the **imparfait**. For more on **si** clauses and conditional sentences, see Chapter 15.

Si tu visitais Paris, qu'est-ce que tu ferais?	If you went to Paris, what would you do?
Je visiterais tous les musées, je me promènerais aux Champs-Elysées, et je mangerais à tous les grands restaurants.	I would go to all the museums, walk down the Champs-Elysées, and eat at all the fine restaurants.
Je ne mangerais pas chez MacDo.	I wouldn't eat at McDonald's.

Using the *conditionnel*: what if . . . ?

B. **Quel verbe?** Complete each sentence with the **conditionnel** form of an appropriate verb from the list.

manger	pouvoir	faire
avoir	aller	être
acheter	vouloir	rester

1. Si nous étions plus intelligents, nous _____ devenir médecins.

2. Jacques et Claudie ne/n'_____ probablement pas de voiture s'ils habitaient à Paris.

3. **Si je ne voulais pas perdre des kilos, je** _____ **plus de desserts.**

4. **Que** _____ **-vous si vous aviez plus de temps libre?**

5. **Si ton mari avait une maîtresse,** _____ **-tu avec lui?**

6. **Si vous pouviez voler (fly), où** _____ **-vous?**

C. Que feriez-vous? Complete the following sentences to indicate what you would do in the following circumstances. Choose a different verb for those in each sentence. Don't forget to use the **conditionnel**.

acheter	apprendre	voyager
aller	trouver	être
travailler	écrire	habiter
offrir	envoyer	quitter
partir	essayer	sortir

1. **Si je gagnais à la loterie, je/j'** . . .

    _____

2. **Si j'étais marié(e) / célibataire, je/j'** . . .

    _____

3. **Si j'habitais en France, je/j'** . . .

    _____

4. **Si mes collègues n'étaient pas gentils, ils** . . .

    _____

5. **Si mon patron m'appréciait plus, il** . . .

    _____

6. **Si j'avais plus de temps libre, je/j'** . . .

    _____

The **conditionnel** is often used to express requests and to make suggestions. Verbs used in the **conditionnel** make the request or suggestion more tactful and polite than a direct statement in the present tense.

Je voudrais vous parler de mon examen.	I would like to speak with you about my exam.
Pourriez-vous m'aider avec cet exercice?	Could you help me with this exercise?
Il faudrait faire un peu plus d'effort.	You should try a little harder.

D. Plus poli? Change the following sentences into more polite requests by using the **conditionnel**.

Modèle: Peux-tu m'aider?   →   *Pourrais-tu m'aider?*

1. Je veux un sandwich au jambon et une bière.

   _____

2. Mon ami veut un croque-monsieur et un verre de rouge.

   _____

3. Nous voulons de l'eau.

   _____

4. Pouvez-vous me dire où sont les toilettes?

   _____

5. Il faut étudier plus.

   _____

6. Peux-tu m'emprunter (to loan) un peu d'argent?

   _____

As in English, use the **conditionnel** to express what someone stated, thought, hoped, or decided (in the past) would happen (in the future).

Marianne a dit qu'elle ferait ses devoirs après le dîner.	Marianne said that she would do her homework after dinner.
Luc pensait que tu sortirais avec lui.	Luc thought that you would go out with him.
Le prof a décidé qu'il n'y aurait plus d'examens.	The prof decided that there would be no more exams.

E. Qu'est-ce qu'il a dit? You have a nasty habit of eavesdropping. Report what people said to a gossip-loving friend.

Modèle: Sandrine: "Je serai journaliste."
               Sandrine a dit qu'elle serait journaliste.

1. Yves: "Je pars en Hongrie mardi."

   _____

2. Mme Riband: "Je ne vais pas au mariage de Julien."

   _____

3. Thomas: "Quentin ne sortira pas avec Gilberte."

   _____

4. Alice: "Il fera beau demain."

_____

5. M. Menant: "Il y aura un examen vendredi."

_____

6. Patrice: "Jules ne sera jamais professeur."

_____

In addition to these uses, you will find the **conditionnel** in journalism, relating facts or events that are reported, but may not have been confirmed. Be sure not to translate these as conditional sentences with "would" in English.

Dans l'accident de ce matin, il y aurait deux morts et plusieurs blessés.	There were [reportedly] two people killed and several injured in this morning's accident.
Selon les études, les routes deviendraient de plus en plus dangereuses.	According to studies, the highways are becoming more and more dangerous.

F. **A la une (On the front page).** You are a newspaper editor. The following information has not yet been confirmed. Indicate this by changing the verbs to the **conditionnel**.

Modèle: Le Président voyage en Israël cette semaine.
                 Le Président voyagerait en Israël cette semaine.

1. **Il y a une bombe à l'intérieur du Palais royal.**

_____

2. **Les manifestants sont prêts à aller en prison.**

_____

3. **Le chocolat est bon pour la santé.**

_____

4. **Les employés de la RATP[1] font grève.**

_____

5. **Céline Dion a un nouveau bébé.**

_____

6. **Les soldats sont mécontents (discontented) des conditions de guerre.**

_____

---

[1] La RATP is the **Régie autonome des transports parisiens**, the national company responsible for public transportation in and around Paris (métro, bus).

Reviewing the *conditionnel*

G. Quel verbe? Choose the best verb for each sentence, and conjugate it in the **conditionnel**.

se nettoyer	parler	vouloir
aimer	avoir	aller

1. Rachel _____ acheter un nouvel ordinateur.

2. Si mes parents habitaient au Maroc, je/j'_____ des vacances plus intéressantes.

3. Rémy a décidé qu'il ne/n'_____ pas au bal sans Béatrice.

4. Nous _____ mieux le français si nous habitions en France!

5. Qu'est-ce que vous _____ manger?

6. Dans un journal: "La nouvelle voiture de Peugeot _____ automatiquement."

H. Questions personnelles. Répondez en phrases complètes.

1. Que feriez-vous si vous pouviez choisir n'importe quelle profession?

   _____

2. Imaginez que vous êtes dans un café parisien. Que dites-vous pour commander?

   _____

3. Comment est-ce que votre vie serait différente si vous habitiez dans un autre pays?

   _____

   _____

Les mots croisés 13

Use the **conditionnel** to complete the crossword puzzle.

Horizontal

4   **Ils ___ (préférer) rester à la maison.**

7   You should use the computer: **Vous ___ vous servir de l'ordinateur.**

11   I would see the Eiffel Tower: **Je/J' ___ la Tour Eiffel.**

13   They would eat oysters: **Ils ___ des huîtres.**

14   You would buy oranges: **Tu ___ des oranges.**

15   **Qu'est-ce que tu ___ (faire) si tu avais un million d'euros?**

16   We would receive many letters: **Nous ___ beaucoup de lettres.**

Vertical

1   **La vie ne ___ (être) pas très intéressante sans amour.**

2   **Nous ___ (vendre) nos actions si nous avions besoin d'argent.**

3   **Il ___ (voyager) en Italie s'il avait le temps et l'argent.**

5   **Si vous saviez toute l'histoire, vous ___ (rire).**

6   **Est-ce que Vincent ___ (venir) si Laure ne venait pas?**

8   You would want some water: **Vous ___ de l'eau.**

9   **Si tu savais faire la cuisine, tu ___ (pouvoir) économiser beaucoup d'argent.**

10   **Je/J' ___ (jouer) au football si j'étais plus en forme.**

12   She would go to India: **Elle ___ en Inde.**

14
Le Conditionnel Passé

The **conditionnel passé**, or past conditional tense, expresses what would have happened (but didn't) or how things would have been (but weren't).

A ta place, je n'aurais jamais fait cela!	I would never have done that if I were you!
Ces exercices auraient été plus faciles à faire avec un dictionnaire.	These exercises would have been easier to do with a dictionary.
Nous serions arrivés à 15.00 heures si le train était parti à l'heure.	We would have arrived at 3:00 if the train had left on time.

As you see in the last example, when there is an "if" clause, its verb is in the **plus-que-parfait (si le train était parti)**. We will tell you about how this works in the following chapter on conditional sentences.

How to form the *conditionnel passé*

The **conditionnel passé** is a compound tense like the **passé composé**. The auxiliary verb is in the **conditionnel**.

an **avoir** verb: **parler**

j'aurais parlé	I would have spoken
tu aurais parlé	you would have spoken
il/elle/on aurait parlé	he/she/one would have spoken; we would have spoken
nous aurions parlé	we would have spoken
vous auriez parlé	you would have spoken
ils/elles auraient parlé	they would have spoken

an **être** verb: **partir**

je serais parti(e)	I would have left
tu serais parti(e)	you would have left
il serait parti	he would have left
elle serait partie	she would have left
on serait parti	one would have left; we would have left
nous serions parti(e)s	we would have left
vous seriez parti(e)(s)	you would have left
ils seraient partis	they would have left
elles seraient parties	they would have left

a pronominal verb: **se lever**

je me serais levé(e)	I would have gotten up
tu te serais levé(e)	you would have gotten up
il se serait levé	he would have gotten up
elle se serait levée	she would have gotten up
on se serait levé	one would have gotten up; we would have gotten up
nous nous serions levé(e)s	we would have gotten up
vous vous seriez levé(e)(s)	you would have gotten up
ils se seraient levés	they would have gotten up
elles se seraient levées	they would have gotten up

As in all compound tenses, the past participle in the **conditionnel passé** agrees in gender and in number:

- with the subject of a verb conjugated with **être**

- with a preceding direct object of verbs conjugated with **avoir**

- with the reflexive pronoun (a preceding direct object) of pronominal verbs

Special meanings: *devoir* and *pouvoir*

The verbs **devoir** and **pouvoir** have special meanings in the **conditionnel passé**. They state what should or shouldn't have happened—or what could have happened.

devoir: should have

Tu aurais dû étudier plus pour l'examen!	You should have studied more for the exam!
Léa n'aurait pas dû acheter cette nouvelle voiture.	Léa shouldn't have bought that new car.

pouvoir: could have

Nous aurions pu rester plus longtemps à la plage.	We could have stayed longer at the beach.
Tu aurais pu me le dire plus tôt.	You could have told me that sooner.

Using the *conditionnel passé*

A. Conjugaisons. Write the correct form of the **conditionnel passé**. Then write its translation in English.

Modèle: trouver: je/j'*aurais trouvé*   *I would have found*

1. **attendre: tu** _____ _____
2. **faire: Marc** _____ _____
3. **partir: nous** _____ _____
4. **se détendre: ils** _____ _____
5. **remplir: vous** _____ _____

6. **voir: je** _____ _____

7. **se doucher: Rachel** _____ _____

8. **acheter: elles** _____ _____

9. **rester: vous** _____ _____

10. **être: je** _____ _____

11. **devoir: tu** _____ _____

12. **pouvoir: ils** _____ _____

B. What is the correct form? Conjugate the verb in parentheses so that it agrees with the subject. Then read the completed sentences aloud.

Si le chien n'avait pas aboyé (barked) . . .

les voleurs (thieves) _____[1] **(ne pas être) surpris et** . . .

les Grimaud _____[2] **(ne pas se réveiller) et** . . .

les voleurs _____[3] **(prendre) l'ordinateur et** . . .

Nicole Grimaud _____[4] **(ne pas pouvoir) finir ses devoirs sur l'ordinateur et** . . .

le professeur _____[5] **(ne pas croire) son histoire de voleurs et** . . .

le professeur _____[6] **(se fâcher) avec Nicole et** . . .

Nicole _____[7] **(recevoir) une mauvaise note et** . . .

M. et Mme Grimaud _____[8] **(être) déçus et** . . .

ils _____[9] **(ne pas emmener) Nicole au restaurant pour fêter ses bonnes notes et** . . .

Nicole _____[10] **(ne pas manger) de viande pourrie** (rotten meat) **et** . . .

elle _____[11] **(ne pas tomber) malade et** . . .

elle _____[12] **(ne pas mourir) le jour suivant.**

Heureusement que (thank goodness) **le chien a aboyé!**

C. Which verb? For each sentence, choose the verb that makes the best sense, and conjugate it so that it agrees with the subject. When you've completed each sentence, read it aloud! Then translate into English.

ne pas être	se coucher	emmener
faire	avoir	rouspéter
voir	partir	apprendre
ne pas se réveiller	recevoir	ne pas grossir

Modèle: **Si j'avais appris à faire la cuisine, je/j'***aurais fait* **un gâteau pour ce soir.**
If I had learned to cook, I would have made a cake for tonight.

1. **Si Monique avait fait ses devoirs, elle** _____ **une meilleure note.**

_____

2. **Si le professeur était arrivé en retard, les étudiants** _____ **.**

_____

3. Si mes parents m'avaient fait prendre des leçons, je/j'_____ à jouer du piano.

_____

4. Les filles _____ autant (as much) si elles avaient fait du sport à l'école.

_____

5. Si vous aviez mis le réveil (set the alarm), vous _____ en retard.

_____

6. Thomas et Michel _____ déçus de leur note s'ils avaient étudié pour l'examen.

_____

7. Nos parents nous _____ à EuroDisney si nous avions réussi au baccalauréat.

_____

8. Si nous étions allés à EuroDisney, nous _____ Mickey.

_____

9. Je/J'_____ une augmentation de salaire si j'avais fait le rapport à temps.

_____

D. Comment dit-on? Write these sentences in French. Read them aloud when you have finished translating.

1. I should've called my mother yesterday.

_____

2. If I had known the truth, I would have spoken to the police.

_____

3. Yves could've arrived on time if he had wanted to.

_____

4. We would've won the match, if only we had scored a goal.

_____

5. If she had seen the ice cream, she would've ordered it.

_____

6. If you (**vous**) could've had the answers, would you have cheated?

_____

7. She should've given a better present to her husband.

_____

Les mots croisés 14

Use the **conditionnel passé** to complete the crossword puzzle.

Horizontal

1   Tu ___ (devenir) archéologue si tu étais plus aventureux.

8   I could've loved you: **Je/J'___ t'aimer.**

10   **Les enfants ___ (apprendre) l'espagnol s'ils avaient habité au Mexique pendant quelques mois.**

12   **Madeleine ___ (dire) la vérité, mais elle savait qu'elle serait punie.**

13   **Renée ___ (se maquiller) si elle s'était réveillée un peu plus tôt.**

14   **Mes collègues ___ (aller) au match de baseball s'ils avaient fini leur travail plus vite.**

Vertical

2   **Je/J'___ (être) plus heureux si mes parents n'avaient pas déménagé.**

3   **Nous ___ (prendre) la voiture si on nous l'avait laissée.**

4   **La mère ___ (faire) un gâteau si elle avait su que ses enfants venaient.**

5   **Est-ce que vous ___ (écrire) un meilleur essai si vous aviez plus de temps?**

6   **Pauline ___ (s'habiller) plus élégamment si on lui avait dit que le Président serait à la soirée.**

7   **Julien ___ (chanter) "Je ne regrette rien" si on lui avait donné le microphone.**

9   You should've called: **Vous ___ téléphoner.**

11   **Qu'est-ce que tu ___ (dire) si le patron t'avait demandé pourquoi tu n'étais pas venu au bureau hier?**

15
Conditional Sentences

Conditional sentences have an "if" clause and a "result" clause: if X, then Y. As you will see in these examples, the verb tenses in conditional sentences are parallel in French and English.

S'il fait beau, nous ferons un pique-nique.	If the weather is nice, we'll have a picnic.
S'il faisait beau, nous ferions un pique-nique.	If the weather were nice, we would have a picnic.
S'il avait fait beau, nous aurions fait un pique-nique.	If the weather had been nice, we would have had a picnic.

The "if" clause can come either before or after the "result" clause.

Nous ferons un pique-nique s'il fait beau.	We'll have a picnic if the weather is nice.
Nous ferions un pique-nique s'il faisait beau.	We would have a picnic if the weather were nice.
Nous aurions fait un pique-nique s'il avait fait beau.	We would have had a picnic if the weather had been nice.

Conditional sentences: present + future

When the "if" clause is in **présent**, the "result" clause is usually in the **futur**: if X happens, Y will happen.

Si tu étudies, tu auras une bonne note.	If you study, you will get a good grade.
Si nous allons en France l'été prochain, nous visiterons le Musée du Louvre.	If we go to France next summer, we'll go to the Louvre Museum.
On ira au restaurant si je peux finir mes devoirs.	We will go out to eat if I can finish my homework.

Perspective personnelle

Vrai ou faux? Indicate whether each sentence is true (**vrai**) or false (**faux**). Remember to read each sentence aloud to practice speaking.

_____ **Si j'ai le temps, j'irai au musée demain.**

_____ **Je démissionerai (resign) si mes collègues ne sont pas gentils.**

_____ **Si j'ai besoin d'aide, mes amis m'aideront.**

_____ **Si je ne travaille pas bien, mon patron me renvoiera (fire).**

_____ **J'apprendrai le français si je fais bien mes exercices.**

A. What is the correct form? Conjugate the verb in parentheses to agree with the subject. Then read the completed sentence aloud. Finally, translate the sentence into English.

1. S'il fait beau, nous _____ (aller) à la plage.

   _____

2. Patrick fera le voyage au Sénégal l'année prochaine s'il _____ (avoir) assez d'argent.

   _____

3. Que _____ (faire)-vous si vous gagnez à la loterie ?

   _____

4. Si on _____ (écrire) un livre important, on pourra recevoir le prix Goncourt.

   _____

5. Si tu nourris le chien tous les jours et tu joues avec lui, il _____ (être) content.

   _____

6. On n'aura pas de bonnes notes si on n'_____ (étudier) pas.

   _____

7. Les jeunes filles ne trouveront pas de travail au magasin de musique si elles ne _____ (connaître) pas Édith Piaf.

   _____

8. Si mes parents me donnent de l'argent, j'_____ (acheter) un cadeau d'anniversaire pour ma sœur.

   _____

B. Now, make sentences of your own! Complete each sentence in one or two different ways by choosing one expression from each column and conjugating the verb accordingly. Read your sentences aloud to practice speaking.

1. S'il neige demain . . .

je les enfants mon frère / ma sœur	être	triste(s) déçu(e)(s) ravi(e)(s)

   _____

   _____

2. S'il fait beau demain . . .

nous vous tu	aller	à la piscine au marché en plein air à la montagne

   _____

   _____

3. **Si on n'a pas cours demain . . .**

mes amis		le ménage
je	faire	la sieste
nous		un voyage

_____

_____

4. **Si j'ai assez d'argent . . .**

		un ordinateur
je	acheter	une bague de fiançailles
		une nouvelle voiture

_____

_____

5. **J'irai en France si . . .**

	apprendre le français
je	avoir assez d'argent
	gagner une bourse

_____

_____

Conditional sentences: *imparfait + conditionnel*

When the "if" clause is in the **imparfait**, the "result" clause is in the **conditionnel**: if X happened, Y would happen.

Si tu étudiais, tu aurais une bonne note.	If you studied, you would get a good grade.
Si nous allions en France l'été prochain, nous visiterions le Musée du Louvre.	If we went to France next summer, we would go to the Louvre Museum.
On irait au restaurant si je pouvais finir mes devoirs.	We would go out to eat if I could finish my homework.

Perspective personnelle

Vrai ou faux? Indicate whether each sentence is true (**vrai**) or false (**faux**). Remember to read each sentence aloud to practice speaking.

_____ **Si j'avais le temps, je rendrais visite à une vieille personne.**

_____ **J'irais en Europe si j'avais de l'argent.**

_____ **Si j'étais plus intelligent(e), je serais plus heureux / heureuse.**

_____ **J'aurais plus d'amis si j'étais moins rouspéteur / rouspéteuse.**

_____ **Si mon patron ne me traitait pas bien, je trouverais un autre travail.**

C. **What is the correct form?** Conjugate the verb in parentheses to agree with the subject. Then read the completed sentence aloud. Finally, translate the sentence into English.

1. J'achèterais un livre sur le Mali si je _____ (savoir) où le trouver.

_____

2. Si j'avais un chat, je _____ (dormir) avec lui.

_____

3. Si Yves _____ (se doucher) plus, les femmes l'aimeraient plus.

_____

4. Les enfants _____ (regarder) moins la télévision si leurs parents jouaient avec eux.

_____

5. Jean _____ (être) plus heureux s'il n'était pas toujours au régime.

_____

6. Si je _____ (faire) de la gymnastique, j'aurais plus d'énergie.

_____

7. Si tu travaillais plus, tu _____ (avoir) de meilleures notes.

_____

8. Si vous me téléphoniez de temps en temps, je _____ (sortir) avec vous.

_____

9. Nous _____ (faire) moins de fautes si nous faisions attention.

_____

D. **Que ferait-on?** What would the people below do in these situations? Use one of the verbs listed in each response. You may need to add words after the verb to complete your meaning.

aller . . .	jouer . . .	acheter . . .
être . . .	s'amuser	se préoccuper (to worry)
faire . . .	démissionner	
déménager (to move)	se perdre (to get lost)	

1. Si mes parents allaient en Europe, ils . . .

_____

2. Si j'avais beaucoup d'argent, je/j' . . .

_____

3. Si mes collègues n'avaient pas besoin de travailler, ils/elles . . .

_____

4. Si j'avais des enfants (si je n'avais pas d'enfants), je/j' . . .

_____

5. Si mon meilleur ami (ma meilleure amie) n'était pas en forme (était en forme), il/elle . . .

_____

Conditional sentences: *plus-que-parfait* + *conditionnel passé*

When the "if" clause is in the **plus-que-parfait**, the "result" clause is usually in the **conditionnel passé**: if *X* had happened, *Y* would have happened.

Si tu avais étudié, tu aurais eu une bonne note.	If you had studied, you would have gotten a good grade.
Si nous étions allés en France, nous aurions visité le Musée du Louvre.	If we had gone to France, we would have gone to the Louvre Museum.
On serait allé au restaurant si j'avais pu finir mes devoirs.	We would have gone out to eat if I had been able to finish my homework.

Notice that a "si" clause with the **plus-que-parfait** always expresses a contrary-to-fact statement, usually a regret: **si tu avais étudié . . . (mais tu n'as pas étudié), si nous étions allés en France . . . (mais nous n'y sommes pas allés), si j'avais pu finir mes devoirs . . . (mais je ne les ai pas finis).**

E. **What is the correct form?** Conjugate the verb in parentheses to agree with the subject. Then read the completed sentence aloud. Finally, translate the sentence into English.

1. **Si Richard _____ (ne pas manger) autant de bonbons, il n'aurait pas grossi.**

   _____

2. **Qu'est-ce que vous _____ (faire) si vos parents vous avaient quitté(e)(s) à l'âge de 16 ans?**

   _____

3. **J'aurais pu acheter une maison si je/j'_____ (épargner) mon argent.**

   _____

4. **Si nous ne nous étions pas connus, nous _____ (ne pas se marier).**

   _____

5. **Si nous _____ (ne pas se marier), nous ne nous serions pas divorcés.**

   _____

6. **Tu _____ (réussir) à l'examen si tu avais étudié avec moi.**

   _____

7. **Si Béatrice _____ (ne pas venir) à la soirée, on se serait amusé.**

   _____

8. **Où est-ce que tu _____ (aller) à l'université si tu avais pu choisir?**

   _____

Conditional sentences: other patterns are possible!

The three patterns of conditional sentences we've shown you are the most frequent ones, but there are others that are determined by the context. Logic best determines the sequence of tenses in conditional sentences. In French, a conditional or future tense is never used in a **si** clause. Here are some common patterns. Remember that the verb tenses are parallel in French and English—let your English ear be your guide.

S'il fait (*présent*) **beau, on fait** (*présent*) **une promenade.**	If the weather is nice, we're taking a walk. (**[O]n fait une promenade** is a future action expressed in the present tense.)
S'il fait (*présent*) **beau, on fait** (*présent*) **souvent une promenade.**	If the weather is nice (or when the weather is nice), we often take a walk. (This sentence makes a generalization.)
Si tu avais étudié (*plus-que-parfait*)**, tu pourrais** (*conditionnel*) **répondre à ces questions.**	If you had studied, you would be able to answer these questions. (You could do it now.)
On pourrait (*conditionnel*) **aller au restaurant si j'avais fini** (*plus-que-parfait*) **mes devoirs.**	We could go out to eat if I had finished my homework. (We could go out now.)

Using conditional sentences

F. **Which verb?** For each sentence, choose an appropriate verb and conjugate it to agree with the subject. When you've completed each sentence, read it aloud!

être	**pleuvoir**	**s'arrêter**
pleurer	**recommander**	**avoir**
revenir	**pouvoir**	**dire**

1. **Si j'avais vu le panneau** (sign), **je** _____ .

2. **S'il ne reçoit pas de cadeaux, il** _____ .

3. **S'il y a des nuages** (clouds) **noirs, il** _____ **bientôt.**

4. **Si vous** _____ **voir le futur, voudriez-vous le voir?**

5. **Que ferais-tu pour t'amuser si tu** _____ **aveugle** (blind)**?**

6. **Les garçons auraient mangé toute la glace si leurs parents** _____ .

7. **Pourquoi** _____ **que j'aille voir cette pièce si elle ne l'avait pas aimée?**

8. **Si nous** _____ **un cheval** (horse)**, nous ferions de l'équitation régulièrement.**

G. Comment dit-on? How would you say these sentences in French? Read them outloud when you have finished translating.

to hurry	**se dépêcher**	red light	**feu (m) rouge**
cavity	**carie (f)**	Geneva	**Genève**
police car	**voiture (f) de police**	to pay for	**payer**
to ignore	**ignorer**		

1. If I had known that you **(vous)** were waiting, I would have hurried.

   _____

2. We will go skiing if it snows.

   _____

3. If you **(tu)** brushed your teeth, you wouldn't have cavities.

   _____

4. If Sylvain had seen the police car, he wouldn't have ignored the red light.

   _____

5. Will you **(tu)** eat the cake if I make it?

   _____

6. Would you **(vous)** go to Geneva if your boss paid for the ticket?

   _____

7. If I hadn't read the book, I would've liked the movie better.

   _____

Les mots croisés 15

Use the **présent**, **imparfait**, **futur**, **conditionnel**, **conditionnel passé**, or **plus-que-parfait** to complete the following clues.

Horizontal

3 　Si vous ___ (étudier) plus, vous auriez de meilleures notes.

6 　Si j'avais acheté des actions de cette compagnie en 2001, je/j'___ (pouvoir) vivre sans travailler maintenant.

7 　Si tu ___ (vouloir) recevoir une augmentation de salaire, tu travaillerais plus.

11 　Je/j'___ (aller) en Irlande si tu allais avec moi.

12 　Si tu ne t'étais pas couché si tard, tu ___ (gagner) le match.

14 　Tu gagneras beaucoup d'argent si tu ___ (devenir) médecin.

15 　Le patron ___ (se fâcher) s'il avait vu le bureau pendant son absence.

Vertical

1 　Si vous ___ (être) trop timide, vous ne réussirez pas aux interviews.

2 　Jeannine et Denis ___ (vendre) leur maison s'ils pouvaient trouver un acheteur.

4 　Si je vais au concert, je/j' ___ (s'amuser).

5 　Est-ce que vous ___ (partir) si je ne vous avais pas demandé de rester?

8 　Si nous ___ (voir) le journal ce matin, nous ne serions pas venus à ce restaurant.

9 　Ma mère ___ (mourir) si elle savait ce que mon frère fait le weekend.

10 　Si les enfants jouent dehors, ils ___ (devoir) se baigner ce soir.

13 　Nous ___ (être) contents si le patron aime le projet que nous avons fait.

Part Four
The Subjunctive Tenses

The Subjunctive: an Overview

The *subjunctive* is the mood that allows you to express a point of view, fear, doubt, hope, possibility—in other words, anything that is not viewed as a factual statement. The subjunctive is a counterpart to the *indicative*, the mood that conveys facts, objective statements, and information.

The main point to note about the subjunctive is that it is used, mainly, in a *subordinate clause*. What, then, is a subordinate clause? We're glad you asked.

A *complex sentence* has at least one subordinate clause. A clause, by the way, is a group of related words containing a subject and a predicate (see our Overview for Part One) but, rather than standing by itself, the clause is part of the main sentence. The subjunctive is used, as we mentioned, mainly in a subordinate clause, generally introduced by **que** (that). So, when you express a wish, an emotion, an obligation, a doubt, or a possibility, put the verb in the subordinate clause (after **que**) in the subjunctive.

Je veux	que tu viennes avec moi.	I want you to come with me.
a wish	subordinate clause with a verb in the subjunctive	

Subjunctive vs. Indicative

Not all verbs in subordinate clauses (those after **que**) are necessarily stated in the subjunctive, only those connected to a main clause that expresses a wish, an emotion, an obligation, a doubt, or a possibility.

Indicative	Subjunctive
Elle sait que c'est la vérité. She knows that it's the truth.	**Elle doute que ce soit la vérité.** She doubts that it's the truth.
Il est certain que le train ne partira pas à l'heure. It's certain that our train will not leave on time.	**Il est possible que le train ne parte pas à l'heure.** It's possible that our train will not leave on time.

16
Le Présent du Subjonctif

The subjunctive is a form of the verb that is used to express

- wishes, desires, requests, expectations, and preferences

- opinions and emotions

- obligations and requirements

- doubt, denial, uncertainty, and possibility

There are two main subjunctive tenses, present and past. We will talk about the past subjunctive in the next chapter.

Je veux que tu saches la vérité. (un désir)	I want you to know the truth.
Hélène est triste que je parte pour la France. (une émotion)	Hélène is sad that I'm leaving for France.
Il faut que vous fassiez ces exercices pour demain. (une obligation)	You have to do these exercises for tomorrow. (It is necessary that you do these exercises . . .)
Je ne crois pas que le subjonctif soit trop difficile. (un doute)	I don't think the subjunctive is very difficult.

The subjunctive is also used in clauses after specific conjunctions.

La prof expliquera la grammaire pour que tu la comprennes mieux.	The professor will explain the grammar so that you will understand it better.
Bien que nous ayons déjà nos billets, nous devons tout de même faire la queue!	Although we already have our tickets, we still have to stand in line!

How to form the present subjunctive

Verbs in the present subjunctive, except **avoir** and **être**, have the following endings with the subjunctive stem:

-e	**-ions**
-es	**-iez**
-e	**-ent**

For regular **-er**, **-re**, and **-ir** verbs, the subjunctive stem comes from the third person plural (**ils/elles**) stem of the present tense indicative. (The indicative is the form of the verb you have been using up to this point.)

Here's how some common verbs look in the present subjunctive. We show these verbs with the phrase **il faut que . . .** (it is necessary that . . .) as an example of how verbs in the subjunctive are used in a sentence.

parler: subjunctive stem **parl-**

il faut que je parle	il faut que nous parlions
il faut que tu parles	il faut que vous parliez
il faut qu'il/elle/on parle	il faut qu'ils/elles parlent

étudier: subjunctive stem **étudi-**

il faut que j'étudie	il faut que nous étudiions*
il faut que tu étudies	il faut que vous étudiiez*
il faut qu'il/elle/on étudie	il fait qu'ils/elles étudient

*The letter *i* appears twice, once in the verb stem and once in the ending.

rendre: subjunctive stem **rend-**

il faut que je rende	il faut que nous rendions
il faut que tu rendes	il faut que vous rendiez
il faut qu'il/elle/on rende	il faut qu'ils/elles rendent

finir: subjunctive stem **finiss-**

il faut que je finisse	il faut que nous finissions
il faut que tu finisses	il faut que vous finissiez
il faut qu'il/elle/on finisse	il faut qu'ils/elles finissent

partir: subjunctive stem **part-**

il faut que je parte	il faut que nous partions
il faut que tu partes	il faut que vous partiez
il faut qu'il/elle/on parte	il faut qu'ils/elles partent

Verbs with two subjunctive stems

If a verb has a second stem for **nous** and **vous** in the present indicative (see Chapters 1 and 2), it maintains this second stem for **nous** and **vous** in the present subjunctive. This includes verbs like **tenir** and **venir** (indicative: **je tiens, nous tenons**) and verbs with spelling changes like **acheter** (indicative: **j'achète, nous achetons**) and **appeler** (indicative: **j'appelle, nous appelons**). Here are the forms for the present subjunctive.

tenir: subjunctive stems **tienn-, ten-**

que je tienne	que nous tenions
que tu tiennes	que vous teniez
qu'il/elle/on tienne	qu'ils/elles tiennent

venir: subjunctive stems **vienn-, ven-**

que je vienne	que nous venions
que tu viennes	que vous veniez
qu'il/elle/on vienne	qu'ils/elles viennent

acheter: subjunctive stems **achèt-, achet-**

que j'achète	que nous achetions
que tu achètes	que vous achetiez
qu'il/elle/on achète	qu'ils/elles achètent

appeler: subjunctive stems **appell-, appel-**

que j'appelle	que nous appelions
que tu appelles	que vous appeliez
qu'il/elle/on appelle	qu'ils/elles appellent

Irregular verbs

Many verbs have irregular subjunctive stems. Some irregular verbs have two subjunctive stems, and some have just one. If there are two stems, the **nous** and **vous** stem, as usual, is different from the rest of the forms.

Irregular verbs with two subjunctive stems

aller: subjunctive stems **aill-, all-**

que j'aille	que nous allions
que tu ailles	que vous alliez
qu'il/elle/on aille	qu'ils/elles aillent

vouloir: subjunctive stems **veuill-, voul-**

que je veuille	que nous voulions
que tu veuilles	que vous vouliez
qu'il/elle/on veuille	qu'ils/elles veuillent

The verbs **avoir** and **être** have two irregular subjunctive stems. Many of the subjunctive *endings* for these verbs are irregular, as well.

avoir: subjunctive stems **ai-, ay-**

que j'aie	que nous ayons
que tu aies	que vous ayez
qu'il/elle/on ait	qu'ils/elles aient

être: subjunctive stems **soi-, soy-**

que je sois	que nous soyons
que tu sois	que vous soyez
qu'il/elle/on soit	qu'ils/elles soient

Irregular verbs with one subjunctive stem

faire: subjunctive stem **fass-**

que je fasse	que nous fassions
que tu fasses	que vous fassiez
qu'il/elle/on fasse	qu'ils/elles fassent

pouvoir: subjunctive stem **puiss-**

que je puisse	que nous puissions
que tu puisses	que vous puissiez
qu'il/elle/on puisse	qu'ils/elles puissent

savoir: subjunctive stem **sach-**

que je sache	que nous sachions
que tu saches	que vous sachiez
qu'il/elle/on sache	qu'ils/elles sachent

Perspective personnelle

Vrai ou faux? Indicate whether each sentence is true (**vrai**) or false (**faux**) for you. Remember to read each sentence aloud for practice.

_____   **Je doute que le président des États-Unis soit honnête (honest).**
_____   **Il faut que j'aille au supermarché bientôt.**
_____   **Je travaille afin que ma famille puisse prendre des vacances.**
_____   **Je suis triste que mes parents vieillissent.**
_____   **Mes collègues exigent que je fasse leur travail.**

A. What is the correct form? Conjugate the verb in parentheses in the present subjunctive so that it agrees with the subject. Then read the completed sentence aloud. Finally, translate the sentence into English.

1. **Nous craignons que Philippe _____ (ne pas venir) à la cérémonie.**

   _____

2. **Il est possible qu'il _____ (neiger) demain.**

   _____

3. **Le professeur exige que les étudiants _____ (écrire) leur nom sur leur projet.**

   _____

4. Êtes-vous surpris que je/j' _____ (avoir) une petite voiture?

   _____

5. Marie est ravie (delighted) que vous _____ (venir) à la soirée.

   _____

6. Il faut que nous _____ (finir) ce rapport.

   _____

7. Je ne pensais pas que nous _____ (pouvoir) finir ce travail à temps.

   _____

8. Nous avons peur que Josianne _____ (ne pas faire) de son mieux.

   _____

9. Il vaut mieux que nous _____ (travailler) beaucoup.

   _____

10. Nous ne croyons pas que nos collègues _____ (vouloir) travailler le weekend.

    _____

11. Notre mère voulait que nous _____ (nettoyer) notre chambre.

    _____

12. Je ne veux pas que vous _____ (tolérer) cette insolence.

    _____

13. Il est impossible que je/j' _____ (aller) à Paris cet été.

    _____

14. Je viendrai à la soirée pourvu que vous _____ (être) là (there).

    _____

15. Mon patron demande que je _____ (choisir) un nouvel assistant.

    _____

16. Les étudiants préfèrent que le professeur _____ (lire) leurs essais tout de suite.

    _____

17. Les Dupont souhaitent que Thomas _____ (dire) la vérité.

    _____

18. Tu es heureux que nous _____ (aller) en France?

    _____

19. René veut que je _____ (être) au musée avec lui.

    _____

20. La femme fâchée (angry) exige que son mari _____ (dormir) sur le canapé.

    _____

21. **Le patron de Ghislaine veut qu'elle** _____ (apprendre) l'italien.

_____

22. **Je doute que M. Troude** _____ (boire) du citron pressé.

_____

23. **Le médecin ne croit pas que Sylvie** _____ (avoir) une angine.

_____

24. **Je te dirai la nouvelle** (the news) **avant que je la** _____ (dire) **à mes parents.**

_____

B. **Now, write sentences of your own!** For each box, create one or two sentences by choosing one expression from each column and conjugating the verb accordingly. Read your sentences aloud for practice.

Maman veut que	**nous** **vous** **ses enfants**	**nettoyer la maison** **faire la vaisselle** **être heureux**

1. _____

_____

Je suis triste que	**tu** **mes amis** **mon/ma collègue**	**attendre le bus** **aller à Tahiti sans moi** **avoir une pneumonie**

2. _____

_____

Il faut que	**je** **nous** **les employé(e)s**	**prendre des vacances** **lire un bon livre** **se détendre**

3. _____

_____

When do you use the subjunctive?

The subjunctive is a special form of the verb that frequently indicates the speaker's or writer's attitude about something stated or expected. It is used after expressions of wishing, opinion, obligation, and doubt. The subjunctive almost always appears in a subordinate clause—the separate part of a sentence that begins with the conjunction **que** (but not all clauses that start with **que** include a verb in the subjunctive). The subjects of the main verb and the subjunctive verb are not the same.

Wishes, desires, requests, expectations, and preferences

vouloir que, désirer que, suggérer que, souhaiter que, attendre que, préférer que, aimer mieux que, il vaut mieux que, permettre que, demander que, and so on.

Le prof voulait que nous fassions un peu plus d'effort.	The professor wanted us to try a little harder.
Dorothée aurait préféré que Toto reste dans le Kansas.	Dorothy would have preferred that Toto stay in Kansas.
Il vaut mieux que nous partions tout de suite.	It's better that we leave right away.

Exception: The subjunctive is not used with the verb **espérer**.

Nous espérons que tu reviendras bientôt au pays d'Oz.	We hope that you will come back soon to the Land of Oz.
J'espère que le cours n'a pas été annulé.	I hope class hasn't been cancelled.

The subjunctive is also found occasionally all by itself in short sentences that express a wish or suggestion. These sentences are often proverbial in nature.

Vive le roi!	Long live the king!
Vive les vacances!	Let's hear it for vacation!
Que la force soit avec toi.	May the force be with you.
Advienne que pourra. (a proverbial expression)	Come what may.

Opinions and emotions

être heureux(se), triste, content(e), ravi(e), surpris(e), désolé(e), étonné(e) que, and so on

il est bon, étonnant, intéressant, utile, triste, regrettable, curieux que, and so on

regretter que, avoir peur que, craindre que, and so on

il est dommage que, c'est dommage que, and so on

Mes amis sont tristes que je parte pour la France sans eux.	My friends are sad that I'm leaving for France without them.
Il est bon que je comprenne le français.	It's a good thing I understand French.
Il est dommage que vous ne puissiez pas m'accompagner.	It's a shame you can't come with me.

Obligations and requirements

il faut que, il est nécessaire que, and so on

exiger que, and so on

Est-ce qu'il faut que nous sachions les verbes irréguliers?	Do we have to know the irregular verbs? (Is it necessary that we know . . . ?)
La loi exige qu'on ne dépasse pas la limite de vitesse.	The law requires that you not exceed the speed limit.

Doubt, denial, uncertainty, and possibility

douter que, il est peu probable que, il est possible que, il semble que, and so on

Je doute que l'examen soit très difficile.	I doubt that the test will be very difficult.
Il est possible que nous n'ayons pas de devoirs à faire pour demain.	It's possible that we won't have any homework to do for tomorrow.
Il semble que tu sois un petit peu fatigué.	It seems that you're a little tired.

Note: **il est probable que** is an expression of probability, not possibility, so it is followed by the indicative.

Il est probable que notre vol aura un retard de trente minutes.	It's likely that our flight will be thirty minutes late.

Expressions of doubt vs. expressions of certainty

Expressions like **je pense que, je crois que,** and **je trouve que** do not show doubt or uncertainty, and so they are *not* followed by the subjunctive. But when they are negative (**je ne pense/crois/trouve pas que**) or interrogative (**est-ce que vous pensez/croyez/trouvez que**), they show uncertainty on the part of the speaker and may be followed by a verb in the subjunctive.

Est-ce que vous croyez que le français soit facile?	Do you believe that French is easy?
Non, je trouve qu'il est quelquefois un peu difficile, mais je ne pense pas qu'on puisse trouver une langue plus belle. Alors voilà!	No, I find that it's a little difficult sometimes, but I don't think you can find a language more beautiful. So there!

Expressions of certainty such as **il est sûr/vrai/clair/évident que** and **je suis sûr(e)/certain(e) que** are followed not by the subjunctive, but by the indicative.

Il est clair que Jean a triché sur l'examen.	It's obvious that Jean cheated on the exam.
Nous sommes certains que le prof va être fâché.	We're sure that the prof will be angry.

The subjunctive with certain conjunctions

As we mentioned at the beginning of this chapter, subjunctive verbs are used after certain conjunctions that include **que**. In this case, the sentence does not necessarily have a subjunctive meaning of wishing, opinion, obligation, or doubt.

Conjunctions followed by the subjunctive

afin que, pour que	so that, in order that	**bien que, quoique**	although
à moins que, sans que	unless	**jusqu'à ce que**	until
avant que	before	**pourvu que**	provided that

Here's how these work:

J'ai déjà acheté les billets pour que nous ayons de bonnes places.	I've already bought the tickets so we would have good seats.
Je ne partirai pas sans que tu m'accompagnes.	I won't leave unless you come with me.
Bien qu'elle soit malade, Aline est venue au cours aujourd'hui.	Although she's sick, Aline came to class today.
Nous resterons au café jusqu'à ce que tu arrives.	We'll stay at the café until you arrive.

C. Subjonctif ou indicatif? Decide whether the following expressions should be followed by the subjunctive (S) or the indicative (I).

Modèle: _I_   **Je crois que**

1. _____ **Je doute que**
2. _____ **Il est sûr que**
3. _____ **pourvu que**
4. _____ **Il est possible que**
5. _____ **Il est probable que**
6. _____ **Ils ne pensent pas que**
7. _____ **Il vaut mieux que**
8. _____ **Elles sont certaines que**
9. _____ **Je souhaite que**
10. _____ **J'espère que**
11. _____ **Nous voulons que**
12. _____ **Elle exige que**
13. _____ **Je ne crois pas que**
14. _____ **pour que**
15. _____ **parce que**
16. _____ **Elle est surprise que**
17. _____ **Nous craignons que**

18. _____ **avant que**
19. _____ **Il préfère que**
20. _____ **Il est vrai que**
21. _____ **Nous demandons que**
22. _____ **Il est clair que**
23. _____ **bien que**
24. _____ **Il est important que**
25. _____ **Il est dommage que**
26. _____ **Nous sommes ravis que**
27. _____ **Il est nécessaire que**
28. _____ **On ne doute pas que**
29. _____ **Je veux que**
30. _____ **Je dis que**
31. _____ **Vous regrettez que**
32. _____ **Il est évident que**
33. _____ **jusqu'à ce que**
34. _____ **Il faut que**

D. **What is the correct form?** Conjugate the verb in parentheses in either the present subjunctive *or* the present indicative to agree with the subject. Then read the completed sentence aloud.

1. **Il ne faut pas que nous _____ (jeter) du papier par terre.**

2. **Il vaut mieux que nous _____ (recycler) le papier.**

3. **Henri va au théâtre à moins que sa fille _____ (être) toujours malade.**

4. **Je souhaite que mes enfants _____ (lire) le journal.**

5. **Nous croyons que tu _____ (aller) venir avec nous.**

6. **Marc et Camille pensent que le soleil _____ (avoir) des pouvoirs magiques.**

7. **Je travaille afin que ma famille _____ (pouvoir) prendre des vacances.**

8. **Je travaille parce que ma famille _____ (vouloir) prendre des vacances.**

9. **Henriette exige que ses collègues _____ (faire) son travail pendant son absence.**

10. **Elle est surprise qu'ils _____ (ne pas être) contents.**

11. **Il est vrai que les Martin _____ (aller) aux Antilles.**

12. **Il est possible que les Capoulade _____ (aller) au Maroc.**

13. **Nous craignons que vous _____ (ne pas répondre) au téléphone.**

14. **Le patron dit que nous _____ (devoir) finir ce travail avant la fin de la journée.**

15. **Les enfants jouent dehors jusqu'à ce qu'il _____ (faire) nuit.**

16. **J'essaie de manger avant que je/j'_____ (avoir) faim.**

17. **Mes parents auraient voulu que je _____ (devenir) médecin.**

18. **Ma mère exige que je _____ (faire) mes devoirs avant de regarder la télé.**

19. **Je suis étonné que Paul _____ (avoir) des enfants.**

20. **Mathilde voulait que Thomas lui _____ (rendre) visite.**

E. **Now, write sentences of your own!** Complete each sentence in one or two different ways by choosing one expression from each column and conjugating the verb accordingly. Read your sentences aloud for practice.

Il est possible que	**je**	**aller au restaurant**
Il est vrai que	**nous**	**faire du ski**
Il faut que	**les enfants**	**s'amuser au parc**

1. _____

   _____

Je doute que	**le prof**	**vouloir de la glace**
Est-il vrai que	**vous**	**dormir jusqu'à midi**
Je crois que	**tu**	**prendre le dîner à 22h**

2. _____

   _____

Nous sommes content(e)s que	le patron	être malade(s)
Nous sommes tristes que	vous	ne pas avoir de rhume
Nous sommes certain(e)s que	les filles	acheter un bateau

3. _____

_____

F. Comment dit-on? Write these sentences in French. Read them aloud when you have finished translating.

German	**allemand (m)**	to please	**plaire à**
cute	**mignon (mignonne)**	dentist	**dentiste (m/f)**
apologize	**s'excuser**		

1. We want you **(tu)** to go to the store.

_____

2. It is necessary that I sell the car.

_____

3. My boss wants me to understand German.

_____

4. I think Alain is handsome.

_____

5. Do you **(tu)** think he's cute?

_____

6. I don't think he has a girlfriend.

_____

7. I wish he would go out with me.

_____

8. It is obvious that Roxanne wants to please the boss.

_____

9. I hope you **(vous)** brush your teeth every day.

_____

10. The dentist requires you **(vous)** to brush your teeth every day.

_____

11. Élise studies a lot, although she doesn't want to go to college.

_____

12. I won't be happy unless you **(vous)** apologize.

_____

A last word: the subjunctive with two subjects

In all of the examples we have showed you in this chapter, whenever there are two clauses, the subjects of the main verb and the subjunctive verb are different. When the subject of the two verbs is the same, the second verb is an infinitive, often introduced by the preposition **de**.

Different Subjects: *que* with the subjunctive	Same Subject: the second verb is an infinitive
Je suis triste que tu partes.	**Je suis triste de partir.**
Nous voulons qu'Alain rentre à la maison.	**Nous voulons rentrer à la maison.**

With impersonal constructions with **il**, the second verb in the infinitive makes a generalization, as a specific verb subject is not stated.

Il faut que tu étudies beaucoup.	**Il faut étudier beaucoup.**
Il est bon que je comprenne le français.	**Il est bon de comprendre le français.**

G. **Le rabat-joie (*party pooper*).** Marc never wants people to do what they want to do. In each item below, first state what each person wants to do. Then state that Marc doesn't want the person to do that activity. Remember to use the infinitive when you only have one subject and the subjunctive when there are two.

Modèle: Patrick (sortir à la discothèque)

Patrick veut sortir à la discothèque.

Marc ne veut pas que Patrick sorte à la discothèque.

1. **nous (aller au bord de la mer)**

   _____

   _____

2. **vous (écrire un roman)**

   _____

   _____

3. **Hélène et Céline (faire un pique-nique)**

   _____

   _____

4. **je (être avocat)**

   _____

   _____

5. **les employés (demander une augmentation)**

   _____

   _____

6. **Gérard (finir ses devoirs)**

_____

_____

7. **Quentin (rendre visite à sa grand-mère)**

_____

_____

8. **je (prendre un pot avec mes amis)**

_____

_____

Les mots croisés 16

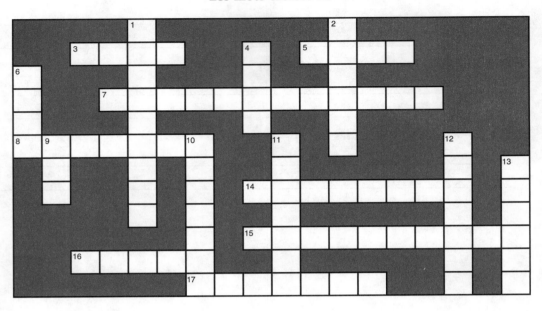

Use the present subjunctive, present indicative, or the infinitive of the verbs given to complete the crossword puzzle.

Horizontal

3   Il est nécessaire que tu ___ (avoir) un stylo en classe.

5   La mère espère que son fils ___ (pouvoir) trouver une femme gentille.

7   Il est bon que nous ___ (réussir) aux examens.

8   Nous allons à Londres sans que nos amis le ___ (savoir).

14   Il est sûr que nous ___ (arriver) à l'heure.

15   Nous sommes très déçus que Céline et Alice ___ (s'en aller).

16   Les employés veulent bien ___ (faire) leur travail.

17   Hélène est triste que vous ne ___ (rester) pas plus longtemps.

Vertical

1   Nous ne sommes pas sûrs que Jacqueline ___ (se détendre) pendant ses vacances.

2   Il faut que vous ___ (venir) aussi tôt que possible.

4   Je crois qu'on ___ (devoir) s'excuser auprès de Mme LeBlanc.

6   Je vais continuer à jouer au foot pourvu que je/j' ___ (être) en bonne santé.

9   Je doute qu'il y ___ (avoir) de la neige sur les montagnes au mois d'août.

10   Samuël était étonné de ___ (trouver) un travail si vite.

11   La maîtresse exige que les enfants ne ___ (perdre) pas leur stylo.

12   Le patron veut que ses employés ___ (faire) bien leur travail.

13   Je voudrais que tu ___ (partir) toute de suite.

17
Le Passé du Subjonctif

The **passé du subjonctif**, or past subjunctive, is used in the contexts for the present subjunctive described in the previous chapter, but it refers to events that happened in the past. Compare the following:

Je suis étonné que Martin vende sa nouvelle voiture. *(présent du subjonctif)*	I'm surprised that Martin is selling his new car.
Je suis étonné que Martin ait vendu sa nouvelle voiture. *(passé du subjonctif)*	I'm surprised that Martin has sold his new car.
Mes amis sont tristes que je parte sans eux. *(présent du subjonctif)*	My friends are sad that I'm leaving without them.
Mes amis sont tristes que je sois parti sans eux. *(passé du subjonctif)*	My friends are sad that I left without them.

The **passé du subjonctif** is a compound tense. You can think of this tense as the **passé composé**, but in the subjunctive. In the **passé du subjonctif**, **avoir** or **être** is in the **présent du subjonctif**.

A Verb Conjugated with **avoir: vendre**

que j'aie vendu	**que nous ayons vendu**
que tu aies vendu	**que vous ayez vendu**
qu'il/elle/on ait vendu	**qu'ils/elles aient vendu**

A Verb Conjugated with **être: partir**

que je sois parti(e)	**que nous soyons parti(e)s**
que tu sois parti(e)	**que vous soyez parti(e)(s)**
qu'il soit parti	**qu'ils soient partis**
qu'elle soit partie	**qu'elles soient parties**
qu'on soit parti	

A Pronominal Verb: **s'amuser**

que je me sois amusé(e)	**que nous nous soyons amusé(s)**
que tu te sois amusé(e)	**que vous vous soyez amusé(e)(s)**
qu'il se soit amusé	**qu'ils se soient amusés**
qu'elle se soit amusé(e)	**qu'elles se soient amusées**
qu'on se soit amusé	

As in all compound tenses, the past participle in the **passé du subjonctif** agrees in gender and in number:

- with the subject of a verb conjugated with **être**

- with a preceding direct object of verbs conjugated with **avoir**

- with the reflexive pronoun (a preceding direct object) of pronominal verbs

Using the *passé du subjonctif*

Perspective personnelle

Vrai ou faux? Indicate whether each sentence is true (**vrai**) or false (**faux**) for you. Remember to read each sentence aloud to practice speaking.

_____   Je doute que le président des États-Unis ait fait la sieste aujourd'hui.

_____   Je suis déçu(e) que les Américains aient élu (elected) ce président.

_____   Je regrette que l'hiver se soit terminé.

_____   Il est possible que Gérard Depardieu ait fait un nouveau film cette année.

_____   Mes parents sont contents que je sois né(e).

A. What is the correct form? Conjugate the verb in parentheses in the **passé du subjonctif** to agree with the subject. Then read the completed sentence aloud. Finally, translate the sentence into English.

1. **Nous craignons que Philippe _____ (ne pas aller) à la cérémonie.**

    _____

2. **Il est possible qu'il _____ (neiger) hier soir.**

    _____

3. **Le professeur est content que les étudiants _____ (écrire) leur nom sur leur projet.**

    _____

4. **Êtes-vous surpris que je/j' _____ (acheter) une petite voiture?**

    _____

5. **Marie est ravie que vous _____ (venir) à la soirée.**

    _____

6. **Est-il possible que nous _____ (finir) ce rapport.**

    _____

7. **Je ne pense pas que Raoul _____ (pouvoir) finir ce rapport.**

    _____

8. **Nous avons peur que Josianne _____ (ne pas faire) de son mieux.**

    _____

9. **Je suis fier (proud) que nous _____ (travailler) beaucoup.**

    _____

10. Nous ne croyons pas que nos collègues _____ (voir) notre rapport.
_____

11. Ta mère est étonnée (surprised) que tu _____ (se réveiller) de bonne heure.
_____

12. Je ne crois pas que les filles _____ (partir) sans leurs parents.
_____

13. Il est impossible que je/j' _____ (aller) chez Lise hier soir. J'étais chez moi toute la soirée!
_____

14. Mon patron est fâché que je _____ (choisir) un nouvel assistant.
_____

15. Les étudiants sont choqués que leur professeur _____ (lire) leurs essais tout de suite.
_____

16. Les Dupont doutent que Thomas _____ (dire) la vérité.
_____

17. Tu es heureux que nous _____ (aller) en France?
_____

18. La femme est horrifiée que son mari _____ (s'endormir) pendant l'opéra.
_____

19. Le patron de Ghislaine doute qu'elle _____ (apprendre) l'italien.
_____

20. Je ne suis pas sûr que M. Troude _____ (boire) du citron pressé à la soirée.
_____

B. **Now, write sentences of your own!** For each box, create one or two sentences by choosing one expression from each column and conjugating the verb accordingly. Read your sentences aloud for practice.

Maman doute que	nous ses filles ses fils	nettoyer la maison faire la vaisselle aller à l'église

1. _____
_____

| Je suis triste que | tu
mes amis
mon/ma collègue | attendre le bus
aller à Tahiti sans moi
avoir une pneumonie |

2. _____

_____

| Il est possible que | Madeleine
les Robichard
Hervé | partir en vacances
lire un bon livre
se coucher |

3. _____

_____

C. **What is the correct form?** Conjugate the verb in parentheses in either the **passé du subjonctif** *or* the **passé composé** to agree with the subject. Then read the completed sentence aloud.

1. Il est triste que ces touristes _____ (jeter) du papier par terre.

2. Je crains que mes amis _____ (se perdre).

3. Je crois que mes amis _____ (se perdre).

4. Je doute que mes enfants _____ (lire) le journal.

5. Nous croyons que tu _____ (aller) avec eux.

6. Marc et Camille pensent que le soleil _____ (causer) la mort de leur mère.

7. Je suis sûr que ma famille _____ (pouvoir) prendre des vacances.

8. Ma mère est choquée que je _____ (rentrer) avant minuit.

9. Henriette est embarrassée que ses collègues _____ (faire) son travail pendant son absence.

10. Elle est surprise qu'ils _____ (se fâcher).

11. Il est vrai que les Martin _____ (aller) aux Antilles.

12. Il est possible que les Capoulade _____ (aller) au Maroc.

13. Nous craignons que vous _____ (ne pas réparer) le téléphone.

14. Le patron dit que nos collègues _____ (finir) leur travail hier.

15. Je suis étonné que Paul _____ (faire) une erreur de calcul.

D. **Now, write sentences of your own!** Complete each sentence in one or two different ways by choosing one expression from each column and conjugating the verb accordingly (**passé du subjonctif** or **passé composé**). Read your sentences aloud for practice.

| Il est possible que
Il est vrai que
Il est clair que | je
nous
les enfants | aller au restaurant
faire du ski
s'amuser au parc |

1. _____

_____

Je doute que	le prof	manger de la glace
Est-il vrai que	vous	dormir jusqu'à midi
Je crois que	tu	prendre le dîner à 22h

2. _____

_____

Nous sommes content(e)s que	le patron	devenir malade(s)
Nous sommes tristes que	vous	s'enrhumer
Nous sommes certain(e)s que	les filles	acheter un bateau

3. _____

_____

E. **Comment dit-on?** Write these sentences in French. Read them aloud when you have finished translating.

to kiss   **s'embrasser**   in order to   **pour (+ infinitif)**

1. It is good that you **(tu)** went to the store.

_____

2. Mireille doubts that I sold the car.

_____

3. It is true that I sold it (the car).

_____

4. I think Alain went out with Sophie last night.

_____

5. Do you **(tu)** think they had fun?

_____

6. I think they liked the movie they saw.

_____

7. I don't think they kissed.

_____

8. It is obvious that Roxanne arrived early (in order) to please the boss.

_____

9. I hope you **(vous)** brushed your teeth this morning.

_____

10. The dentist is happy that you **(vous)** brushed your teeth this morning.

_____

Les mots croisés 17

Use the **passé du subjonctif** to complete the crossword puzzle.

Horizontal

3	**savoir: qu'ils ___**
5	**mettre: qu'il ___**
9	**surprendre: qu'il ___**
10	**tenir: que tu ___**
12	**confondre: qu'elles ___**
13	**guérir: qu'ils ___**
14	**revenir: que vous ___**
15	**boire: qu'on ___**
16	**se rappeler: qu'elle ___**
17	**pouvoir: que tu ___**

Vertical

1	**tomber: que vous ___**
2	**vérifier: que je/j' ___**
4	**descendre: que nous ___**
5	**craindre: que je/j___**
6	**offrir: que nous ___**
7	**connaître: qu'elle ___**
8	**suivre: que je/j' ___**
11	**naître: qu'elles ___**

18

The Literary Subjunctive Tenses: *l'Imparfait du Subjonctif, le Plus-que-parfait du Subjonctif*

There are two subjunctive tenses in French that are used in highly formal literary style. They are the **imparfait du subjonctif** and the **plus-que-parfait du subjonctif**.

The *imparfait du subjonctif*

The **imparfait du subjonctif**, or imperfect subjunctive, is found in very formal literary style in place of the present subjunctive. It is used only in formal writing, and it may be used in all the contexts for the subjunctive (see Chapter 16) when the main verb is in any past tense or in the conditional. Like the literary past tenses (see Chapter 10), the **imparfait du subjonctif** is not used in everyday writing, and it is never used in conversation.

How to recognize the imparfait du subjonctif

The forms of the **imparfait du subjonctif** are similar to the forms for the **passé simple**, which we show you again here for reference.

aller: *passé simple*		aller: *imparfait du subjonctif*	
j'allai	nous allâmes	que j'allasse	que nous allassions
tu allas	vous allâtes	que tu allasses	que vous allassiez
il/elle/on alla	ils/elles allèrent	qu'il/elle/on allât	qu'ils/elles allassent

partir: *passé simple*		partir: *imparfait du subjonctif*	
je partis	nous partîmes	que je partisse	que nous partissions
tu partis	vous partîtes	que tu partisses	que vous partissiez
il/elle/on partit	ils/elles partirent	qu'il/elle/on partît	qu'ils/elles partissent

courir: passé simple		courir: imparfait du subjonctif	
je courus	nous courûmes	que je courusse	que nous courussions
tu courus	vous courûtes	que tu courusses	que vous courussiez
il/elle/on courut	ils/elles coururent	qu'il/elle/on courût	qu'ils/elles courussent

Note that the endings for the **imparfait du subjonctif** include **ss**, except for the third person singular (**il/elle/on**), in which a circumflex is added to the vowel before the ending: **-ât, -ît, -ût**. Be sure that when reading French, you can distinguish between these two tenses.

Two verbs you may see fairly often in the **imparfait du subjonctif** are **avoir** and **être**. Except for their endings, these verbs also resemble the **passé simple** forms.

avoir: passé simple		avoir: imparfait du subjonctif	
j'eus	nous eûmes	que j'eusse	que nous eussions
tu eus	vous eûtes	que tu eusses	que vous eussiez
il/elle/on eut	ils/elles eurent	qu'il/elle/on eût	qu'ils/elles eussent

être: passé simple		être: imparfait du subjonctif	
je fus	nous fûmes	que je fusse	que nous fussions
tu fus	vous fûtes	que tu fusses	que vous fussiez
il/elle/on fut	ils/elles furent	qu'il/elle fût	qu'ils/elles fussent

As in the **passé simple**, several verbs have **imparfait du subjonctif** stems ending in **-u-** that resemble their past participles.

Infinitive	Past Participle	imparfait du subjonctif
connaître	connu	qu'il/elle connût, ils/elles connussent
courir	couru	qu'il/elle courût, ils/elles courussent
croire	cru	qu'il/elle crût, ils/elles crussent
devoir	dû	qu'il/elle dût, ils/elles dussent
lire	lu	qu'il/elle lût, ils/elles lussent
pouvoir	pu	qu'il/elle pût, ils/elles pussent

Meanings of the imparfait du subjonctif

As we have mentioned, the **imparfait du subjonctif** is found in place of the present subjunctive in very formal (literary style) written French. There is no difference in meaning between the **imparfait du subjonctif** and the present. In the following pairs of sentences, the verbs in the subjunctive may be translated in the same way, and the difference between the two tenses is one of style, rather than meaning. Remember that the **imparfait du subjonctif** is used only when the main verb in the sentence is in a past tense or in the conditional. Otherwise, only the present subjunctive is used.

L'éditeur voulait que le journaliste expliquât la situation encore une fois. *(imparfait du subjonctif)* **L'éditeur voulait que le journaliste explique la situation encore une fois.** *(présent du subjonctif)*	The editor wanted the reporter to explain the situation again.
Il a fallu que le Président partît pour l'étranger. *(imparfait du subjonctif)* **Il a fallu que le Président parte pour l'étranger.** *(présent du subjonctif)*	The president had to leave on a trip abroad.
Le patron voulait que ses employés fussent capables de l'aider. *(imparfait du subjonctif)* **Le patron voulait que ses employés soient capables de l'aider.** *(présent du subjonctif)*	The boss wanted his employees to be able to help him.
Il faudrait que ces ouvriers fissent la grève pour se faire entendre. *(imparfait du subjonctif)* **Il faudrait que ces ouvriers fassent la grève pour se faire entendre.** *(présent du subjonctif)*	Those workers should go on strike in order to make themselves heard.

Le plus-que-parfait du subjonctif

The **plus-que-parfait du subjonctif**, or pluperfect subjunctive, is used like the **imparfait du subjonctif**. In written and formal literary style, it may replace the **passé du subjonctif** (see Chapter 17) when the main verb of the sentence is in a past tense or in the conditional.

How to recognize the plus-que-parfait du subjonctif

As a compound tense, the **plus-que-parfait du subjonctif** is conjugated like the **passé du subjonctif**, except that **avoir** or **être** is in the **imparfait du subjonctif**.

A Verb Conjugated with **avoir**: **vendre**

que j'eusse vendu	**que nous eussions vendu**
que tu eusses vendu	**que vous eussiez vendu**
qu'il/elle/on eût vendu	**qu'ils/elles eussent vendu**

A Verb Conjugated with **être: partir**

que je fusse parti(e)	que nous fussions parti(e)s
que tu fusses parti(e)	que vous fussiez parti(e)(s)
qu'il fût parti	qu'ils fussent partis
qu'elle fût partie	qu'elles fussent parties
qu'on fût parti	

A Pronominal Verb: **s'amuser**

que je me fusse amusé(e)	que nous nous fussions amusé(s)
que tu te fusses amusé(e)	que vous vous fussiez amusé(e)(s)
qu'il se fût amusé	qu'ils se fussent amusés
qu'elle se fût amusé(e)	qu'elles se fussent amusées
qu'on se fût amusé	

As in the other compound tenses, the past participle in the **plus-que-parfait du subjonctif** agrees in gender and in number:

- with the subject of a verb conjugated with **être**

- with a preceding direct object of verbs conjugated with **avoir**

- with the reflexive pronoun (a preceding direct object) of pronominal verbs

Meanings of the plus-que-parfait du subjonctif

Like the **passé du subjonctif** (which it replaces), the **plus-que-parfait du subjonctif** refers to an action in the subjunctive that took place before the time expressed by the main verb in the sentence. The **plus-que-parfait du subjonctif** is used only when the main verb is in a past tense or in the conditional.

J'étais étonné que Martin eût vendu sa nouvelle voiture. *(plus-que-parfait du subjonctif)*	I was surprised that Martin had sold his new car.
Mes amis étaient tristes que je fusse parti sans eux. *(plus-que-parfait du subjonctif)*	My friends were sad that I had left without them.

In the same way that the **présent du subjonctif** replaces the **imparfait du subjonctif** in everyday (non-literary) writing, the **passé du subjonctif** is used in place of the **plus-que-parfait du subjonctif**. The meaning is the same.

J'étais étonné que Martin ait vendu sa nouvelle voiture. *(passé du subjonctif)*	I was surprised that Martin had sold his new car.
Mes amis étaient tristes que je sois parti sans eux. *(passé du subjonctif)*	My friends were sad that I had left without them.

Using the Literary Subjunctive Tenses

Because these tenses are only used in literature, we don't think it's important that you be able to produce the forms. It is, however, important to be able to recognize and distinguish these verbs when you encounter them in your reading.

A. Identifiez et changez. Imagine that you are "editing" *Les Liaisons dangereuses* (1782) by Pierre Choderlos de Laclos to make it more understandable for those unfamiliar with the literary subjunctive tenses. In each passage,* mark through occurrences of the **imparfait du subjonctif**, and write the more standard (non-literary) form of the subjunctive (i.e., **présent du subjonctif** or **passé du subjonctif**) on the line below.

*All citations are from Laclos, Pierre Choderlos de. *Les Liaisons dangereuses*. GF Flammarion, Paris. 1981. P.D.

Modèle:

Cependant Maman m'a dit si souvent qu'une Demoiselle devait rester au Couvent jusqu'à ce qu'elle ~~se mariât~~ . . . (p. 20)
se marie

1. **Cela me contrarie; mais cela me fait espérer que nous aurons le plaisir de vous voir à la noce, et j'étais fâchée qu'elle se fît sans vous.** (p. 34)

   _____

2. **Enfin, si j'avais un frère, je désirerais qu'il fût tel que M. de Valmont se montre ici.** (p. 39)

   _____

3. **Je voudrais bien le consoler; mais je ne voudrais rien faire qui fût mal.** (p. 45)

   _____

4. **Un instant après il me demanda si je voulais qu'il allât chercher ma harpe.** (pp. 47–48)

   _____

5. **J'avais bien peur qu'il ne s'en allât en même temps; mais il revint.** (p. 48)

   _____

6. **Je craignis un moment que ses ordres ne fussent révoqués, et que sa délicatesse ne me nuisît.** (p. 52) **(Attention: Deux occurrences de l'imparfait du subjonctif!)**

   _____;

   _____

7. **Eh bien! j'ai voulu que ce moyen scandaleux tournât à l'édification publique . . .** (p. 52)

   _____

8. **Mais on m'avertit que le souper est servi, et il serait trop tard pour que cette Lettre partît si je ne la fermais qu'en me retirant.** (p. 54)

   _____

9. . . . je serais vraiment peinée qu'il restât aucune trace d'un événement qui n'eût jamais dû exister. (p. 64)

_____

10. Elle m'avait demandé de lui rendre sa Lettre: je lui donnai la mienne en place, sans qu'elle eût le moindre soupçon. (p. 75)

_____

11. Je ne fus pas très étonné qu'elle ne voulût pas recevoir cette Lettre que je lui offrais tout simplement . . . (p. 75)

_____

12. . . . il faudrait qu'elle se trouvât seule avec moi . . . (pp. 75–76)

_____

13. . . . et le jour même, sans qu'elle s'en doutât, je lui ai ménagé un tête-à-tête avec son Danceny. (p. 84)

_____

14. Il est en Corse à présent, bien loin d'ici; je voudrais qu'il y restât dix ans. (p. 85)

_____

15. Je voulais, ou qu'il obtînt de cette fille de faire ce que je lui avais demandé, ou au moins qu'il s'assurât de sa discrétion . . . (pp. 94–95) (Attention: Deux occurrences de l'imparfait du subjonctif!)

_____ ;

_____

16. Il serait honteux que nous ne fissions pas ce que nous voulons, de deux enfants. (p. 110)

_____

17. Il me semble que je l'aime plus comme Danceny que comme toi, et quelquefois je voudrais qu'elle fût lui. (p. 116)

_____

18. Tout a réussi à merveille: ma seule inquiétude était que Madame de Volanges ne profitât de ce moment pour gagner la confiance de sa fille . . . (p. 128)

_____

19. J'ai donné mes ordres pour qu'on tînt ici un déjeuner prêt . . . (p. 164)

_____

20. Pour qu'elle s'en ressouvînt mieux . . . (p. 253)

_____

21. Je voudrais pour beaucoup qu'il ne vous en devînt que plus attaché . . . (p. 265)

_____

22. . . . il serait possible que nous eussions quelques droits auprès de lui . . . (p. 281)

_____

B. Identifiez et changez. Continue your "editing" job, now eliminating occurrences of the **plus-que-parfait du subjonctif** and writing the more standard (non-literary) form of the subjunctive (i.e., **présent du subjonctif** or **passé du subjonctif**) on the line below.

1. . . . **il se pourrait que tout s'y fût passé à notre satisfaction** . . . (p. 113)

   _____

2. **Vous m'aviez pourtant bien assuré, avant que je vous l'eusse dit, que cela suffisait pour vous rendre heureux.** (p. 179)

   _____

3. . . . **il ne serait pas vraisemblable que vous eussiez été témoin de ce tracas sans en demander la cause.** (p. 184)

   _____

4. . . . **j'aimerais mieux qu'il ne fût venu que ma femme de chambre** . . . (p. 196)

   _____

5. **Ah! ne croyez pas que je l'eusse laissée partir** . . . (p. 224)

   _____

6. **Elles tomberaient d'elles-mêmes, s'il se trouvait, comme il est vraisemblable, que MM. de Valmont et Danceny ne se fussent point parlé depuis leur malheureuse affaire, et qu'il n'y eût pas eu de papiers remis.** (p. 365) **(Attention: Deux occurrences du plus-que-parfait du subjonctif!)**

   _____;

   _____

7. **Ne voulant pas qu'elle pût douter que j'eusse remarqué ses divers mouvements** . . . (p. 156) **(Attention: Éliminez l'imparfait _et_ le plus-que-parfait du subjonctif dans ce passage!)**

   _____;

   _____

Part Five
Additional Topics

Additional Topics: an Overview

What is the imperative?

The *imperative* is the verbal mood that allows you to express a suggestion, a command, or a warning.

Dis toujours la vérité!	Always tell the truth!
Ne faites pas cela!	Don't do that!
Envoyons un e-mail au professeur.	Let's send the professor an e-mail.

What is the passive?

All of the sentences and exercises in the book up to this point have been *active* in their form. The verb in such sentences expresses the action that the subject performs. For many active sentences, there are corresponding *passive* sentences in which the subject of the sentence (for example, **la lettre** in the passive sentence below) does not perform the action at all: The action is expressed as being performed by someone or something.

Active	Passive
Marie a écrit cette lettre. Mary wrote that letter.	**Cette lettre a été écrite par Marie.** That letter was written by Mary.

How do negative sentences work?

You can make a sentence negative in French by placing **ne** before the verb and another negative word or expression, usually **pas**, after the verb.

Je n'aime pas me lever très tôt le matin.	I don't like to get up too early in the morning.
Désolé, je ne sais pas la réponse.	Sorry, I don't know the answer.

In the compound tenses, **ne** precedes the auxiliary verb, and **pas** (or another negative word) follows the auxiliary and comes before the past participle. In all cases, **ne** precedes the conjugated verb.

Hélène n'a pas encore fini ses devoirs.	Helen hasn't finished her homework yet.
Nous ne sommes pas partis à l'heure.	We didn't leave on time.

How are infinitives used in a sentence?

An *infinitive* may be used to complete the meaning of the main verb in a sentence. The infinitive immediately follows the verb, or it may be followed by either **à** or **de**.

Le cycliste adore gagner le Tour de France.	The cyclist adores winning the Tour de France.
Il continue à participer à la course tous les ans.	He continues to participate in the race every year.
Il refuse de se reposer sur ses lauriers.	He refuses to rest on his laurels.

What is the causative?

A *causative* verbal construction expresses an idea that relates to influencing someone to do something or to have something done. This is achieved in French through use of the verb **faire** and a second verb in the infinitive form.

Je ferai venir le médecin à la maison.	I'll get the doctor to come to the house.
Maman a fait faire la vaisselle aux enfants.	Mom had the kids wash the dishes.

19
L'impératif

The *imperative* form of the verb (in French: **l'impératif**) makes suggestions and requests. This is the form used to give orders, directions, advice, and warnings.

Regarde ces photos de mon chien.	Look at these pictures of my dog.
Lisez le chapitre 2 pour demain.	Read Chapter 2 for tomorrow.
Allons au café après la classe.	Let's go to the café after class.
N'éveillez pas le chat qui dort. (proverbe)	Let sleeping dogs lie. (Literally: "Don't wake up a sleeping cat!")

How to form the imperative

The imperative corresponds in almost all cases to the present-tense indicative form of the verb, but with the subject omitted. Use the second-person singular (the **tu** form) to address informally one person you know well, someone to whom you would say **tu**. Use the second-person plural (the **vous** form) to address more than one person or someone you don't know well.

Anne, aide-moi avec ces exercices, s'il te plaît.	Anne, please help me with these exercises.
Nous allons à la plage ce week-end. Sarah et Denis, venez avec nous!	We're going to the beach this weekend. Sarah and Denis, come with us!

Use the first-person plural (the **nous** form) to make a suggestion that includes yourself.

Invitons Sarah et Denis à nous accompagner à la plage.	Let's invite Sarah and Denis to go to the beach with us.

Exception: The second-person singular form of **-er** verbs ends in **s**, but in the imperative, this ending is dropped.

Parle français, s'il te plaît.	Speak French, please.
Ne va jamais au centre commercial sans ta carte de crédit.	Never go to the mall without your credit card.

As you see in this last example, a negative imperative sentence includes negative phrases, such as **ne . . . pas**, **ne . . . jamais**, and **ne . . . plus** in the usual place, surrounding the verb. The word order is the same as that of a declarative sentence, except that the subject pronoun is not expressed.

Ne mangeons pas à ce restaurant-là. **C'est trop cher.**	Let's not eat at that restaurant. It's too expensive.
Ne faites pas de bêtises, les enfants!	Don't get into any trouble, kids!

Irregular imperatives

The verbs **avoir**, **être**, and **savoir** have irregular imperative forms. **L'impératif** resembles the **présent du subjonctif**—no surprise, really, since you know that the subjunctive can be used to express a wish or desire. This is related to making a suggestion or giving an order.

avoir	*être*	*savoir*
aie	sois	sache
ayez	soyez	sachez
ayons	soyons	sachons

Sache que je te suivrai jusqu'au bout du monde.	Know that I will follow you to the ends of the earth.
Ayez un peu de patience, s'il vous plaît.	Please have a little patience.
Soyons raisonnables!	Let's be reasonable!

Object pronouns in imperative sentences

In the imperative, object pronouns follow the verb and are connected to the verb and to each other with a hyphen. This happens with direct and indirect object pronouns (including reflexive pronouns) and with the pronouns **y** and **en**.

Tu aimes cette robe? Achète-la!	Do you like that dress? Buy it!
Dépêchez-vous, sinon vous allez manquer votre vol.	Hurry up, or else you'll miss your flight.
La Belgique, tu dis? Oui, allons-y!	Belgium, you say? Yes, let's go there!
Si tu veux des bonbons, prends-en.	If you want some candy, take some.

If there happen to be two object pronouns in a sentence, they follow the order in the chart below. The pronouns **me** and **te** become **moi** and **toi** (their accented forms) when they appear at the end of a sentence.

-le	-moi (-m'en)	y	en
-la	-toi (t'en)		
-les	-lui		
	-nous		
	-vous		
	-leur		

Here's how this works:

Voilà mon ordinateur. Sers-t'en.	Here's my computer. Help yourself. (Use it.)
Les enfants veulent aller au zoo. D'accord, emmenons-les-y.	The kids want to go to the zoo. OK, let's take them there.
Voyez-vous ce livre-là? Donnez-le-moi, s'il vous plaît.	Do you see that book? Give it to me, please.

Do you remember the exception we mentioned, that in the imperative of **-er** verbs, the second-person singular ending **s** is dropped? When followed by **y** or **en**, though, this form maintains the **s** ending. You will see this most often in the idiomatic expression **vas-y**, which means "go ahead."

Ça va si je change le programme à la télé?	OK if I change the channel on the TV?
Oui, vas-y!	Sure, go ahead!
Des bonbons? Oui, achètes-en!	Some candy? Yes, buy some!

In negative imperatives, object pronouns take their usual place before the verb. **Ne** precedes the object pronouns. Here's their order:

me	le	lui	y	en	(verb)
te	la	leur			
se	les				
nous					
vous					

Oops, now our friends have changed their minds. Here are the imperatives from before, but they're in the negative this time.

Ne t'en sers pas, s'il te plaît.	Don't use it, please.
Ne les y emmenons pas aujourd'hui. Il va pleuvoir.	Let's not take them there today. It's going to rain.
Ne me le donnez pas, merci. Je n'en ai plus besoin.	Don't give it to me, thanks. I don't need it any longer.

Using *l'impératif*

A. **Une mère polie.** A particular mother makes many polite requests of her daughter. But when the daughter fails to respond, the mother changes to the imperative for a bit more force. Below are her original requests. Change each to the imperative (**tu** form). Then imagine that the daughter passes along the orders to all of the children in the family (**vous** form).

Modèle: Tu veux mettre la table?   *Mets la table!   Mettez la table!*

1. **Tu veux te brosser les dents?**

   _____

   _____

2. **Tu devrais avoir de la patience.**

   _____

   _____

3. **Tu pourrais m'aider?**

   _____

   _____

4. **Veux-tu sortir la poubelle?**

   _____

   _____

5. **Il vaut mieux que tu fasses les devoirs.**

   _____

   _____

6. **Tu devrais penser aux autres.**

   _____

   _____

7. **Je voudrais que tu manges les petits pois.**

   _____

   _____

8. **Veux-tu te réveiller?**

   _____

   _____

9. **Tu pourrais aller au supermarché?**

   _____

   _____

10. **Tu devrais être sage.**

_____

_____

11. **Tu veux lire le journal?**

_____

_____

12. **J'aimerais que tu apprennes à nager.**

_____

_____

B. Des ordres négatives. Now the mother (from Exercise A) is telling her daughter (**tu**) what _not_ to do. The daughter again passes the orders along to the other children (**vous**).

Modèle: **Il ne faut pas regarder la télé.** _Ne regarde pas la télé._ _Ne regardez pas la télé._

1. **Je ne veux pas que tu te battes (avec ton frère).**

_____

_____

2. **Je ne veux pas que tu écrives sur les murs.**

_____

_____

3. **Il ne faut pas que tu dises des bêtises** (stupid things)**.**

_____

_____

4. **Tu ne dois pas fumer.**

_____

_____

5. **Il ne faut pas que tu rentres après minuit.**

_____

_____

6. **Je ne veux pas que tu te fâches.**

_____

_____

7. **Tu ne dois pas vendre ma voiture.**

_____

_____

8. Je ne veux pas que tu perdes les livres.

_____

_____

9. Je n'aime pas que tu me désobéisses.

_____

_____

10. Je ne veux pas que tu maigrisses trop.

_____

_____

11. Tu ne dois pas tutoyer les professeurs.

_____

_____

12. Il ne faut pas que tu prennes des drogues.

_____

_____

13. Il ne faut pas rouspéter.

_____

_____

14. Je ne veux pas que tu ailles en vacances sans moi.

_____

_____

15. Je ne veux pas que tu te maries avant l'âge de 20 ans.

_____

_____

16. Tu ne dois pas boire de bière avant l'âge de 21 ans.

_____

_____

17. Je ne veux pas que tu te moques de moi.

_____

_____

18. Il ne faut pas que tu deviennes un acteur médiocre.

_____

_____

C. Des suggestions. You are always suggesting things to do and not to do. For each situation, suggest that the group do an appropriate activity from the list. Then suggest that the group *not* do another activity. Use the **nous** form of the **impératif**.

voir un film	**travailler dur**	**se coucher tôt**
faire un pique-nique	**se reposer**	**manger au café**
aller au restaurant	**réfléchir**	**apprendre les leçons**
finir notre travail	**jouer au football**	**étudier**
lire un bon livre	**se détendre**	**prendre un pot**

Modèle: **Il fait beau.**   *Jouons au football. N'étudions pas.*

1. **Il pleut.**

2. **Il est minuit.**

3. **Nous avons faim.**

4. **Nous voulons nager.**

5. **Nous sommes fatigués.**

6. **Nous avons envie de nous amuser.**

7. **Nous avons un examen difficile demain.**

8. **Le patron pense que nous sommes paresseux.**

D. La soupe. You love onion soup, but don't like to cook. So, you have found the following recipe on the Internet (www.recettes-cuisine.org) for your friend to cook for you. You will read the instructions and tell your friend what to do. As in many recipes written in French, the verbs are all in the infinitive form. You will need to change them to the **tu** form of the imperative. Don't forget the object pronouns! We have started for you.

Recette de gratinée au champagne (www.recettes-cuisine.org)

Pour 8 personnes :

500 g d'oignons (onions),
300 g de gruyère râpé,
3 jaunes d'oeufs,
50 g de beurre,
1 verre de porto,
1 cuillerée à soupe d'Armagnac,

sel, poivre de Cayenne,
pain grillé (toast),
1 bouteille (bottle) de champagne.

1. **Éplucher** (peel) **les oignons et les couper en tranches fines.**

2. **Dans une casserole, mettre le beurre et y faire doucement colorer**[1] **les oignons; lorsqu'ils brunissent** (get brown), **leur ajouter trois quarts (3/4) de litre d'eau, saler (peu), poivrer puis verser les deux tiers (2/3) de la bouteille de champagne.**

3. **Porter à ébullition** (bring to a boil), **laisser ensuite cuire doucement pendant 1 heure environ puis retirer du feu** (remove from heat)·

4. **Battre les jaunes d'oeufs dans le porto et les incorporer doucement** (gently) **au bouillon** (broth) **qui ne doit plus bouillir** (boil), **ajouter l'Armagnac.**

5. **Disposer le pain grillé dans des petites marmites** (pots, bowls) **individuelles, les saupoudrer** (sprinkle) **largement** (generously) **de gruyère râpé, puis recouvrir** (cover) **avec le bouillon.**

6. **Dès que le pain remonte** (comes back up) **à la surface, le saupoudrer avec le reste du fromage râpé puis mettre à four préalablement** (already) **très chaud (260°C, 8 du thermostat) pour faire gratiner quelques minutes.**

1. *Épluche* **les oignons et** *coupe-les* **en tranches fines.**

2. **Dans une casserole, _____ le beurre et _____ doucement color-er les oignons; lorsqu'ils brunissent, _____ trois quarts de litre d'eau, _____ (peu), _____ puis _____ les deux tiers de la bouteille de champagne.**

3. **_____ à ébullition, _____ ensuite cuire doucement pendant 1 heure environ puis _____ du feu.**

4. **_____ les jaunes d'oeufs dans le porto et _____ doucement au bouillon qui ne doit plus bouillir, _____ l'Armagnac.**

5. **_____ le pain grillé dans des petites marmites individuelles, _____ largement de gruyère râpé, puis _____ avec le bouillon.**

6. **Dès que le pain remonte à la surface, _____ avec le reste du fromage râpé puis _____ à four préalablement très chaud (260°C, 8 du thermostat) pour faire gratiner quelques minutes.**

[1] See Chapter 20 for a discussion of the **faire causatif** construction.

Les mots croisés 19

Use the **impératif** to solve this puzzle.

Horizontal

5   Don't go there.
7   Do your work: ___ **votre travail.**
9   Let's buy it (**la voiture**).
12 Listen to your mother: ___ **ta mère.**
14 Be good: ___ **sages.**
16 Wait for the bus: ___ **le bus.**
17 Finish your homework: ___ **tes devoirs.**
18 ___ (**savoir**) **que je t'aime.**
19 Don't say it!
20 Repeat them (**les mots de vocabulaire**).
21 ___ (**avoir**) **un peu de patience.**
22 Give them to me.
23 ___ (**réflechir**) **à votre problème.**

Vertical

1   Sleep!
2   Get up!
3   Let's invite them.
4   Do it (**ton travail**).
6   Let's relax!
8   Don't worry about it (**ne pas s'en faire**)!
10 Sing!
11 Let's have fun!
13 Wake up!
15 Get dressed!

20
The Passive Voice, Negation, and Infinitive Constructions

The passive voice

In a sentence in the active voice, the *subject of the sentence* performs the action of the verb.

Tous les enfants chantent cette chanson-là.	All children sing that song.
Le professeur expliquera la leçon.	The professor will explain the lesson.
Onze pays membres ont ratifié la nouvelle constitution.	Eleven member states ratified the new constitution.

In the passive voice, the action of the verb is performed *by* someone or something.

Cette chanson-là est chantée par tous les enfants.	That song is sung by all children.
La leçon sera expliquée par le professeur.	The lesson will be explained by the professor.
La nouvelle constitution a été ratifiée par onze pays membres.	The new constitution was ratified by eleven member states.

Notice that there is no difference in meaning between these pairs of active and passive sentences. The difference is one of style and emphasis.

How to form the passive voice

In English, the passive is formed with the verb *to be* and the past participle (e.g., "the passive is formed"). French, likewise, forms the passive voice with the verb **être**—in any tense or mood—and the past participle. The verb **aimer** looks like this in the passive voice, present tense:

je suis aimé/aimée	I am loved
tu es aimé/aimée	you are loved
il est aimé	he is loved
elle est aimée	she is loved
on est aimé	one is loved, we are loved
nous sommes aimés/aimées	we are loved
vous êtes aimé/aimée/aimés/aimées	you are loved
ils sont aimés	they are loved
elles sont aimées	they are loved

The past participle of a passive verb agrees in gender and in number with the subject of the sentence, just as an adjective does. All the other tenses can be formed simply by using the appropriate corresponding tense of **être**.

j'étais aimé(e), etc. *(imparfait)*	I was loved
j'ai été aimé(e), etc. *(passé composé)*	I was loved, I have been loved
je serai aimé(e), etc. *(futur)*	I will be loved
je serais aimé(e), etc. *(conditionnel)*	I would be loved
j'aurais été aimé(e), etc. *(passé du conditionnel)*	I would have been loved
je fus aimé(e), etc. *(passé simple)*	I was loved

Often, the performer of the action (the agent) is not identified. This happens in sentences that make general statements or in other cases where the identity of the agent(s) is not relevant.

La porte a été fermée à clé.	The door was locked.
S'il neige demain, le cours sera annulé.	If it snows tomorrow, class will be cancelled.
Les voitures sont fabriquées dans plusieurs pays.	Cars are manufactured in several countries.

Generally, the agent is introduced by the preposition **par**.

Les meilleurs chocolats sont fabriqués par les Belges.	The best chocolates are manufactured by the Belgians.
Ces photos ont été prises par un photographe célèbre.	These photos were taken by a famous photographer.

In passive sentences that describe emotions and conditions rather than actions, the agent, if there is one, is introduced by **de**, rather than by **par**.

Le français est très apprécié des étudiants partout dans le monde.	French is highly esteemed by students everywhere in the world.
Les montagnes étaient couvertes de neige.	The mountains were covered with snow.

In French, only transitive verbs (verbs that have a direct object) are used in the passive voice because the *direct object* of an active verb is the *subject* of a passive verb. If there is no direct object, the sentence cannot be made passive.

La Maison Blanche reçoit des centaines de lettres.	The White House receives hundreds of letters.
Des centaines de lettres sont reçues par la Maison Blanche.	Hundreds of letters are received by the White House.
Mais:	But:
La Maison Blanche répond à des centaines de lettres.	The White House answers hundreds of letters.
(no passive: The phrase à **des centaines de lettres** is an indirect object and cannot become the subject of a passive sentence.)	Hundreds of letters are answered by the White House. (The passive is acceptable for this sentence in English, but not in French.)

Other ways to express the passive voice

After all this, we need to tell you that in fact, the passive voice is not used very often in French, and it is very often avoided when possible. If the agent is not stated, you can use a sentence in the active voice with *on* as the subject. This only works when the agent is not stated. The following sentences are "*on*" versions of the passive sentences without agents that we showed you above. These are still best translated with a passive verb in English, but other translations are possible.

On a fermé la porte à clé.	The door was locked. (Someone locked the door.)
S'il neige demain, on annulera le cours.	If it snows tomorrow, class will be cancelled.
On fabrique les voitures dans plusieurs pays.	Cars are manufactured in several countries. (They make cars in several countries.)

Another way to avoid using the passive voice is to use a reflexive verb. This construction is used only in the third person (with **se**) with inanimate objects. As sentences such as this make a generalization, they are often, but not always, stated in the present tense.

Les journaux se vendent partout.	Newspapers are sold everywhere.
Les voitures se fabriquent dans plusieurs pays.	Cars are manufactured in several countries.
Le vin blanc se boit frais.	White wine is drunk chilled.
Ça se comprend.	That's easily understood. (That makes sense.)
Rome ne s'est pas fait en un jour.	Rome was not built in a day.

Using the passive voice

Perspective personnelle

Vrai ou faux? Indicate whether each sentence is true (**vrai**) or false (**faux**) for you. Remember to read each sentence aloud for practice.

_____ **Je suis aimé(e) de mon patron (professeur).**
_____ **Toutes mes factures ont été payées le mois dernier.**
_____ **La terre est couverte de neige aujourd'hui.**
_____ **Mes cours sont annulés fréquemment.**
_____ **L'histoire de Blanche Neige** (*Snow White*) **est connue de tous les enfants.**
_____ **Mon travail est bien fait.**
_____ **Je suis bien payé(e).**

A. **À l'actif.** Change each sentence from passive to active voice. Remember that the verb in the active sentence should be stated in the same tense as the verb **être** is stated in the passive sentence.

Modèle: **Les frites sont aimées des enfants.**   *Les enfants aiment les frites.*

1. **Les employés sont bien payés par la compagnie.**

2. Les devoirs seront faits par les étudiants.

_____

3. Une gaffe a été faite par Guy.

_____

4. Ce film a été vu par mes collègues.

_____

5. La Suisse était aimée de mes grands-parents.

_____

6. Mes clés auraient été perdues par mon fils.

_____

7. Mes clés seront trouvées par ma fille.

_____

8. Les règles du jeu sont comprises par les filles.

_____

9. Le nouveau roman de Laurent Gaudé a été lu par Paul.

_____

B. **Au passif.** Now, change these active sentences into the passive voice. If an agent (**le patron** in the model) is mentioned, incorporate the agent into the passive sentence. Remember that the past participle (**offerte** in the model) must agree with the subject of the passive sentence.

Modèle: Le patron a offert une boîte de chocolats à la secrétaire.
                 Une boîte de chocolats a été offerte à la secrétaire par le patron.

1. Est-ce que l'espagnol se parle au Brésil?

_____

2. Le professeur rendra les essais aux étudiants.

_____

3. On nettoie les rues de Paris chaque nuit.

_____

4. Le magicien a ensorcelé la belle princesse.

_____

5. On m'a suivi dans la rue hier soir.

_____

6. On emploie les ordinateurs pour communiquer.

_____

7. **Arthur Rimbaud a écrit ces poèmes.**

_____

8. **On vend les tee-shirts partout.**

_____

C. Comment dit-on? Write these sentences in French. Translate them, using the passive voice; then rewrite them in the active voice in French. Read the sentences aloud when you have finished translating.

1. French is spoken in Cameroun.

_____

_____

2. This painting was created by Paul Gauguin.

_____

_____

Negative sentences and expressions

As we have seen throughout this book, you can express the negative form of a sentence in French by inserting **ne** before the verb and **pas** after the verb. Here are some other negative expressions with **ne** that work the same way.

ne . . . jamais	never, not ever
ne . . . plus	no more, no longer, not anymore
ne . . . pas encore	not yet
ne . . . pas du tout	not at all
ne . . . que	nothing but, no one but, only
ne . . . rien	nothing, not anything
ne . . . personne	nobody, no one, not anybody

Here's how these look in a sentence. **Ne** always becomes **n'** before a word beginning with a vowel sound.

Mes parents ne téléchargent jamais les mp3.	My parents never download MP3s.
Je n'étudie plus le piano.	I'm not studying piano anymore.
Nous ne savons pas encore tous les verbes.	We don't know all the verbs yet.
Je n'aime pas du tout les escargots!	I don't like snails at all!
On ne parlera que français en classe.	Only French (Nothing but French) will be spoken in class.
«Non, je ne regrette rien.» (titre d'une chanson très connue d'Edith Piaf)	"No, I have no regrets [I don't regret anything]." (Title of a famous song by Edith Piaf)

Rien and **personne** are pronouns, so they can be the subject of a sentence. When this happens, they are in normal subject position at the beginning of the sentence. If one serves as the object of a preposition, it appears after the preposition. Remember not to confuse **personne** (no one) with **une personne** (a person).

«Je dis que rien ne m'épouvante.» (Air de l'opéra *Carmen* de Georges Bizet)	"I say that nothing frightens me." (Aria from Georges Bizet's opera *Carmen*)
Personne n'a été absent aujourd'hui.	Nobody was absent today.
De quoi as-tu besoin? Je n'ai besoin de rien.	What do you need? I don't need anything.
Nous n'avons parlé à personne ce matin.	We haven't spoken to anyone this morning.

We said earlier that you can make a sentence negative in French by placing **ne** before the verb and **pas** (**jamais, plus . . .**) after the verb. It's more accurate to say that the two negative expressions are placed around the *conjugated* verb. This means that, in the compound tenses, the negative expressions surround the auxiliary verb, and if the verb occurs with an infinitive, the negative words surround the main verb.

Nous n'avons jamais visité la Tour Eiffel.	We've never been to the Eiffel Tower.
L'avion ne va pas arriver avant 13.00 heures.	The plane will not be arriving before 1:00 p.m.
Hélène ne veut pas partir tout de suite.	Hélène doesn't want to leave right away.

Using negation

Perspective personnelle

Vrai ou faux? Indicate whether each sentence is true (**vrai**) or false (**faux**). Remember to read each sentence aloud for practice.

_____ Je ne pleure jamais.
_____ Je ne m'entends avec personne.
_____ Je n'aime pas du tout la musique classique.
_____ Je n'ai rien fait hier.
_____ Je n'ai pas encore mangé aujourd'hui.

D. Réponses négatives. A particular father always says, "No." Give his answers to his children's questions below. Use negations *other than* **ne . . . pas.**

Modèle: **Est-ce que tu as vu Pierre?**
Non, je n'ai vu personne.

1. **Est-ce qu'il fait toujours beau en avril?**

_____

2. **Est-ce que Maman a déjà acheté nos cadeaux de Noël?**

_____

3. **Est-ce que tu aimes beaucoup les pommes de terre?**

_____

4. **Est-ce qu'on a tout fait pour préparer notre voyage?**

   _____

5. **Est-ce que tout le monde aime chanter?**

   _____

6. **Est-ce que nous avons vu tout le monde à la soirée?**

   _____

7. **Est-ce que tout t'intéresse?**

   _____

8. **Est-ce que Mamie fume toujours?**

   _____

E. Comment dit-on? Write these sentences in French. Read them aloud when you have finished translating.

1. We don't like yellow apples. We only want the red ones.

   _____

2. No one makes his/her own pies.

   _____

3. I don't play the violin any more.

   _____

4. He never makes his bed.

   _____

5. We didn't do anything yesterday.

   _____

6. Guy hasn't finished his homework yet.

   _____

Constructions with infinitives

The infinitive is the non-conjugated form of the verb: It has no person and no number. It cannot function as the main verb in a sentence, but it often complements the meaning of the main verb, which, of course, is always conjugated.

When an infinitive completes the meaning of a main verb, it may follow the main verb directly, or it may be preceded by **à** or **de**. There is no way to predict which of these structures a verb will follow—but it will always use the same structure to introduce an infinitive. It's the main verb, and not the infinitive, that determines the structure.

Verbs that are followed directly by an infinitive

adorer	détester	laisser	sembler	vouloir
aimer	devoir	penser	valoir mieux (il	
aller	espérer	pouvoir	vaut mieux)	
désirer	falloir (il faut)	savoir	venir	

Marc adore faire de la planche à voile.	Marc loves to go windsurfing.
Nous espérons aller en Europe l'été prochain.	We hope to go to Europe next summer.
«Je suis venu te dire que je m'en vais.» (Titre d'une chanson de Serge Gainsbourg)	"I've come to tell you that I'm leaving." (Serge Gainsbourg song title)

Verbs that are followed by à + infinitive

aider à	commencer à	s'habituer à	s'occuper à
s'amuser à	continuer à	hésiter à	réussir à
apprendre à	encourager à	inviter à	songer à
chercher à	enseigner à	se mettre à	tenir à

Nous apprenons à utiliser les verbes français.	We're learning how to use French verbs.
Je ne m'habituerai jamais à me lever si tôt le matin.	I'll never get used to getting up so early in the morning.
David a réussi à trouver un nouvel emploi.	David succeeded in finding a new job.

Verbs that are followed by de + infinitive

accepter de	avoir peur de	se dépêcher de	négliger de	refuser de
s'arrêter de	cesser de	empêcher de	offrir de	regretter de
avoir besoin de	choisir de	essayer de	oublier de	remercier de
avoir envie de	craindre de	finir de	parler de	rêver de
avoir l'intention de	décider de	manquer de	prier de	tenter de

J'ai l'intention de me spécialiser en français.	I intend to major in French.
Mes parents ont choisi de vivre à la campagne.	My parents chose to live in the country.
N'oubliez pas de rendre vos devoirs.	Don't forget to turn in your homework.

The causative construction

French uses the verb **faire** with an infinitive (French: **faire causatif**) to express the idea of causing something to happen—making someone do something or having something done (by someone else). In **faire causatif** expressions with a reflexive verb, the reflexive pronoun precedes the verb **faire**.

Ce prof-là fait travailler ses étudiants.	That professor makes his students work.
J'ai fait réparer ma voiture hier.	I had my car repaired yesterday.
Elle se fera faire une robe de mariée.	She will have her wedding dress made.
Tu t'es fait couper les cheveux! Très chic!	You got your hair cut! Very chic!

If the causative construction with **faire** has two objects, the person performing the action "caused" by **faire** is preceded by the preposition **à**.

Ces profs ont fait ecrire une rédaction à leurs étudiants.	These professors have had their students write an essay.
On faisait toujours faire la vaisselle à notre petit frère.	We would always get our little brother to do the dishes.

In case the expression with **à** is ambiguous, **par** may be used instead for the person performing the caused action.

Tous les soirs, Maman faisait lire une histoire aux enfants.	Every night, Mom would have a story read by the children / to the children.
Tous les soirs, Maman faisait lire une histoire par les enfants.	Every night, Mom would have a story read by the children (would have the children read a story).

Often, you "cause something to happen" when you are cooking, and **faire causatif** is used in French recipes to reflect this.[1]

faire bouillir	to boil
faire cuire	to cook
faire fondre	to melt
faire frire	to fry
faire gratiner	to brown (in the oven)
faire revenir, faire colorer	to brown (in a frying pan), to sauté

[1] See Chapter 19, exercise D.

Using infinitive constructions

Perspective personnelle

Vrai ou faux? Indicate whether each sentence is true (**vrai**) or false (**faux**) for you. Remember to read each sentence aloud to practice.

_____ **Je fais laver ma voiture.**
_____ **Je m'amuse à conjuguer les verbes français.**
_____ **J'ai l'intention de partir en vacances cet été.**
_____ **Quand j'étais à l'école, j'oubliais régulièrement de faire mes devoirs.**
_____ **J'ai fait réparer ma voiture récemment.**

F. **Quelle préposition?** Complete the following sentences with **à**, **de**, **d'**, or X (if no preposition is required).

1. **Pierre veut _____ déménager, mais sa femme préfère _____ rester dans la même maison, et son fils refuse absolument _____ bouger.**

2. **J'ai enfin réussi _____ trouver un appartement disponible et pas trop cher!**

3. **Tu ne veux pas t'arrêter _____ chanter?**

4. **Est-ce que vous allez _____ parler au patron à propos du problème avec Geneviève?**

5. **Je voudrais apprendre _____ parler italien.**

6. Mon frère espère _____ recevoir le prix Nobel pour son nouveau roman.

7. Tu dois _____ offrir un cadeau à ton frère pour son anniversaire. Est-ce que tu as commencé _____ réfléchir aux possibilités?

8. Mes collègues s'occupent _____ finir le projet.

9. Est-ce que les enfants savent _____ nager tout seules?

10. Jeannine a invité ses amies _____ venir chez elle. Elles vont s'amuser _____ jouer aux cartes.

11. Mes fils s'habituent _____ faire leur propre lessive. Mais ils oublient parfois _____ enlever les vêtements du séchoir (dryer).

12. Mon mari a l'intention _____ trouver un nouvel emploi.

13. Jérôme et Sylvie regrettent _____ avoir insulté le prof. Ils ont envie _____ quitter l'école maintenant.

14. Il ne faut pas _____ fumer à moins que vous désiriez _____ mourir très jeune.

15. Avez-vous essayé _____ lire À *la recherche du temps perdu?* Je tiens _____ le finir, mais je crains _____ ne rien comprendre!

16. Mon cousin a décidé _____ divorcer sa femme. Il a peur _____ lui en parler pourtant.

G. Now, write sentences of your own! For each box, create two sentences by choosing one expression from each column and conjugating the verb accordingly. Read your sentences aloud for practice.

Maman	vouloir	à	jouer du piano
Papa	hésiter	de	préparer le dîner
les enfants	refuser	(no preposition)	danser

1. _____

   _____

Je	rêver	à	voyager en Chine
vous	songer	de	se marier
nous	espérer	(no preposition)	devenir célèbre(s)

2. _____

   _____

Marie-Hélène	détester	à	confronter son époux/épouse
mon ami	avoir peur de	de	se plaindre au patron
tu	hésiter	(no preposition)	démissionner

3. _____

   _____

H. Comment dit-on? Write these sentences in French. Read them aloud when you have finished translating.

   1. I refuse to work on Sundays.

   _____

2. I'm learning to play the piano.

_____

3. Do you **(tu)** want to use the computer?

_____

4. They are afraid to speak to the boss.

_____

5. Are you **(vous)** going to resign?

_____

I. Un tyran implacable. Your boss is a real taskmaster. Below is a list of things done in the office. Indicate what the boss has everyone do.

Modèle: **faire du café (Richard)**   *Le patron fait faire du café à Richard.*

1. **taper les rapports (les secrétaires)**

_____

2. **essuyer les fenêtres (Victor)**

_____

3. **répondre au téléphone (Yves)**

_____

4. **examiner les budgets (Alex)**

_____

5. **téléphoner aux clients (Hervé)**

_____

6. **vérifier les stocks (Xavier)**

_____

J. Comment dit-on? Write these sentences in French. Read them aloud when you have finished translating.

1. My mother makes my father do the dishes every night.

_____

2. Melt the butter in a small saucepan.

_____

3. The professor made his students write a five-page essay.

_____

4. She has her hair cut by Mme Siseaux.

_____

5. I had my hair cut.

_____

Les mots croisés 20

Finish the translations to complete the puzzle.

Horizontal

6   No one loves me: ___ m'aime.
8   Cookies make you (one) get fat: **Les biscuits ___.**
9   The teacher makes us write papers: **Le prof ___ écrire des dissertations.**
10 We haven't seen that exposition yet: **Nous n'avons ___ vu cette exposition.**
16 He's afraid of making his boss mad: **Il ___ fâcher son patron.**
17 You don't like pizza at all?: **Vous n'aimez ___ la pizza?**
18 He only eats salmon: **Il ___ du saumon.**

Vertical

1   I hesitate to do it: **Je/j'___ le faire.**
2   That woman makes her husband wait: **Cette femme ___ son mari.**
3   Children make themselves loved: **Les enfants ___ aimer.**
4   I'm not saying anything: **Je/J' ___.**
5   I've never eaten snails: **Je/J' ___ mangé d'escargots.**
7   Vivienne doesn't smoke (fumer) anymore: **Vivienne ___.**
11 She doesn't speak with anyone: **Elle ne parle ___.**
12 You're starting to irritate me: **Vous ___ m'énerver.**
13 We forgot to make the cake: **Nous avons ___ faire le gâteau.**
14 They are afraid to fail: **Ils ___'échouer.**
15 They never drink: **Elles ne boivent ___.**

Appendix

A Summary of Tenses

Here are all the verb tenses presented in this book, shown together for quick reference and review.

The indicative tenses

Le présent (the present tense)
J'apprends les verbes français.

I'm learning French verbs.

Le passé composé (the compound past tense)
J'ai appris les verbes français.

I learned French verbs.

L'imparfait (the imperfect tense)
J'apprenais les verbes français.

I was learning French verbs.

Le plus-que-parfait (the pluperfect tense)
J'avais appris les verbes français.

I had [already] learned French verbs.

Le futur (the future tense)
J'apprendrai les verbes français.

I will learn French verbs.

Le futur antérieur (the future perfect tense)
J'aurai appris les verbes français.

I will have learned French verbs.

Le conditionnel (the conditional tense)
J'apprendrais les verbes français.

I would learn French verbs.

Le conditionnel passé (the past conditional tense)

J'aurais appris les verbes français.   I would have learned French verbs.

L'impératif (the imperative)

Alex, apprends les verbes français!   Alex, learn French verbs!
Alex et Chloë, apprenez les verbes français!   Alex and Chloë, learn French verbs!
Apprenons les verbes français!   Let's learn French verbs!

The subjunctive tenses

Le présent du subjonctif (the present subjunctive tense)

Il faut que j'apprenne les verbes français.   I have to learn French verbs.

Le passé du subjonctif (the past subjunctive tense)

Le prof veut que nous ayons appris les verbes avant l'examen.   The teacher wants us to have learned the verbs before the test.

The literary tenses, indicative and subjunctive

Le passé simple (the simple past tense)

Frédéric apprit les verbes français.   Fred learned French verbs.

Le passé antérieur (the past anterior tense)

Quand il eut appris les verbes, Frédéric décida qu'ils n'étaient pas trop difficiles.   When he had learned the verbs, Fred decided that they weren't very difficult.

L'imparfait du subjonctif (the imperfect subjunctive tense)

Il fallait que Frédéric apprît les verbes français.   It was necessary that Fred learn French verbs.

Le plus-que-parfait du subjonctif (the pluperfect subjunctive tense)

Le prof était étonné que Frédéric eût appris les verbes si vite.   The teacher was astonished that Fred had learned the verbs so quickly.

Proverbs and Expressions

Here are some well-known French proverbs and expressions. See if you can guess what their English equivalents are. Some are close, and others express the same idea quite differently. The answers are on page 298.

1. **Le chat parti, les souris dansent.**

   _____

2. **La fin justifie les moyens.**

   _____

3. **Chat échaudé craint l'eau froide.**

   _____

4. **Comme on fait son lit, on se couche.**

   _____

5. **Il n'y a pas de fumée sans feu.**

   _____

6. **Qui se ressemble s'assemble.**

   _____

7. **Rome ne s'est pas fait en un jour.**

   _____

8. **L'appétit vient en mangeant.**

   _____

9. **Deux avis valent mieux qu'un.**

   _____

10. **L'enfer est pavé de bonnes intentions.**

   _____

11. **C'est en forgeant qu'on devient forgeron.**

   _____

12. **Des goûts et des couleurs, il ne faut pas discuter.**

   _____

13. **Heureux au jeu, malheureux en amour.**

   _____

14. **Un «tiens» vaut mieux que deux «tu l'auras».**

   _____

15. **Il faut battre le fer pendant qu'il est chaud.**

_____

16. **Déshabiller Pierre pour payer Paul.**

_____

17. **Loin des yeux, loin du coeur.**

_____

18. **Mains froides, coeur chaud.**

_____

19. **Il n'y a que le premier pas qui coûte.**

_____

20. **Mieux vaut tard que jamais.**

_____

21. **N'éveillez pas le chat qui dort.**

_____

22. **Un homme averti en vaut deux.**

_____

23. **Pas de nouvelles, bonnes nouvelles.**

_____

24. **Pierre qui roule n'amasse pas mousse.**

_____

25. **Plus on est de fous, plus on rit.**

_____

26. **Mettre la charrue devant les boeufs.**

_____

27. **Qui ne risque rien n'a rien.**

_____

28. **Tel père, tel fils.**

_____

29. **Tous les chemins mènent à Rome.**

_____

30. **Rira bien qui rira le dernier.**

_____

For More Practice

Here are some additional exercises to give you more practice in conjugating and using French verbs.

Chapter 1

I. Supply the missing pronoun. Choose from **tu, il, nous, vous, elles**.

Modèle: _____ parlent arabe couramment.
           <u>Elles</u> parlent arabe couramment.

1. _____ déjeunent au restaurant le dimanche.
2. _____ vends ta moto?
3. _____ mangeons de la dinde aux marrons à Noël.
4. _____ vouvoyez vos grands-parents?
5. _____ trouves intéressant le professeur d'histoire?
6. _____ pars en vacances bientôt?
7. _____ achetons notre pain dans cette boulangerie.
8. _____ adore la classe de biologie.
9. _____ discutons des problèmes au Moyen Orient.
10. _____ nettoie la cuisine pour ses parents.
11. _____ répondons aux courriels tout de suite.
12. _____ promènent leur chien tous les matins.
13. _____ parlez anglais, n'est-ce pas?
14. _____ travaille beaucoup le matin.
15. _____ détestons les concombres.
16. _____ dort souvent en classe.
17. _____ envoient des lettres au président.
18. _____ étudies à la bibliotheque?
19. _____ désobéit à ses parents.
20. _____ finissons cet exercice.
21. _____ jouent au football avec leurs amis.
22. _____ essayons de comprendre nos enfants adolescents.
23. _____ sortent avec leurs amies le samedi soir.
24. _____ préfères le chocolat ou la vanille?
25. _____ aimez le cinéma italien?

II. For each verb, supply the form requested and give the English equivalent.

Modèle: parler: elle _____   =   _____

           elle <u>parle</u>   =   <u>she speaks, she is speaking, she does speak</u>

1. servir: tu _____   =   _____

2. entrer: je _____   =   _____

3. travailler: ils _____   =   _____

4. dessiner: tu _____   =   _____

5. obéir: il _____   =   _____

6. répondre: je _____   =   _____

7. regarder: vous _____   =   _____

8. téléphoner: on _____   =   _____

9. souffrir: elle _____   =   _____

10. vendre: tu _____   =   _____

11. nager: nous _____   =   _____

12. acheter: je _____   =   _____

13. finir: nous _____   =   _____

14. entendre: on _____   =   _____

15. parler: il _____   =   _____

16. ouvrir: nous _____   =   _____

17. exagérer: tu _____   =   _____

18. demander: elles _____   =   _____

19. attendre: nous _____   =   _____

20. balayer: tu _____   =   _____

21. couvrir: vous _____   =   _____

22. sécher: elles _____   =   _____

23. jouer: je _____   =   _____

24. rougir: vous _____   =   _____

25. arriver: tu _____   =   _____

26. jeter: je _____   =   _____

27. commencer: nous _____   =   _____

28. finir: ils _____   =   _____

29. grossir: nous _____   =   _____

30. défendre: elle _____   =   _____

31. chercher: on _____   =   _____

32. tolérer: nous _____   =   _____

33. danser: elles _____   =   _____

34. **finir: je** _____ = _____

35. **effrayer: vous** _____ = _____

36. **dormir: ils** _____ = _____

37. **étudier: vous** _____ = _____

38. **partir: je** _____ = _____

39. **servir: elles** _____ = _____

40. **employer: elles** _____ = _____

Chapter 2

I. Supply the missing pronoun. Choose from **tu, il, nous, vous, elles**.

Modèle: _____ **parlent arabe couramment.**
Elles parlent arabe couramment.

1. _____ **conduit très prudemment.**
2. _____ **suivez un cours de psychologie?**
3. _____ **sont assez perspicaces.**
4. _____ **vis avec tes parents?**
5. _____ **sommes ravis de vous voir!**
6. _____ **mourons de faim!**
7. _____ **vont à l'église tous les dimanches.**
8. _____ **prend trop de médicaments à mon avis.**
9. _____ **lisent l'allemand et le français.**
10. _____ **font leurs devoirs après le dîner.**
11. _____ **apprends à danser le tango?**
12. _____ **ont un chien qui s'appelle Éros.**
13. **Qu'est-ce que** _____ **buvez?**
14. _____ **devons rendre visite à notre grand-mère.**
15. **Est-ce que** _____ **connais Richard François?**
16. _____ **vaut mieux acheter une maison que louer un appartement.**
17. _____ **rit trop facilement.**
18. _____ **ne crois pas que je t'aime?**
19. _____ **mettent du beurre sur leur pain.**
20. _____ **allons au théâtre. Veux-**_____ **aller avec nous?**

II. For each verb, supply the form requested and give the English equivalent.

Modèle: parler: elle _____   =   _____
elle parle   =   she speaks, she is speaking, she does speak

1. **suivre: je** _____   =   _____
2. **être: je** _____   =   _____
3. **courir: tu** _____   =   _____
4. **faire: ils** _____   =   _____
5. **comprendre: elle** _____   =   _____
6. **voir: vous** _____   =   _____
7. **écrire: ils** _____   =   _____

8. **avoir: je** _____ = _____
9. **lire: tu** _____ = _____
10. **aller: elles** _____ = _____
11. **savoir: je** _____ = _____
12. **croire: vous** _____ = _____
13. **recevoir: iis** _____ = _____
14. **mettre: tu** _____ = _____
15. **devoir: on** _____ = _____
16. **vouloir: tu** _____ = _____
17. **pouvoir: nous** _____ = _____
18. **venir: il** _____ = _____
19. **dire: vous** _____ = _____
20. **apprendre: je** _____ = _____
21. **boire: nous** _____ = _____
22. **connaître: vous** _____ = _____
23. **mourir: il** _____ = _____
24. **prendre: elles** _____ = _____
25. **rire: nous** _____ = _____

Chapter 3

I. Supply the missing present tense forms of the verb **s'habiller** and give their English equivalents.

Modèle: Il _____ = _____

Il <u>s'habille</u> = <u>He gets dressed, he is getting dressed, he does get dressed.</u>

je _____ = _____

nous _____ = _____

elles _____ = _____

vous _____ = _____

tu _____ = _____

elle _____ = _____

II. Supply the missing present tense forms of the verb **se détendre** and give their English equivalents.

Modèle: Nous _____ = _____

Nous <u>nous détendons</u> = <u>We relax, we are relaxing, we do relax.</u>

elle _____ = _____

vous _____ = _____

ils _____ = _____

tu _____ = _____

je _____ = _____

il _____ = _____

III. Supply the missing present tense forms of the verb **s'endormir** and give their English equivalents.

Modèle: Elles _____ = _____

Elles <u>s'endorment</u> = <u>They fall asleep, they are falling asleep, they do fall asleep.</u>

nous _____ = _____

ils _____ = _____

tu _____ = _____

vous _____ = _____

je _____ = _____

elle _____ = _____

IV. **Comment dit-on?** Give a French translation of the following sentences. Use pronominal verbs wherever possible!

1. I remember Rachel.

   _____

2. Georges gets up, gets dressed, shaves, and leaves.

   _____

3. Go to bed!

   _____

4. We talk to each other every day.

   _____

5. My parents get along well.

   _____

6. Don't worry!

   _____

7. Yvonne is taking care of the dog.

   _____

8. Cécile and Rodrigue are getting married Saturday.

   _____

9. Are you interested in history?

   _____

10. Let's rest a little.

   _____

11. I get bored in Philosophy class.

   _____

214 FRENCH VERB WORKBOOK

Chapter 4

I. **Quelle heure est-il?** When after 12 pm, give the 24-hour version as well.

1. 12:00 am   _____

2. 3:00 am   _____

3. 4:30 am   _____

4. 8:45 am   _____

5. 10:50 am   _____

6. 12:00 pm   _____

                    _____

7. 1:05 pm   _____

                    _____

8. 2:15 pm   _____

                    _____

9. 4:40 pm   _____

                    _____

10. 7:20 pm   _____

                    _____

11. 10:30 pm   _____

                    _____

12. 11:45 pm   _____

                    _____

II. **Comment dit-on?** Translate the following sentences into French.

1. What's the weather like? _____

2. It's raining cats and dogs! _____

3. It's foggy and freezing. _____

4. Is it nice out? _____

5. No, it's windy and raining. _____

III. Say what each person has just done using the expression **venir de**.

Modèle: se réveiller (Marc)   <u>**Marc vient de se réveiller.**</u>

  1. **manger (Jérôme et ses parents)** _____.
  2. **faire la vaisselle (nous)** _____.
  3. **partir (Francine)** _____.
  4. **aller au cinéma (je)** _____.
  5. **prendre des photos (vous)** _____.
  6. **écrire un poème (tu)** _____.

IV. Say what each person is in the middle of doing using the expression **être en train de** + infinitif.

Modèle: étudier les verbes français (nous)   <u>Nous sommes en train d'étudier les verbes français.</u>

  1. **jouer au tennis (Bertrand)** _____.
  2. **discuter de la politique (Hervé et Alice)** _____.
  3. **lire (tu)** _____.
  4. **écrire (nous)** _____.
  5. **apprendre le français (je)** _____.
  6. **écouter de la musique (vous)** _____.

V. Say what each person is going to do using the expression **aller** + infinitif.

Modèle: faire les courses (je)   <u>Je vais faire les courses.</u>

  1. **se déguiser (les enfants)** _____.
  2. **téléphoner à ses parents (Robert)** _____.
  3. **faire une promenade (nous)** _____.
  4. **divorcer (les Dupont)** _____.
  5. **attendre le bus (tu)** _____.
  6. **faire de l'exercice (vous)** _____.
  7. **aller au marché (je)** _____.

Chapter 5

I. Jeopardy! Write an appropriate question that would elicit the underlined part of each answer. Write both the inversion and the **est-ce que** versions. Use the *tu* form when addressing one person (as in the model).

Modèle: **QUESTION:** _____

   QUESTION: _____

   RÉPONSE: J'ai <u>34 ans</u>.

   QUESTION: <u>**Quel âge est-ce que tu as?**</u>

   QUESTION: <u>**Quel âge as-tu?**</u>

   RÉPONSE: J'ai <u>34 ans.</u>

1. **QUESTION:** _____

   QUESTION: _____

   RÉPONSE: J'ai mon cours de français <u>dans le bâtiment Furman</u>.

2. **QUESTION:** _____

   QUESTION: _____

   RÉPONSE: Nous avons cours <u>le lundi, le mardi, le jeudi et le vendredi</u>.

3. **QUESTION:** _____

   QUESTION: _____

   RÉPONSE: Marc est content <u>parce qu'il voyage en France</u>.

4. **QUESTION:** _____

   QUESTION: _____

   RÉPONSE: Il y a <u>deux</u> chocolats dans la boîte.

5. **QUESTION:** _____

   QUESTION: _____

   RÉPONSE: Jérôme déjeune <u>à 11h30</u>.

6. **QUESTION:** _____

   QUESTION: _____

   RÉPONSE: <u>Josette</u> aime chanter.

7. **QUESTION:** _____

   QUESTION: _____

   RÉPONSE: Je dîne avec <u>mes amis</u>.

8. **QUESTION:** _____
    QUESTION: _____
    RÉPONSE: Nous étudions <u>le français</u>.

9. **QUESTION:** _____
    QUESTION: _____
    RÉPONSE: J'aime faire <u>la lessive</u>.

10. **QUESTION:** _____
    QUESTION: _____
    RÉPONSE: Je vais <u>à New York</u> ce weekend.

11. **QUESTION:** _____
    QUESTION: _____
    RÉPONSE: Suzanne est déçue <u>parce qu'elle vient de rompre avec son copain</u>.

12. **QUESTION:** _____
    QUESTION: _____
    RÉPONSE: <u>Jacques Chirac</u> est président de la France.

13. **QUESTION:** _____
    QUESTION: _____
    RÉPONSE: Paul voit <u>son acteur préféré</u> à la télé.

14. **QUESTION:** _____
    QUESTION: _____
    RÉPONSE: Jacques Chirac téléphone à <u>George Bush</u>.

15. **QUESTION:** _____
    QUESTION: _____
    RÉPONSE: Nous avons besoin de <u>nos amis</u>.

16. **QUESTION:** _____
    (There is no inversion form for this question.)
    RÉPONSE: <u>Les films d'épouvante</u> donnent peur aux enfants.

17. **QUESTION:** _____
    QUESTION: _____
    RÉPONSE: Les garçons aiment <u>les chocolats</u>.

18. **QUESTION:** _____
    QUESTION: _____
    RÉPONSE: J'aime faire <u>de la natation</u>.

19. **QUESTION:** _____
    QUESTION: _____
    RÉPONSE: Hélène a peur des <u>monstres</u>.

20. **QUESTION:** _____
    QUESTION: _____
    RÉPONSE: Elle s'intéresse à <u>la danse</u>.

21. **QUESTION:** _____
    QUESTION: _____
    RÉPONSE: Je visite <u>Paris, Lyon et Marseille</u>.

22. **QUESTION:** _____
    QUESTION: _____
    RÉPONSE: J'admire <u>Paul McCartney</u>.

23. **QUESTION:** _____
    QUESTION: _____
    RÉPONSE: Elle est en train de regarder <u>"King Kong"</u>.

24. **QUESTION:** _____
    QUESTION: _____
    RÉPONSE: J'ai <u>un</u> enfant.

25. **QUESTION:** _____
    QUESTION: _____
    RÉPONSE: Oui, <u>je suis américaine</u>.

26. **QUESTION:** _____

    QUESTION: _____

    RÉPONSE: **Nous dînons <u>à 19 heures</u>.**

27. **QUESTION:** _____

    QUESTION: _____

    RÉPONSE: **Mes parents <u>regardent la télé</u> le soir.**

28. **QUESTION:** _____

    QUESTION: _____

    RÉPONSE: **J'aime le français <u>parce que c'est une belle langue</u>.**

29. **QUESTION:** _____

    QUESTION: _____

    RÉPONSE: **Mon fils joue avec <u>son père</u>.**

30. **QUESTION:** _____

    QUESTION: _____

    RÉPONSE: **Le soir <u>j'écoute de la musique</u>.**

31. **QUESTION:** _____

    QUESTION: _____

    RÉPONSE: **<u>Mon mari</u> aime le cinéma.**

32. **QUESTION:** _____

    QUESTION: _____

    RÉPONSE: **J'aime <u>dîner au restaurant</u>.**

Chapter 6

I. Give the past participle of each verb.

1. **écouter** _____
2. **tomber** _____
3. **finir** _____
4. **entendre** _____
5. **venir** _____
6. **avoir** _____
7. **naître** _____
8. **chanter** _____
9. **réussir** _____
10. **prendre** _____
11. **rire** _____
12. **lire** _____
13. **attendre** _____
14. **surprendre** _____
15. **cacher** _____
16. **chérir** _____
17. **savoir** _____
18. **connaître** _____
19. **manger** _____
20. **descendre** _____

II. Give the requested **passé composé** form of the following verbs. Then give the possible English translations.

Modèle: boire: je _____ = _____
boire: j'ai bu = <u>I drank, I have drunk, I did drink</u>

1. **danser: les garçons** _____ = _____
2. **travailler: Isabelle** _____ = _____
3. **finir: je** _____ = _____
4. **réfléchir: tu** _____ = _____
5. **attendre: nous** _____ = _____
6. **téléphoner: vous** _____ = _____

7. **dormir:** les enfants _____ = _____

8. **prendre:** je _____ = _____

9. **lire:** Mme Villard _____ = _____

10. **sourire:** nous _____ = _____

11. **recevoir:** tu _____ = _____

12. **offrir:** ma mère _____ = _____

13. **répondre:** vous _____ = _____

14. **choisir:** je _____ = _____

15. **essayer:** Véronique _____ = _____

16. **fondre:** le beurre _____ = _____

17. **chercher:** nous _____ = _____

18. **perdre:** vous _____ = _____

19. **vivre:** je _____ = _____

20. **écrire:** tu _____ = _____

III. Give the requested **passé composé** form of the following verbs. Remember to make the past participle agree when the verb is conjugated with **être**. Then give the possible English translations.

Modèle: revenir: je _____ = _____

revenir: je suis revenu(e) = <u>I came back, I have come back, I did come back</u>

1. **tomber:** elle _____ = _____

2. **sortir:** nous _____ = _____

3. **devenir:** Albert _____ = _____

4. **venir:** vous _____ = _____

5. **arriver:** ils _____ = _____

6. **partir:** tu _____ = _____

7. **descendre:** je _____ = _____

8. **rester:** vous _____ = _____

9. **aller:** je _____ = _____

10. **entrer:** nous _____ = _____

11. **naître:** elle _____ = _____

12. **mourir:** ils _____ = _____

IV. Give the requested **passé composé** form of the following pronominal verbs. Be careful to follow the rules for agreement of the past participle. Then give the possible English translations.

Modèle: se lever: je _____   = _____

   se lever: je <u>me suis levé(e)</u>   = <u>I got up, I have gotten up, I did get up</u>

1. **se parler: elles** _____   = _____

2. **se réveiller: nous** _____   = _____

3. **se maquiller: les acteurs** _____   = _____

4. **se laver le visage: je** _____   = _____

5. **se doucher: Charles** _____   = _____

6. **se brosser les dents: Marianne** _____   = _____

7. **s'embrasser: ils** _____   = _____

8. **s'amuser: vous** _____   = _____

9. **s'en aller: tu** _____   = _____

10. **se tromper: je** _____   = _____

11. **s'évanouir: ma grand-mère** _____   = _____

12. **se disputer: nous** _____   = _____

13. **s'endormir: elles** _____   = _____

14. **s'écrire: ils** _____   = _____

15. **se raser les jambes: elle** _____   = _____

Chapter 7

I. Give the requested **imparfait** form of the following verbs. Then give the possible English translations.

Modèle: boire: je _____ = _____

boire: je <u>buvais</u> = <u>I drank, I was drinking, I used to drink</u>

1. **danser: les garçons** _____ = _____
2. **travailler: Isabelle** _____ = _____
3. **finir: je** _____ = _____
4. **être: tu** _____ = _____
5. **attendre: nous** _____ = _____
6. **téléphoner: vous** _____ = _____
7. **dormir: les enfants** _____ = _____
8. **prendre: je** _____ = _____
9. **lire: Mme Villard** _____ = _____
10. **sourire: nous** _____ = _____
11. **recevoir: tu** _____ = _____
12. **offrir: ma mère** _____ = _____
13. **répondre: vous** _____ = _____
14. **choisir: je** _____ = _____
15. **essayer: Véronique** _____ = _____
16. **fondre: le beurre** _____ = _____
17. **chercher: nous** _____ = _____
18. **perdre: vous** _____ = _____
19. **vivre: je** _____ = _____
20. **écrire: tu** _____ = _____

II. **Comment dit-on?** Give a French translation of the following sentences. The verbs will be in the **imparfait**.

1. It was hot on July 14.

    _____

2. We used to go to church every Sunday.

    _____

3. Élisabeth was very happy.

    _____

4. It would always start to rain when I had a day off.

    _____

5. When I was young, I would do the dishes every night.

   _____

6. Pauline used to run ten kilometers per day.

   _____

7. They used to be best friends.

   _____

8. Did you play soccer when you were little?

   _____

9. We used to eat oysters every year at Christmas.

   _____

10. He used to eat candies.

    _____

11. Roxanne had blue eyes when she was a child.

    _____

12. It was raining and windy.

    _____

Chapter 8

I. **Passé composé ou imparfait?** In the story below, determine which verbs should be in the **imparfait** and which should be in the **passé composé.** Then conjugate them appropriately.

Hier soir je _____ (devoir) appeler ma mère au téléphone, mais il _____
(y avoir) un problème . . . Mes chats _____ (être) dehors pendant l'après-midi.
Normalement, ils reviennent avant qu'il ne fasse noir. Gogo (la femelle) _____
(rentrer) pendant que nous _____(dîner). Mais Didi (le mâle) _____
(ne pas rentrer). Après le dîner, on _____ (commencer) à s'inquiéter parce qu'on
_____ (ne pas savoir) où il _____ (être). Jacques (mon mari)
_____ (sortir) le chercher. Il _____ (appeler) Didi pendant dix
minutes, mais il _____ (n'entendre aucune réponse). Enfin, il _____
(savoir) où Didi _____ (être). Le chat _____ (être) très haut
dans un arbre, et il _____ (ne pas pouvoir) descendre. Normalement, il ne monte pas
dans les arbres, mais un autre chat _____ (devoir) l'effrayer (to scare). Le pauvre
_____ (miauler) désespérément. Nous _____ (téléphoner) aux
pompiers, mais ils _____ (ne pas vouloir) venir. Par contre, ils nous _____
(donner) le numéro de téléphone d'un monsieur avec une grande échelle (ladder). Alors, on
_____ (appeler) le monsieur. Il _____ (ne pas vouloir) venir parce qu'il
_____ (faire) déjà nuit, mais on le _____ (persuader) de venir.
Il _____ (arriver) une demi-heure plus tard avec son échelle et sa femme. Pendant
que le monsieur _____ (tenir) l'échelle, la dame _____ (monter)
chercher Didi. Mais Didi _____ (ne pas vouloir) aller à la dame. Alors, Jacques
_____ (monter) l'échelle, _____ (prendre) Didi dans ses bras, et
_____ (redescendre). Nous _____ (devoir) payer le monsieur
très cher. Quelle soirée! Et ma mère? Je lui _____ (téléphoner) ce matin.

II. **Comment dit-on?** Translate the following sentences into French. Be careful: some verbs should be in the **imparfait**; others should be in the **passé composé!**

1. When we arrived at the theater, there were no tickets (places) left.

_____

2. It was raining when I left this morning.

_____

3. Then it started to snow.

_____

4. Her name was Rio, and she danced on the sand.

_____

5. Where were you when I called?

   _____

6. We were fishing at the lake.

   _____

7. Gisèle waited an hour.

   _____

8. Paul was late.

   _____

9. When he showed up (**se présenter**), she was crying.

   _____

10. Then she yelled for five minutes.

    _____

11. He apologized and said he loved her.

    _____

12. She took her coat and left.

    _____

Chapter 9

I. Give the requested **plus-que-parfait** form of the following verbs. Then give the possible English translations.

Modèle: boire: je _____ = _____

boire: j'<u>avais bu</u> = <u>I had drunk</u>

1. **danser: les garçons** _____ = _____

2. **travailler: Isabelle** _____ = _____

3. **finir: je** _____ = _____

4. **réfléchir: tu** _____ = _____

5. **attendre: nous** _____ = _____

6. **téléphoner: vous** _____ = _____

7. **dormir: les enfants** _____ = _____

8. **prendre: je** _____ = _____

9. **lire: Mme Villard** _____ = _____

10. **sourire: nous** _____ = _____

11. **recevoir: tu** _____ = _____

12. **offrir: ma mère** _____ = _____

13. **répondre: vous** _____ = _____

14. **choisir: je** _____ = _____

15. **essayer: Véronique** _____ = _____

16. **fondre: le beurre** _____ = _____

17. **chercher: nous** _____ = _____

18. **perdre: vous** _____ = _____

19. **vivre: je** _____ = _____

20. **écrire: tu** _____ = _____

II. Give the requested **plus-que-parfait** form of the following verbs. Remember to make the past participle agree when the verb is conjugated with **être**. Then give the possible English translations.

Modèle: revenir: je _____ = _____

revenir: j'étais <u>revenu(e)</u> = <u>I had come back</u>

1. **tomber: elle** _____ = _____

2. **sortir: nous** _____ = _____

3. **devenir: Albert** _____ = _____

4. **venir: vous** _____ = _____

5. **arriver: ils** _____ = _____

6. **partir: tu** _____ = _____

7. **descendre: je** _____   = _____

8. **rester: vous** _____   = _____

9. **aller: je** _____   = _____

10. **entrer: nous** _____   = _____

11. **naître: elle** _____   = _____

12. **mourir: ils** _____   = _____

III. Give the requested **plus-que-parfait** form of the following pronominal verbs. Be careful to follow the rules for agreement of the past participle. Then give the possible English translations.

Modèle: se lever: je _____   = _____

    se lever: je m'étais levé(e)   = I had gotten up

1. **se parler: elles** _____   = _____

2. **se réveiller: nous** _____   = _____

3. **se maquiller: les acteurs** _____   = _____

4. **se laver le visage: je** _____   = _____

5. **se doucher: Charles** _____   = _____

6. **se brosser les dents: Marianne** _____   = _____

7. **s'embrasser: ils** _____   = _____

8. **s'amuser: vous** _____   = _____

9. **s'en aller: tu** _____   = _____

10. **se tromper: je** _____   = _____

11. **s'évanouir: ma grand-mère** _____   = _____

12. **se disputer: nous** _____   = _____

13. **s'endormir: elles** _____   = _____

14. **s'écrire: ils** _____   = _____

15. **se raser les jambes: elle** _____   = _____

Chapter 10

I. For each of the phrases in the **passé simple** below, identify the verb and write its infinitive. Then write the corresponding form of the **passé composé**.

passé simple	*infinitif*	*passé composé*
1. les garçons dansèrent		
2. Isabelle travailla		
3. je finis		
4. tu réflechis		
5. nous attendîmes		
6. vous téléphonâtes		
7. les enfants dormirent		
8. je pris		
9. Mme Villard lut		
10. nous sourîmes		
11. tu reçus		
12. ma mère offrit		
13. vous répondîtes		
14. je choisis		
15. Véronique essaya		
16. le beurre fondit		
17. nous cherchâmes		
18. vous perdîtes		
19. je vécus		
20. tu écrivis		
21. nous eûmes		
22. je vins		
23. elles furent		
24. tu connus		
25. nous tînmes		
26. ils durent		
27. je pus		
28. il mourut		
29. elles naquirent		
30. vous vous levâtes		

Chapter 11

I. Supply the missing pronoun. Choose from **je, tu, il, nous, vous, elles**.

Modèle: _____ iront au Sénégal en février.

      <u>Elles</u> iront au Sénégal en février.

1. _____ achèterai mon billet d'avion demain.

2. _____ chantera avec la chorale l'année prochaine.

3. _____ essaieront de tricher pendant l'examen.

4. _____ viendras au concert avec moi?

5. _____ serons ravis de vous voir.

6. Ferez-_____ une promenade dimanche?

7. _____ faudra se dépêcher.

8. _____ pourrai éventuellement vous aider.

9. _____ auras du temps libre ce weekend?

10. _____ dirons la vérité au juge.

11. _____ partiront mardi pour le Japon.

12. Quand saurez-_____ la réponse?

13. _____ répéterai les directifs une fois seulement.

14. Écris-moi quand _____ voudras.

15. _____ lirons ce roman pour la classe d'anglais.

16. _____ finirez les devoirs à temps?

II. For each verb, supply the **futur** form requested and give the English equivalent.

Modèle: parler: elle _____   = _____

      elle <u>parlera</u>   = <u>she will speak</u>

1. **servir: tu** _____   = _____

2. **entrer: je** _____   = _____

3. **travailler: ils** _____   = _____

4. **venir: je** _____   = _____

5. **dessiner: tu** _____   = _____

6. **obéir: il** _____   = _____

7. **aller: nous** _____   = _____

8. **répondre: je** _____   = _____

9. **regarder: vous** _____   = _____

10. **valoir: il** _____   = _____

11. **téléphoner: on** _____   = _____

12. **recevoir: je** _____   = _____

13. **souffrir: elle** _____   = _____

14. **vendre: tu** _____   = _____

15. **devoir: on** _____   = _____

16. **nager: nous** _____   = _____

17. **voir: vous** _____   = _____

18. **acheter: je** _____   = _____

19. **finir: nous** _____   = _____

20. **entendre: on** _____   = _____

21. **avoir: elles** _____   = _____

22. **parler: il** _____   = _____

23. **ouvrir: nous** _____   = _____

24. **exagérer: tu** _____   = _____

25. **être: je** _____   = _____

26. **demander: elles** _____   = _____

27. **attendre: nous** _____   = _____

28. **balayer: tu** _____   = _____

29. **couvrir: vous** _____   = _____

30. **sécher: elles** _____   = _____

31. **vouloir: tu** _____   = _____

32. **jouer: je** _____   = _____

33. **rougir: vous** _____   = _____

34. **arriver: tu** _____   = _____

35. **jeter: je** _____   = _____

36. **commencer: nous** _____   = _____

37. **finir: ils** _____   = _____

38. **falloir: il** _____   = _____

39. **grossir: nous** _____   = _____

40. **défendre: elle** _____   = _____

41. **chercher: on** _____   = _____

42. **tolérer: nous** _____   = _____

43. **danser: elles** _____   = _____

44. **mourir: ils** _____   = _____

45. **finir: je** _____   = _____

46. **effrayer: vous** _____   = _____

47. **dormir: ils** _____   = _____

48. **étudier: vous** _____   = _____

49. **faire: nous** _____   = _____

50. **partir: je** _____   = _____

51. **servir: elles** _____   = _____

52. **employer: elles** _____   = _____

Chapter 12

I. Give the requested **futur antérieur** form of the following verbs. Then give the possible English translations.

Modèle: boire: je _____   = _____

           boire: j'<u>aurai bu</u>   = <u>I will have drunk</u>

1. **danser: les garçons** _____ = _____

2. **travailler: Isabelle** _____ = _____

3. **finir: je** _____ = _____

4. **réfléchir: tu** _____ = _____

5. **attendre: nous** _____ = _____

6. **téléphoner: vous** _____ = _____

7. **dormir: les enfants** _____ = _____

8. **prendre: je** _____ = _____

9. **lire: Mme Villard** _____ = _____

10. **sourire: nous** _____ = _____

11. **recevoir: tu** _____ = _____

12. **offrir: ma mère** _____ = _____

13. **répondre: vous** _____ = _____

14. **choisir: je** _____ = _____

15. **essayer: Véronique** _____ = _____

16. **fondre: le beurre** _____ = _____

17. **chercher: nous** _____ = _____

18. **perdre: vous** _____ = _____

19. **vivre: je** _____ = _____

20. **écrire: tu** _____ = _____

II. Give the requested **futur antérieur** form of the following verbs. Remember to make the past participle agree when the verb is conjugated with **être**. Then give the possible English translations.

Modèle: revenir: je _____   = _____

           revenir: je <u>serai revenu(e)</u>   = <u>I will have come back</u>

1. **tomber: elle** _____ = _____

2. **sortir: nous** _____ = _____

3. **devenir: Albert** _____ = _____

4. **venir: vous** _____ = _____

5. **arriver: ils** _____ = _____

6. **partir: tu** _____ = _____

7. **descendre: je** _____ = _____

8. **rester: vous** _____ = _____

9. **aller: je** _____ = _____

10. **entrer: nous** _____ = _____

11. **naître: elle** _____ = _____

12. **mourir: ils** _____ = _____

III. Give the requested **futur antérieur** form of the following pronominal verbs. Be careful to follow the rules for agreement of the past participle. Then give the possible English translations.

Modèle: se lever: je _____ = _____

se lever: je <u>me serai levé(e)</u> = <u>I will have gotten up</u>

1. **se parler: elles** _____ = _____

2. **se réveiller: nous** _____ = _____

3. **se maquiller: les acteurs** _____ = _____

4. **se laver les mains: je** _____ = _____

5. **se doucher: Charles** _____ = _____

6. **se brosser les dents: Marianne** _____ = _____

7. **s'embrasser: ils** _____ = _____

8. **s'amuser: vous** _____ = _____

9. **s'en aller: tu** _____ = _____

10. **se tromper: je** _____ = _____

11. **s'évanouir: ma grand-mère** _____ = _____

12. **se disputer: nous** _____ = _____

13. **s'endormir: elles** _____ = _____

14. **s'écrire: ils** _____ = _____

15. **se raser les jambes: elle** _____ = _____

Chapter 13

I. Supply the missing subject. Choose from **je, Vincent, nous, vous, Nicole et Thérèse**.

Modèle: _____ iraient au Sénégal si elles avaient l'argent.

    <u>Nicole et Thérèse</u> iraient au Sénégal si elles avaient l'argent.

Si on avait le temps . . .

1. _____ étudierait plus.

2. _____ passerions plus de temps avec notre famille.

3. _____ jouerais avec mon chien.

4. _____ iriez au musée.

5. _____ feraient le ménage.

6. _____ ferions du jardinage.

Si on avait l'argent . . .

7. _____ achèterions une nouvelle voiture.

8. _____ suivrais des cours de cuisine.

9. _____ verrait tous les films au cinéma.

10. _____ auraient plusieurs maisons.

11. _____ iriez en France tous les étés.

12. _____ mangerais au restaurant tous les soirs.

II. For each verb, supply the **conditionnel** form requested and give the English equivalent.

Modèle: parler: elle _____ = _____

      elle <u>parlerait</u> = <u>she would speak</u>

1. **chanter: nous** _____ = _____

2. **trouver: je** _____ = _____

3. **aller: vous** _____ = _____

4. **acheter: ils** _____ = _____

5. **acheter: nous** _____ = _____

6. **prendre: tu** _____ = _____

7. **voyager: elle** _____ = _____

8. **payer: je** _____ = _____

9. **recevoir: il** _____ = _____

10. **vouloir: vous** _____ = _____

11. **devoir: on** _____   = _____

12. **attendre: nous** _____   = _____

13. **finir: tu** _____   = _____

14. **jeter: elle** _____   = _____

15. **travailler: vous** _____   = _____

16. **faire: je** _____   = _____

17. **courir: tu** _____   = _____

18. **falloir: il** _____   = _____

19. **avoir: nous** _____   = _____

20. **voir: ils** _____   = _____

21. **être: je** _____   = _____

22. **perdre: elle** _____   = _____

23. **réfléchir: vous** _____   = _____

24. **venir: tu** _____   = _____

25. **prendre: ils** _____   = _____

Chapter 14

I. Give the requested **conditionnel passé** form of the following verbs. Then give the possible English translations.

Modèle: boire: je _____ = _____

boire: j'<u>aurais bu</u> = <u>I would have drunk</u>

1. danser: les garçons _____ = _____

2. travailler: Isabelle _____ = _____

3. finir: je _____ = _____

4. réfléchir: tu _____ = _____

5. attendre: nous _____ = _____

6. téléphoner: vous _____ = _____

7. dormir: les enfants _____ = _____

8. prendre: je _____ = _____

9. lire: Mme Villard _____ = _____

10. sourire: nous _____ = _____

11. recevoir: tu _____ = _____

12. offrir: ma mère _____ = _____

13. répondre: vous _____ = _____

14. choisir: je _____ = _____

15. essayer: Véronique _____ = _____

16. fondre: le beurre _____ = _____

17. chercher: nous _____ = _____

18. perdre: vous _____ = _____

19. vivre: je _____ = _____

20. écrire: tu _____ = _____

II. Give the requested **conditionnel passé** form of the following verbs. Remember to make the past participle agree when the verb is conjugated with **être**. Then give the possible English translations.

Modèle: revenir: je _____ = _____

revenir: je <u>serais revenu(e)</u> = <u>I would have come back</u>

1. tomber: elle _____ = _____

2. sortir: nous _____ = _____

3. devenir: Albert _____ = _____

4. venir: vous _____ = _____

5. **arriver: ils** _____   = _____

6. **partir: tu** _____   = _____

7. **descendre: je** _____   = _____

8. **rester: vous** _____   = _____

9. **aller: je** _____   = _____

10. **entrer: nous** _____   = _____

11. **naître: elle** _____   = _____

12. **mourir: ils** _____   = _____

III. Give the requested **conditionnel passé** form of the following pronominal verbs. Be careful to follow the rules for agreement of the past participle. Then give the possible English translations.

Modèle: se lever: je _____   = _____

   se lever: je <u>me serais levé(e)</u> = <u>I would have gotten up</u>

1. **se parler: elles** _____   = _____

2. **se réveiller: nous** _____   = _____

3. **se maquiller: les acteurs** _____   = _____

4. **se laver les mains: je** _____   = _____

5. **se doucher: Charles** _____   = _____

6. **se brosser les dents: Marianne** _____ = _____

7. **s'embrasser: ils** _____   = _____

8. **s'amuser: vous** _____   = _____

9. **s'en aller: tu** _____   = _____

10. **se tromper: je** _____   = _____

11. **s'évanouir: ma grand-mère** _____   = _____

12. **se disputer: nous** _____   = _____

13. **s'endormir: elles** _____   = _____

14. **s'écrire: ils** _____   = _____

15. **se raser les jambes: elle** _____   = _____

Chapter 15

I. **Comment dit-on?** Give a French translation of the following sentences.

1. I would have come if my sister had loaned me her car.

   _____

2. If he had 1000 euros, Martin would take a trip to Florida.

   _____

3. If she hadn't slept in class, Édith would've passed the exam.

   _____

4. I wouldn't go if I were you.

   _____

5. Would you (**tu**) have gotten married if you had known he was a criminal?

   _____

6. Thomas would eat the whole cake if he weren't on a diet.

   _____

7. What would you (**vous**) do if you didn't have to work?

   _____

8. We would have to (it would be necessary to) buy the plate if we broke it.

   _____

9. Wouldn't you (**tu**) want to know?

   _____

10. Wouldn't you (**tu**) have wanted to know?

    _____

Chapter 16

I. Give the correct form of the present subjunctive for the following.

Modèle: parler: que nous _____

          parler: que nous <u>parlions</u>

1. **finir:** que je _____

2. **prendre:** que tu _____

3. **avoir:** qu'il _____

4. **quitter:** que nous _____

5. **habiter:** que vous _____

6. **boire:** que tu _____

7. **être:** que je _____

8. **donner:** que nous _____

9. **mettre:** qu'elle _____

10. **chanter:** que vous _____

11. **attendre:** qu'il _____

12. **choisir:** que je _____

13. **dormir:** que nous _____

14. **appeler:** qu'elle _____

15. **savoir:** que tu _____

16. **connaître:** qu'ils _____

II. **Comment dit-on?** How would you say each of these sentences in French?

1. We want you (**vous**) to sing.

   _____

2. I doubt that he drinks milk.

   _____

3. My mother is afraid I am not doing my homework.

   _____

4. Marc is happy that his sisters can come to the party.

   _____

5. It is possible that Vivianne is pregnant.

   _____

6. It is necessary that we visit Mme Thomas in the hospital.

   _____

7. The law requires that we wear a seat belt.

   _____

Chapter 17

I. Give the requested **passé du subjonctif** form of the following verbs.

Modèle: boire: que je _____
boire: que j'<u>aie bu</u>

1. **danser: que les garçons** _____
2. **travailler: qu'Isabelle** _____
3. **finir: que je** _____
4. **réfléchir: que tu** _____
5. **attendre: que nous** _____
6. **téléphoner: que vous** _____
7. **dormir: que les enfants** _____
8. **prendre: que je** _____
9. **lire: que Mme Villard** _____
10. **sourire: que nous** _____
11. **recevoir: que tu** _____
12. **offrir: que ma mère** _____
13. **répondre: que vous** _____
14. **choisir: que je** _____
15. **essayer: que Véronique** _____
16. **fondre: que le beurre** _____
17. **chercher: que nous** _____
18. **perdre: que vous** _____
19. **vivre: que je** _____
20. **écrire: que tu** _____

II. Give the requested **passé du subjonctif** form of the following verbs. Remember to make the past participle agree when the verb is conjugated with **être**.

Modèle: revenir: que je _____
revenir: que je <u>sois revenu(e)</u>

1. **tomber: qu'elle** _____
2. **sortir: que nous** _____
3. **devenir: qu'Albert** _____
4. **venir: que vous** _____
5. **arriver: qu'ils** _____
6. **partir: que tu** _____
7. **descendre: que je** _____

8. **rester:** que vous _____

9. **aller:** que je _____

10. **entrer:** que nous _____

11. **naître:** qu'elle _____

12. **mourir:** qu'ils _____

III. Give the requested **passé du subjonctif** form of the following pronominal verbs. Be careful to follow the rules for agreement of the past participle.

Modèle: se lever: que je _____
            se lever: que je <u>me sois levé(e)</u>

1. **se parler:** qu'elles _____

2. **se réveiller:** que nous _____

3. **se maquiller:** que les acteurs _____

4. **se laver les mains:** que je _____

5. **se doucher:** que Charles _____

6. **se brosser les dents:** que Marianne _____

7. **s'embrasser:** qu'ils _____

8. **s'amuser:** que vous _____

9. **s'en aller:** que tu _____

10. **se tromper:** que je _____

11. **s'évanouir:** que ma grand-mère _____

12. **se disputer:** que nous _____

13. **s'endormir:** qu'elles _____

14. **s'écrire:** qu'ils _____

15. **se raser les jambes:** qu'elle _____

Chapter 19

I. **Des ordres.** Give orders to a child in your family using the **tu** form of the **impératif**. Then give a translation into English.

Modèle: se dépêcher _____ = _____
                          Dépêche-toi. = <u>Hurry up.</u>

1. **être sage** _____ = _____
2. **manger tes carottes** _____ = _____
3. **essuyer la table** _____ = _____
4. **mettre la table** _____ = _____
5. **ranger ta chambre** _____ = _____
6. **s'habiller** _____ = _____
7. **se laver les mains** _____ = _____
8. **se peigner** _____ = _____
9. **faire tes devoirs** _____ = _____
10. **ne pas embêter ta sœur** _____ = _____
11. **aller dans ta chambre** _____ = _____
12. **venir avec moi** _____ = _____
13. **ne pas chanter à table** _____ = _____
14. **avoir de la patience** _____ = _____

II. **Des ordres.** Now give orders to several children using the **vous** form of the **impératif**.

Modèle: se dépêcher _____
                          Dépêchez-vous.

1. **être sages** _____
2. **manger vos carottes** _____
3. **essuyer la table** _____
4. **mettre la table** _____
5. **ranger votre chambre** _____
6. **s'habiller** _____
7. **se laver les mains** _____
8. **se peigner** _____
9. **faire vos devoirs** _____
10. **ne pas embêter votre sœur** _____
11. **aller dans votre chambre** _____
12. **venir avec moi** _____
13. **ne pas chanter à table** _____
14. **avoir de la patience** _____

Answers

·

Answers to *Chapter Exercises*

CHAPTER 1

A. **What is the correct form?**

1. adore
2. jouent
3. prépare
4. aime
5. écoutent
6. étudient
7. déjeunez
8. détestes
9. lave
10. invitent

B. **Now, write sentences of your own!**

1. J'écoute . . .
   Vous écoutez . . .
   Mon meilleur ami écoute . . .

2. Mes amis travaillent . . .
   Nous travaillons . . .
   Tu travailles . . .

3. Ma collègue déteste . . .
   Ma sœur déteste . . .
   Je déteste . . .
   Vous détestez . . .

C. **Au centre commercial.**

1. Le professeur préfère faire la cuisine. Il achète la poêle. Il paie 24 euros.

2. Les enfants préfèrent jouer. Ils achètent le jouet. Ils paient 8 euros.

3. Sébastien préfère le football. Il achète le ballon. Il paie 12 euros.

4. Julie et Thérèse préfèrent la danse. Elles achètent les chaussons de danse. Elles paient 54 euros.

5. Nous préférons le cinéma. Nous achetons le dvd. Nous payons 27 euros.

6. M. et Mme Robin préfèrent manger. Ils achètent la glace. Ils paient 3 euros.

7. Vous préférez lire. Vous achetez le livre. Vous payez 11 euros.

D. **What is the correct form?**

1. aboie
2. commençons
3. célèbrent
4. pèsent
5. vouvoyons
6. tutoie
7. raie
8. élève
9. répète
10. appelle ; promène
11. sèchent
12. projetez
13. tolère
14. nageons

E. **Now, write sentences of your own!**

1. J'achète . . .
   Mes collègues achètent . . .
   Vous achetez . . .

245

2. Ma mère nettoie . . .
   Tu nettoies . . .
   Nous nettoyons . . .

3. Nous jetons . . .
   Mes enfants jettent . . .
   Mon patron jette . . .

F. What is the correct form?

1. **défend**   4. **attendons**   7. **perds**

2. **revends**   5. **rendent**   8. **prétend**

3. **fond**   6. **Entendez**   9. **répondent**

G. Now, write sentences of your own!

1. Mes collègues vendent . . .
   Tu vends . . .
   Mon fils vend . . .

2. J'attends . . .
   Vous attendez . . .
   Mes amis attendent . . .

3. Mes parents perdent souvent . . .
   Ma femme / Mon mari perd souvent . . .
   Nous perdons souvent . . .

H. What is the correct form?

1. **réusissent**   6. **dorment**   11. **maigrissez**

2. **finis**   7. **rougit**   12. **punissent ; obéissent**

3. **souffre**   8. **fleurissent**   13. **nourit**

4. **choisis**   9. **agit**   14. **sortent**

5. **réfléchissons**   10. **partons**

I. Now, write sentences of your own!

1. Les enfants choisissent . . .
   Maman choisit . . .
   Vous choisissez . . .

2. Tu pars . . .
   Le président part . . .
   Nous partons . . .

3. Le médecin réfléchit . . .
   Je réfléchis . . .
   Les professeurs réfléchissent . . .

J. Which verb?

1. travaillent
2. regarde
3. réussis
4. écoutons
5. parlez
6. guérit
7. appellent ; épelle
8. détestent
9. mangeons ; grossissons
10. vends
11. emploie
12. choisit
13. réfléchis
14. perdez ; maigrissez
15. découvre

K. Change each sentence from singular to plural.

1. Vous rougissez facilement, n'est-ce pas?
2. Si nous mangeons beaucoup de desserts, nous grossissons.
3. Vous regardez la télé le soir?
4. Nous obéissons au professeur.
5. Les étudiantes tutoient leur camarade de classe.
6. Vous descendez l'escalier; puis, vous tournez à gauche.
7. Les Parisiens partent en vacances le premier août.
8. Les soldats confondent l'ennemi.

L. Change each sentence from plural to singular.

1. Elle arrive toujours en retard.
2. Je défends les droits des femmes.
3. Il agit comme un animal.
4. Je réponds tout de suite aux courriels.
5. Tu joues aux échecs?
6. Le professeur vouvoie les étudiants.
7. J'appelle la police quand il y a un problème.
8. Tu obéis au code de la route?

Les mots croisés 1

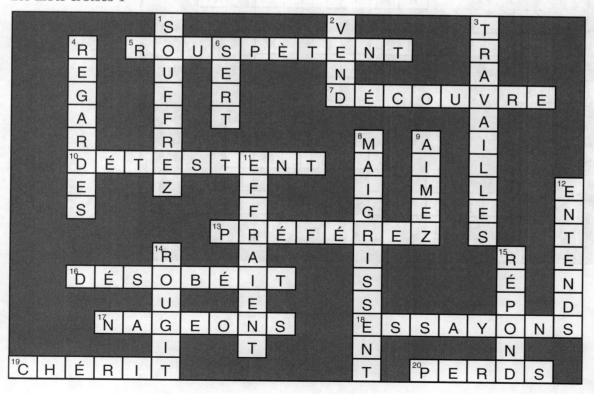

CHAPTER 2

A. What is the correct form?

1. **dites**
2. **ai ; mets**
3. **vont**
4. **est**
5. **a**
6. **sommes**
7. **font**
8. **vas**
9. **disent ; suis ; dis**
10. **faites**
11. **ont**
12. **fais ; vais**

B. Now, write sentences of your own!

1. **On va . . .**
    Vous allez . . .
    Je vais . . .

2. **Tu es sympathique / méchant / méchante / intelligent / intelligente.**
    Mes parents sont sympathiques / méchants / intelligents.
    Mon professeur est sympathique / méchant / intelligent.

3. **Nous faisons . . .**
    Mes amis font . . .
    Mon patron fait . . .

4. **J'ai . . .**
    L'homme idéal a . . .
    La femme idéale a . . .
    Vous avez . . .

Les mots croisés 2.1

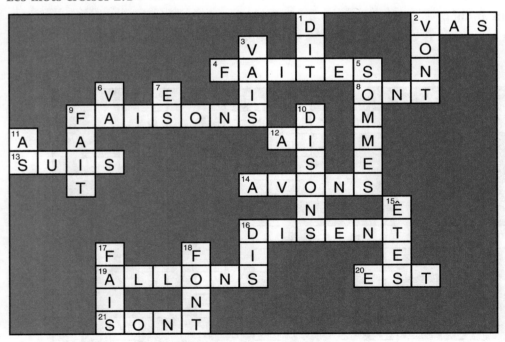

C. What is the correct form?

1. reçoit
2. croyez
3. rient
4. met
5. vaut
6. écrivent
7. connaissons
8. sais
9. vit
10. viennent
11. devons
12. ne peuvent pas
13. tiennent
14. paraît

D. Now, write sentences of your own!

1. Je veux . . .
   Les enfants veulent . . .
   Mon copain veut . . .
   Ma copine veut . . .

2. Tu connais . . .
   Un de mes collègues connaît . . .
   Nous connaissons . . .

3. Vous écrivez . . .
   Le professeur écrit . . .
   Mes amis écrivent . . .

Les mots croisés 2.2

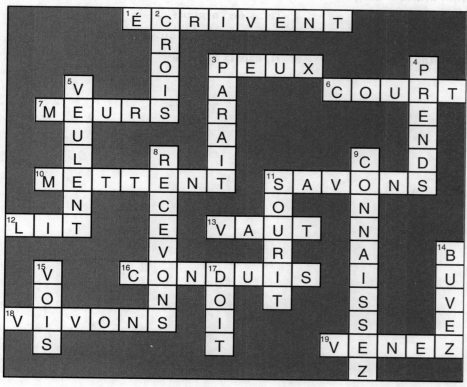

E. Which verb?

1. rient
2. sont
3. vivons / sommes / venons
4. crois / écris ; est
5. conduit
6. as
7. écrit / a
8. plaignez / suivez
9. buvons / faisons
10. comprends
11. suis / fais
12. vaut
13. devez ; êtes
14. comprenons / apprenons

F. Change each sentence from singular to plural.

1. Elles connaissent Irène.
2. Si nous buvons beaucoup de vin, nous devenons bêtes.
3. Vous pouvez conduire la voiture de Thomas?
4. Nous faisons toujours les devoirs.
5. Vous voyez que j'ai (nous avons) des ennuis.
6. Les médecins savent guérir les malades.

G. Change each sentence from plural to singular.

1. Elle doit aller en prison.
2. Je souris quand je suis content(e).
3. Il lit un livre chaque semaine.
4. Tu as de l'argent?
5. Je ne peux pas trouver le chat.
6. Tu sais la réponse?

CHAPTER 3

A. Que fait-on?

1. s'embrassent
2. se douche
3. s'habille
4. se réveille
5. se maquillent
6. se brosse les dents
7. se disputent

B. Pronominal?

1. marie
2. nous détendons
3. se couchent
4. couche
5. intéresse
6. ennuient
7. habillent
8. appelle
9. vous baignez
10. nous promenons
11. m'amuse
12. se sert

C. What is the correct form?

1. s'agit
2. m'appelle ; t'appelles
3. ne se maquille pas
4. se reposent
5. vous brossez
6. s'évanouit ; se lève
7. se marient ; s'aiment ; s'embrassent ; se disputent
8. t'intéresses
9. ne m'entends pas
10. s'ennuient
11. ne peut pas ; s'occupe
12. nous moquons
13. vous trompez
14. me spécialise
15. se souvient

D. Now, make sentences of your own!

1. Je m'amuse . . .
   Mes amis s'amusent . . .
   Vous vous amusez . . .

2. Nous nous détendons . . .
   Le professeur se détend . . .
   Les vieux se détendent . . .

3. Mon frère se brosse . . .
   Ma sœur se brosse . . .
   Tu te brosses . . .

E. Which verb?

1. se passe
2. nous réveillons
3. me détends / m'amuse
4. vous préparez
5. t'arrêtes
6. se parlent
7. se moque
8. t'en vas / te lèves / te couches / te baignes

9. **vous spécialisez**

10. **se disputent / s'en vont / se lèvent / se couchent / se baignent; se disputent / s'en vont / se lèvent / se couchent / se baignent**

11. **nous aimons ; nous disputons**

12. **se sert**

F. Change each sentence from singular to plural.

1. **À mon avis** (in my opinion), **elles se maquillent trop.**

2. **Si nous nous couchons en retard, nous rouspétons le jour suivant.**

3. **Vous vous spécialisez en mathématiques?**

4. **Nous ne nous endormons jamais en classe.**

5. **Vous vous habillez vraiment bien.**

6. **Ils se rasent tous les jours.**

G. Change each sentence from plural to singular.

1. **Elle s'en va rapidement.**

2. **Je m'intéresse au yoga.**

3. **Il s'occupe du chien abandonné.**

4. **Tu te moques de moi?**

5. **Je ne me trompe jamais.**

6. **Tu te lèves à quelle heure?**

Les mots croisés 3

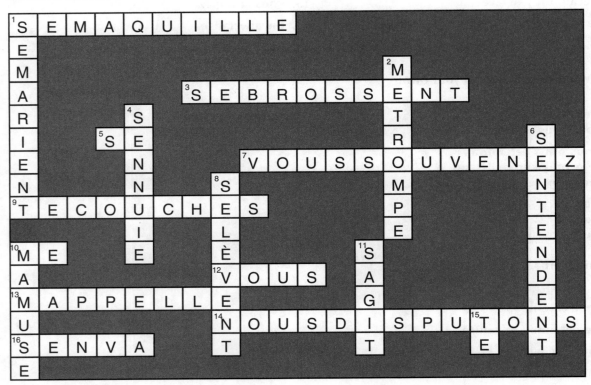

CHAPTER 4

A. Quel temps fait-il? *Answers will vary. These are examples of likely answers.*

1. Il neige. Il fait froid. Il fait du vent. Il gèle.

2. Il fait beau. Il fait du soleil. Il fait du vent.

3. Il pleut. Il fait moche. Il fait mauvais. Il fait un temps de chien!

B. Quelle heure est-il?

1. Il est neuf heures et demie.

2. Il est midi.

3. Il est quatre heures vingt.

4. Il est six heures moins le quart.

5. Il est huit heures et quart.

6. Il est dix heures.

7. Il est onze heures moins le quart.

8. Il est minuit.

C. Idées incomplètes.

1. il s'agit d' / il y a

2. il vaut mieux / il faut

3. il y a

4. il faut

5. il s'agit d'

6. il y a

D. Quel verbe?

1. connaître

2. savoir

3. connaître

4. savoir

5. savoir

6. connaître

7. savoir

8. connaître

9. connaître

10. savoir

E. Savoir ou connaître?

1. sait

2. connaissez

3. savent

4. sais

5. connaissons

6. sais

7. connais

8. savez

9. connaît

10. connais

11. savons

12. connaissent

F. Que fait-on?

1. Julien et Quentin sont en train de lire.

2. Joëlle est en train d'utiliser (de se servir de) l'ordinateur.

3. Véronique est en train d'écouter de la musique.

4. Gabrielle et Gérard sont en train de jouer au basket.

5. Hugo est en train de manger (un sandwich).

6. Paul est en train de boire.

7. Estelle est en train de parler au téléphone (de téléphoner à un ami, and so on).

8. Bernard et Béatrice sont en train de dormir.

G. Qu'est-ce qu'on vient de faire?

1. **Je viens d'acheter une voiture très chère.**

2. **Tu viens de prendre un grand dîner.**

3. **Elles viennent de voir leur mère avec un homme inconnu.**

4. **Nous venons de nous réveiller.**

5. **Vous venez de recevoir un compliment.**

6. **Ils viennent de se baigner.**

7. **Nous venons de voir un concert de rock.**

8. **Il vient de boire de l'eau.**

9. **Vous venez d'être licencié(e).**

10. **Il vient de jouer dans de la boue.**

H. Qu'est-ce qu'on va faire? *Answers may vary. Examples are provided.*

1. **Romain et Vincent vont manger.**

2. **Nous allons voyager (prendre l'avion).**

3. **Vous allez téléphoner (à un ami).**

4. **Je vais lire.**

5. **Tu vas travailler (écrire, te servir de l'ordinateur).**

6. **Denise va conduire (voyager, partir).**

7. **Je vais dormir (me coucher).**

8. **Vous allez regarder la télé.**

I. Des questions! *Answers will vary, but the subject and verb are provided with sample endings in parentheses.*

1. **Je suis en train de/d' (lire).**

2. **Je me lève normalement à (7h).**

3. **Je me couche normalement à (minuit).**

4. **Je vais sortir ce soir à (8h).**

5. **Je vais rentrer à (23h).**

6. **Dans mon sac, il y a (des livres).**

7. **Je préfère (l'hiver).**

8. **Je vais (travailler).**

J. La météo.

1. **À Paris, il va pleuvoir. (Il va faire mauvais.)**

2. **À Marseille, il va faire du vent.**

3. **À Grenoble, il va pleuvoir.**

4. **À Strasbourg, il va faire du brouillard.**

K. Comment dit-on?

1. **Il vaut mieux rester à l'intérieur. Il pleut.**

2. **Je viens d'entendre la météo. Il va faire du vent demain.**

3. **Il faut partir à 4h.**

4. **Chrisine va faire une promenade demain. J'espère qu'il va faire beau.**

5. **Tu sais (vous savez) que je vais partir à six heures et demie?**

6. **Victoria est en train de prendre une douche (de se doucher).**

Les mots croisés 4

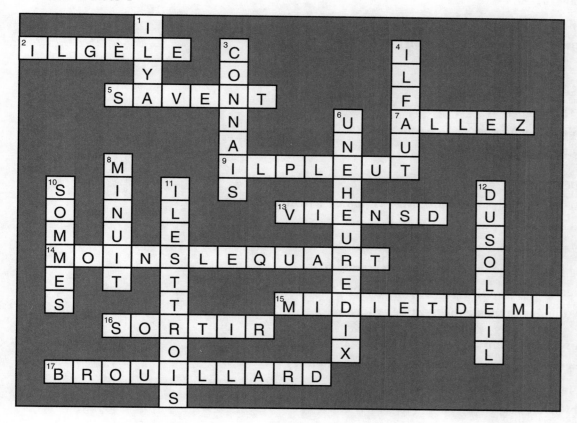

CHAPTER 5

A. Quelle question?

1. Où
2. Pourquoi
3. Quand
4. Où
5. Combien
6. Qui
7. Qu'
8. Quel

B. Plus formel, s'il vous plaît!

1. Comment trouvez-vous la poésie de Nerval?
2. Que fais-tu?
3. Pourquoi Rémy et Sylvie habitent-ils à la campagne?
4. Avec qui vas-tu au cinéma ce soir?
5. Quand part-elle?
6. Qui regardez-vous?
7. Que regardez-vous?
8. Combien de pièces vois-tu chaque mois?
9. Aimes-tu cette jupe?

C. Détendez-vous!

1. Qu'est-ce que ses parents disent à propos de leur mariage?
2. Qu'est-ce qu'il va porter à la cérémonie?
3. Qui est-ce qui vient aux noces de son côté?
4. A quel hôtel est-ce que les invités descendent?
5. Quel genre de musique est-ce qu'ils jouent à la réception?
6. Est-ce que les invités apportent des cadeaux?

D. Mauvaise connection!

1. Qu'est-ce que tu vas acheter? (Que vas-tu acheter?)
2. Pourquoi est-ce que tu le voudrais? (Pourquoi le voudrais-tu?)
3. Combien est-ce que ça coûte? (Combien coûte ça?)
4. Où est-ce que tu vas après? (Où vas-tu après?)
5. Avec qui est-ce que tu as rendez-vous? (Avec qui as-tu rendez-vous?)
6. Qu'est-ce que vous allez faire? (Qu'allez-vous faire?)
7. Où est-ce que vous allez déjeuner? (Où allez-vous déjeuner?)
8. Qu'est-que tu vas manger? (Que vas-tu manger?)

Les mots croisés 5

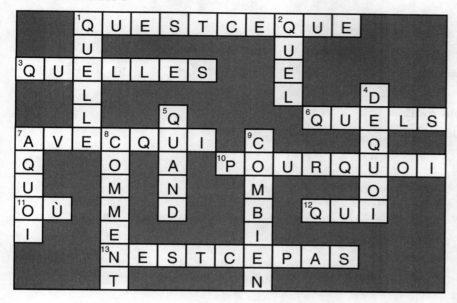

CHAPTER 6

A. What is the correct form?

1. a apprécié	3. as réussi	5. a perdu	7. avez rendu	9. a vécu
2. ai attendu	4. a travaillé	6. ont joué	8. ai offert	10. avons invité

B. Now, write sentences of your own!

1. Une de mes collègues a lu / écrit . . .
Tu as lu / écrit . . .
Nous avons lu / écrit . . .

2. Ma mère a perdu / acheté . . .
Mon copain / Ma copine a perdu / acheté . . .
Vous avez perdu / acheté . . .

3. Vous avez fait . . .
Mes amis ont fait . . .

C. What is the correct form?

1. sont nées

2. sommes resté(e)s (Note that an *e* would indicate that all the people included in *nous* are female.)

3. êtes parti(e)(s) (Note that *vous* can be masculine or feminine [thus, the optional *e*] and singular or plural [thus, the optional *s*].)

4. sont venus

5. est né ; est mort

6. est devenue

7. n'es pas monté(e)

8. suis parti(e) ; suis revenu(e)

9. est sortie

10. est arrivé

D. Être or avoir?

1. as	3. J'ai	5. est	7. as	9. est	11. as
2. est	4. es	6. est	8. J'ai	10. J'ai	12. Je suis

E.

1. Mon patron est allé au musée / au magasin de jouets / à l'hôpital.
Mon patron est entré dans . . .
Mon patron est revenu du musée / du magasin de jouets / de l'hôpital.
Mes collègues sont allé(e)s au musée / au magasin de jouets / à l'hôpital.
Mes collègues sont entré(e)s dans . . .
Mes collègues sont revenu(e)s du musée / du magasin de jouets / de l'hôpital.
Tu es allé(e) au musée / au magasin de jouets / à l'hôpital.
Tu es entré(e) dans . . .
Tu es revenu(e) du musée / du magasin de jouets / de l'hôpital.

2. Je suis arrivé(e) / parti(e) / venu(e) . . .
   Nous sommes arrivé(e)s / parti(e)s / venu(e)s . . .
   Mes parents sont arrivés / partis / venus . . .

3. Mon grand-père est né / mort . . .
   Vous êtes né(e)(s) / mort(e)(s) . . .
   Une de mes cousines est née / morte . . .

F. Agreement of past participle.

1. *X* ; *X* ; es ; *X*   2. *X* ; e ; e   3. s ; *X* ; s

G. What is the correct form?

1. se sont mariés

2. est tombée ; s'est cassé (The past participle does not agree with feminine subject because the direct object is *le bras*.)

3. s'est réveillée

4. t'es levé(e)

5. se sont lavé

6. nous sommes disputés

7. me suis endormi(e) ; s'est fâché ; se sont moqués

8. vous êtes amusé(e)(s)

9. se sont parlé (Note that *se* is an indirect object in this sentence, so there is no agreement.)

10. s'est deshabillée ; s'est douchée ; s'est couchée

H. Way ahead!

1. Il s'est déjà levé.

2. J'ai déjà fait le lit.

3. Nous nous sommes déjà brossé les dents.

4. Elles se sont déjà habillées.

5. J'ai déjà mis un pull chaud.

6. Nous avons déjà pris le petit déjeuner.

7. Il a déjà essuyé la table.

8. Je me suis déjà lavé les mains.

9. Nous sommes déjà allés au magasin.

10. J'ai déjà passé l'aspirateur.

11. Ils ont déjà sorti la poubelle.

12. Nous avons déjà dit la vérité.

13. Elle a déjà fini ses devoirs.

14. Nous avons déjà étudié pour notre examen.

15. Elles ont déjà lu cet article.

16. J'ai déjà ouvert la porte.

17. **Il a déjà fermé la porte.**

18. **J'ai déjà écrit une lettre à ma tante.**

19. **Nous avons déjà répondu à vos questions.**

20. **Je suis déjà allé(e) à l'église.**

21. **Elle est déjà devenue une bonne étudiante.**

22. **Ils sont déjà partis.**

I.   Change each sentence from singular to plural.

1. **Elles ont rougi quand ils sont entrés.**

2. **Nous nous sommes réveillées tôt ce matin.**

3. **Nous avons bu du vin rouge?**

4. **Nous sommes sorties avec Paul.**

5. **Ils sont allés à la discothèque.**

6. **Vous avez suivi une inconnue dans la rue?**

J.   Change each sentence from plural to singular.

1. **Elle est passée par la boulangerie.**

2. **Je me suis reposée au café.**

3. **Tu t'es vu(e) dans le miroir?**

4. **Il a reçu une médaille.**

5. **Tu as vendu la maison?**

6. **Je suis revenu(e) en avion.**

K. Agreement?

1. *X*	4. *X* (***Nous*** is an indirect object, so there is no agreement)	5. *X*	8. **es**	11. **s**
2. **e** ; *X*		6. *X* ; **e**	9. *X*	12. **(e)(s)**
3. **e**		7. *X*	10. **es**	13. **e**

Les mots croisés 6

Across

4. NOUS SOMMES AMUSÉS
5. AVEZ CHOISI
7. AS LU
9. SONT SORTIS
11. EST DEVENU
14. ME SUIS BROSSÉ
17. A FINI
18. AVEZ PU
19. ONT ATTENDU
21. AS MONTÉ
22. A RENDU
23. S'EST LAVÉ

Down

1. ACHETÉE
2. EST ALLÉ
3. AMI
6. SONT CONTENTS
7. AVONS
8. SONT
10. ORIENT
12. EST TOMBÉ
13. A ÉCRIT
14. MANGÉ
15. ME SONT
16. AVONS
20. A AIDI

CHAPTER 7

A. Que faisait-on?

1. mangeait
2. se baignait
3. dormait
4. buvaient

5. faisait du jardinage
6. regardait la télé
7. lisait
8. se brossait les dents

B. What is the correct form?

1. fumait
2. regardait
3. soulevaient
4. laissaient
5. passaient
6. disparaissaient
7. ouvrait

8. fonctionnaient
9. devenaient
10. s'obstinaient
11. avait
12. échangeaient
13. se promettaient
14. remplissaient

C. Interview! *Answers for this exercise will vary greatly, but should follow the form of the sample answers below.*

1. J'habitais (à) Paris.
2. J'habitais avec ma mère et mon frère.
3. Oui, nous avions deux chats.
   Non, nous n'avions pas d'animaux.
4. J'aimais jouer avec mes amies et faire la cuisine avec ma mère.
5. Je jouais au football et je faisais du ski.
   Je ne faisais pas de sport.
6. Oui, je jouais du piano.
   Non, je ne jouais pas de musique.
7. J'aimais manger des bonbons et du gâteau.
8. Je ne mangeais pas de haricots verts ou de pommes de terre.
9. Oui, j'étais très sage.
   Non, je n'étais pas sage.
10. Oui, j'étais content(e).
    Non, je n'étais pas content(e).
11. J'habitais la Nouvelle Orléans.
12. J'habitais avec mon père.
13. Oui, je sortais souvent.
    Non, je ne sortais pas souvent.
14. J'aimais jouer sur l'ordinateur et faire du vélo.
15. Je jouais au football et je faisais du ski.
    Je ne faisais pas de sport.

16. **Oui, je jouais du saxophone.**
   Non, je ne jouais pas de musique.

17. **Oui, j'avais un copain / une copine.**
   Non, je n'avais pas de copain / copine.

18. **Oui, j'étudiais beaucoup.**
   Non, je n'étudiais pas beaucoup.

19. **Oui, je parlais français.**
   Non, je ne parlais pas de langue étrangère.

20. **Oui, j'étais content(e).**
   Non, je n'étais pas content(e).

D. **Which verb?**

1. **habitait**
2. **était**
3. **travaillaient**
4. **lisait**
5. **écrivait**
6. **arrivait**
7. **voulait**
8. **allaient / étaient**
9. **étudiaient**
10. **aimaient**

11. **allaient**
12. **voyaient**
13. **se promenaient**
14. **s'amusaient**
15. **prenaient**
16. **allait**
17. **achetait**
18. **préparait**
19. **faisaient**
20. **emmenaient**

21. **venait**
22. **apportait**
23. **mangeait**
24. **buvait**
25. **commençait**
26. **aimaient**
27. **avait**
28. **s'endormait**

E. **Change each sentence from singular to plural.**

1. **Vous aviez les cheveux courts quand vous étiez jeunes?**
2. **Nous nous couchions à 8h tous les soirs.**
3. **Ils s'ennuyaient en classe.**
4. **Nous faisions de la gymnastique.**
5. **Elles comprenaient tout de suite.**
6. **Vous vouliez être médecin?**

F. **Change each sentence from plural to singular.**

1. **Elle se trompait régulièrement.**
2. **Je savais nager quand j'avais seulement trois ans.**
3. **Tu exagérais beaucoup autrefois.**
4. **Il vouvoyait le professeur.**
5. **Tu balayais la cuisine tous les jours.**
6. **Je voyageais souvent à l'étranger.**

Les mots croisés 7

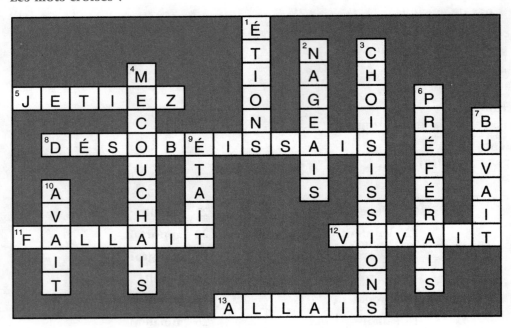

CHAPTER 8

A. Passé composé ou imparfait?

1. a téléphoné; voulait
2. étions; lisions
3. aviez
4. est née
5. ai vu; était
6. était; est arrivé
7. étais; a commencé
8. sommes rentrés; avons ouvert; n'avons rien trouvé; sommes partis
9. sommes allés; avait rien
10. te moquais; étais
11. avais; me brossais pas

B. Passé composé ou imparfait?

1. avait
2. habitaient
3. vivait
4. a dû
5. a réuni
6. a dit
7. ont promis
8. est partie
9. ont entendu
10. a dit
11. allaient
   (They were going to open the door when . . .)
12. ont vu
13. est parti
14. a mis
15. est revenu
16. ont vu
17. ont ouvert
18. est entré
19. ont eu / avaient
20. se sont cachés
21. a trouvés
   (agrees with preceding direct object *les*)
22. a mis
23. était
24. est parti
25. était
26. est devenu
27. s'est arrêté
28. est rentrée
29. était
30. était
31. n'étaient pas
32. a entendu
33. est sorti
34. a raconté
35. est partie
36. a trouvé
37. dormait
38. bougeait
39. rêvait
40. a ouvert
41. sont sortis
42. a rempli
43. a refermé
44. s'est réveillé
45. a pris
46. est rentré
47. marchait
48. pensait
49. imaginait
50. allait
51. est arrivé
52. avait
53. a ouvert
54. était
55. a commencé
56. est rentré
57. n'est jamais revenu

C. Comment dit-on?

1. a quitté; n'était pas

2. s'est fâché; a volé

3. parlait; s'intéressait à

4. neigeait; ai acheté; a commencé

5. était; a travaillé; a fait; a préparé; s'est endormi; a manqué

6. nous promenions; faisions; rentrions

7. aviez; écoutiez; obéissiez

8. est entrée; a répondu; sonnait

D. Du présent au passé.

1. D'habitude, je finissais mes devoirs après le dîner, et ensuite j'écrivais des courriels.

2. Hier, Bertrande est venue chez Louis. Ils sont sortis ensemble, mais ils se sont disputés. Louis s'est mis à pleurer, et Bertrande a commencé à crier. Puis, ils se sont regardés et ont ri.

3. Il faisait beau. Alors, Lilianne a appellé son amie Évelyne et elles sont montées dans la décapotable d'Évelyne et sont allées à la plage où elles ont pris un bain de soleil.

4. Le dimanche, Mme Goudron allait toujours au match de foot de son fils Julien. Julien n'aimait pas ça et il a dit à sa mère de ne pas venir. Mme Goudron ne voulait pas manquer les matchs. Alors après, elle se déguisait chaque semaine, et Julien ne savait pas qu'elle était là!

CHAPTER 9

A. En quel ordre?

1. envoyer
2. dormir
3. se préparer
4. recommander
5. se disputer
6. préparer
7. partir
8. s'amuser

B. Au travail.

1. M. Thomas était déjà allé à l'imprimerie.
2. Mlle Grégoire et M. Bonacieux avaient déjà fini leur projet.
3. Mme Robert et Mme Huchet s'étaient déjà occupées du budget.
4. Mme Bernier avait déjà appris le nouveau logiciel.
5. M. Nicolas avait déjà payé les factures.
6. Mlle Julien avait déjà écrit une lettre au président de la société.
7. M. Troude et M. Quinot avaient déjà réfléchi aux objectifs.
8. Mme Polnichet avait déjà vendu des actions.
9. M. David avait déjà nourri son poisson.

C. En retard.

1. Tu avais offert l'apéritif.
2. Les invités s'étaient mis à table.
3. Julie avait servi l'entrée.
4. Nous avions pris le plat principal.
5. Jacques avait coupé le gâteau.
6. Les adultes avaient bu du champagne.
7. Marie avait ouvert des cadeaux.
8. Thomas avait lu un poème qu'il avait écrit pour Marie.
9. Rachel avait ri des plaisanteries de M. Jacob.
10. Les enfants s'étaient couchés.
11. Vous aviez fait la vaisselle.
12. Tout le monde était parti.

D. Histoire de rupture.

1. s'étaient connus
2. avaient suivi
3. étaient sortis
4. avait rencontré
5. avait offerte (agrees with preceding direct object: **la bague**)
6. avaient achetée (agrees with preceding direct object: **la voiture**)
7. avaient mis
8. avait vécu

E. Un matin occupé? *Answers will vary, but each should contain one of the verbs in the sample sentences below.*

1. **J'étais déjà allé(e) au match de baseball de mon fils.**

2. **Je m'étais déjà réveillé(e).**

3. **J'avais déjà nettoyé le garage.**

4. **J'avais déjà appris que mon équipe préféré de football avait gagné son match hier soir.**

5. **Je m'étais déjà habillé(e).**

6. **J'avais déjà fini mon travail pour la journée.**

7. **J'avais déjà fait de la natation.**

8. **J'avais déjà lu le journal.**

9. **J'avais déjà travaillé sur mon essai pour le cours de philosophie.**

Les mots croisés 9

Across / Down answers:
- 5. SÉTAIENTOUVERTES
- 7. AVAITESSUYÉ
- 9. AVAISEMBRASSÉ
- 10. AVIEZPERDU
- 12. AVIONSÉPELÉ
- 14. SÉTAIENTHABILLÉES
- 15. ÉTAITDESCENDUE
- 16. AVAITEFFRAYÉ

Down:
- 1. ÉTAIENTALLÉES
- 2. AVIONSTRANSFIT (AVIONSTRANSFIT)
- 3. AVAIENTSURPRISE (AVAIENTSURPRIS)
- 4. ÉTAITMONTÉ
- 6. ÉTAITENTÉE
- 8. AVAISDANS
- 11. AVAISPRIS
- 13. AVONSBU

CHAPTER 10

A.

Tout près de la forêt habitait une petite fille qui avait les cheveux si blonds et si bouclés qu'on l'appelait "Boucle d'Or". Dans la forêt, près de la maison de Boucle d'Or, vivait une famille ours.

Il y avait le grand ours, le moyen ours et le petit ours. Comme il faisait très beau ce jour là et parce que la soupe était bien trop chaude pour être mangée tout de suite, les trois ours <u>décidèrent</u> de faire une petite promenade en attendant que le déjeuner refroidisse un peu. Ils <u>sortirent</u> donc tous les trois laissant derrière eux la porte de la maison entrouverte; ils ne craignaient pas les voleurs. Boucle d'Or ce jour là avait aussi eu l'envie de se promener dans la forêt et, chemin faisant, elle <u>arriva</u> près de la maison des trois ours. Elle <u>frappa</u> à la porte mais <u>n'entendit</u> aucune réponse. Alors comme elle était bien curieuse de savoir qui pouvait vivre ici elle <u>entra</u>.

En arrivant dans la salle à manger elle <u>remarqua</u> sur la table trois bols de soupe. Elle <u>s'approcha</u> du grand bol, celui du grand ours, <u>goûta</u> la soupe et la <u>trouva</u> bien trop chaude. Elle <u>s'approcha</u> alors du moyen bol, celui du moyen ours, <u>goûta</u> la soupe et la <u>trouva</u> bien trop salée. Elle <u>s'approcha</u> enfin du petit bol, celui du petit ours, <u>goûta</u> la soupe et la <u>trouva</u> tellement à son goût qu'elle la <u>mangea</u> jusqu'à la dernière goutte. Ensuite elle <u>voulut</u> s'asseoir. Elle <u>s'assit</u> sur la grande chaise, celle du grand ours, mais la <u>trouva</u> bien trop haute. Elle <u>s'assit</u> sur la moyenne chaise, celle du moyen ours, mais la <u>trouva</u> trop bancale. Elle <u>s'assit</u> alors sur la petite chaise, mais comme Boucle d'Or était trop lourde, elle la <u>cassa</u>. "Ce n'est pas grave, <u>se dit</u>-elle, continuons la visite". Elle <u>vit</u> alors un escalier au bout de la pièce et <u>entreprit</u> de le monter. Arrivée en haut elle <u>vit</u> une grande chambre à coucher dans laquelle se trouvaient trois lits: un grand, un moyen et un petit. Elle <u>se coucha</u> sur le grand lit, celui du grand ours évidemment, mais elle le <u>trouva</u> trop dur, alors elle <u>se coucha</u> sur le moyen lit, celui du moyen ours bien entendu, mais elle le <u>trouva</u> trop mou. Enfin elle <u>se coucha</u> sur le petit lit, celui du petit ours, cela va de soi, et elle le <u>trouva</u> tout à fait comme il faut alors elle <u>s'y</u> <u>endormit</u>. Les trois ours, comme ils avaient terminé leur petite promenade, <u>rentrèrent</u> à la maison. Le grand ours voyant son bol <u>s'écria</u>: "quelqu'un a touché à ma soupe!!" Le moyen ours voyant son bol <u>s'exclama</u>: "quelqu'un a touché à ma soupe!!" Le petit ours regardant son bol <u>dit</u>: "quelqu'un a mangé toute ma soupe!!" Le grand ours <u>avança</u> dans la pièce et <u>vit</u> sa chaise: "quelqu'un s'est assis sur ma chaise!!" Le moyen ours, s'avançant alors vers sa chaise <u>affirma</u>: "quelqu'un s'est aussi assis sur ma chaise!!" Et le petit ours, comme il se doit, s'approchant à son tour <u>pleurnicha</u>: "quelqu'un a cassé ma chaise!!" D'un pas décidé le grand ours <u>se dirigea</u> vers l'escalier qu'il <u>grimpa</u> quatre à quatre suivi par le moyen ours et par le petit ours qui séchait ses larmes. Le grand ours une fois dans la chambre <u>avança</u> vers son lit: "quelqu'un s'est couché sur mon lit!!" Le moyen ours s'approchant aussi <u>dit</u> : "quelqu'un s'est couché également sur mon lit!!" Et le petit ours alors <u>s'étonna</u>: "Il y a quelqu'un sur mon lit!!" Boucle d'Or, réveillée par la voix des ours, <u>ouvrit</u> les yeux et <u>vit</u> les trois ours penchés au-dessus d'elle. Elle <u>eut</u> très peur et, voyant la fenêtre ouverte, elle <u>s'y</u> <u>précipita</u> et <u>sauta</u> par dessus pour courir vite jusque chez elle!

B.

Tout près de la forêt habitait une petite fille qui avait les cheveux si blonds et si bouclés qu'on l'appelait "Boucle d'Or". Dans la forêt, près de la maison de Boucle d'Or, vivait une famille ours.

Il y avait le grand ours, le moyen ours et le petit ours. Comme il faisait très beau ce jour là et parce que la soupe était bien trop chaude pour être mangée tout de suite, les trois ours <u>ont décidé</u> de faire une petite promenade en attendant que le déjeuner refroidisse un peu. Ils <u>sont sortis</u> donc tous les trois laissant derrière eux la porte de la maison entrouverte; ils ne craignaient pas les voleurs. Boucle d'Or ce jour là avait aussi eu l'envie de se promener dans la forêt et, chemin faisant, elle <u>est arrivée</u> près de la maison des trois ours. Elle <u>a frappé</u> à la porte mais <u>n'a entendu</u> aucune réponse. Alors comme elle était bien curieuse de savoir qui pouvait vivre ici elle <u>est entrée</u>.

En arrivant dans la salle à manger elle <u>a remarqué</u> sur la table trois bols de soupe. Elle <u>s'est approchée</u> du grand bol, celui du grand ours, <u>a goûté</u> la soupe et l'<u>a trouvée</u> bien trop chaude. Elle <u>s'est approchée</u> alors du moyen bol, celui du moyen ours, <u>a goûté</u> la soupe et l'<u>a trouvée</u> bien trop salée. Elle <u>s'est approchée</u> enfin du petit bol, celui du petit ours, <u>a goûté</u> la soupe et l'<u>a trouvée</u> tellement à son goût qu'elle l'<u>a mangée</u> jusqu'à la dernière goutte. Ensuite elle <u>a voulu</u> s'asseoir. Elle <u>s'est assise</u> sur la grande chaise, celle du grand ours, mais l'<u>a trouvée</u> bien trop haute. Elle <u>s'est assise</u> sur la moyenne chaise, celle du moyen ours, mais l'<u>a trouvée</u> trop bancale. Elle <u>s'est assise</u> alors sur la petite chaise, mais comme Boucle d'Or était trop lourde, elle l'<u>a cassée</u>. "Ce n'est pas grave, <u>s'est</u>-elle <u>dit</u>, continuons la visite". Elle <u>a vu</u> alors un escalier au bout de la pièce et <u>a entrepris</u> de le monter. Arrivée en haut elle <u>a vu</u> une grande chambre à coucher dans laquelle se trouvaient trois lits: un grand, un moyen et un petit. Elle <u>s'est couchée</u> sur le grand lit, celui du grand ours évidemment, mais elle l'<u>a trouvé</u> trop dur, alors elle <u>s'est couchée</u> sur le moyen lit, celui du moyen ours bien entendu, mais elle l'<u>a trouvé</u> trop mou. Enfin elle <u>s'est couchée</u> sur le petit lit, celui du petit ours, cela va de soi, et elle l'<u>a trouvé</u> tout à fait comme il faut alors elle <u>s'y est endormie</u>. Les trois ours, comme ils avaient terminé leur petite promenade, <u>sont rentrés</u> à la maison. Le grand ours voyant son bol <u>s'est écrié</u>: "quelqu'un a touché à ma soupe!!" Le moyen ours voyant son bol <u>s'est exclamé</u>: "quelqu'un a touché à ma soupe!!" Le petit ours regardant son bol <u>a dit</u>: "quelqu'un a mangé toute ma soupe!!" Le grand ours <u>a avancé</u> dans la pièce et <u>a vu</u> sa chaise: "quelqu'un s'est assis sur ma chaise!!" Le moyen ours, s'avançant alors vers sa chaise <u>a affirmé</u>: "quelqu'un s'est aussi assis sur ma chaise!!" Et le petit ours, comme il se doit, s'approchant à son tour <u>a pleurniché</u>: "quelqu'un a cassé ma chaise!!" D'un pas décidé le grand ours <u>s'est dirigé</u> vers l'escalier qu'il <u>a grimpé</u> quatre à quatre suivi par le moyen ours et par le petit ours qui séchait ses larmes. Le grand ours une fois dans la chambre <u>a avancé</u> vers son lit: "quelqu'un s'est couché sur mon lit!!" Le moyen ours s'approchant aussi <u>a dit</u>: "quelqu'un s'est couché également sur mon lit!!" Et le petit ours alors <u>s'est étonné</u>: "Il y a quelqu'un sur mon lit!!" Boucle d'Or, réveillée par la voix des ours, <u>a ouvert</u> les yeux et <u>a vu</u> les trois ours penchés au-dessus d'elle. Elle <u>a eu</u> très peur et, voyant la fenêtre ouverte, elle <u>s'y est précipitée</u> et <u>a sauté</u> par dessus pour courir vite jusque chez elle!

C. Passé composé au passé simple.

1. Les enfants eurent peur.

2. Le messager vint chez le roi.

3. Valmont et la Marquise de Merteuil lurent beaucoup de lettres. Ils en écrirent beaucoup aussi.

4. Albert Camus naquit en 1913 et mourut en 1960.

5. La porte s'ouvra et d'Artagnan et Porthos entrèrent.

6. Swann tomba amoureux d'Odette.

D. Les Trois Mousquetaires.

1. refermèrent ; eurent vu

2. offrit ; s'y suspendit ; gagnèrent

3. écouta ; eut achevé

4. descendit

5. fut-elle sortie ; se dirigea

6. se leva ; prit ; donna

7. l'examina ; devint ; l'essaya

8. tendit ; baisa

9. traversa ; monta ; frappa

CHAPTER 11

A. Un nouveau travail. *The order of sentences may vary, though the order should be logical.*

Il se douchera. Il mettra un nouveau costume. Il prendra un bon petit déjeuner. Il boira un café. Il se brossera les dents. Il achètera le journal. Il attendra le bus. Il lira le journal. Il arrivera au bureau. Il sera un peu nerveux. Il saluera son patron. Il sourira à ses collègues.

B. Votre futur. *Answers will vary, but the verbs should match those given in the sample responses below (except perhaps in #5 and #6, where different verbs could be used).*

1. Je vivrai en Suisse (aux États-Unis, à New York, à Orlando, etc.).

2. Oui, je serai marié(e).
   Non, je ne serai pas marié(e).

3. Oui, j'aurai des chats (des chiens) et des enfants.
   J'aurai des animaux mais je n'aurai pas d'enfants.
   Je n'aurai ni animaux ni enfants.

4. Je ferai la cuisine.
   Je mangerai au restaurant.

5. Je serai professeur (avocat, médecin, coiffeuse, and so on).

6. Je jouerai au foot et je travaillerai dans le jardin.

C. La voyante.

1. Vous vivrez à Tahiti.
2. Vous deviendrez astronaute.
3. Vous aurez 100 chats.
4. Vous découvrirez un remède pour le SIDA.
5. Vous irez en prison.
6. Vous vous marierez.
7. Vous serez millionnaire.
8. Vous tomberez amoureux/euse d'un pingouin.
9. Vous mourrez à l'âge de 120 ans.
10. Vous vous intéresserez à la religion des éléphants.
11. Vous posséderez un avion.
12. Vous essaierez de monter le mont Everest.
13. Vous vendrez des vidéos illégales.
14. Vous étudierez la philosophie chinoise.
15. Vous détiendrez le record du saut en longueur.

D. Quelles vacances?

1. partira
2. irons
3. ferons
4. verrons / découvrirons
5. dormirons
6. découvrirons / verrons
7. faudra
8. devra
9. partirons
10. quittera
11. neigera
12. fera
13. brillera
14. soufflera
15. passeront
16. voudront
17. nageront
18. prendront
19. mangeront
20. danseront
21. pourront
22. aura

23. *(Answers will vary.)* Je choisirai le premier voyage parce que je ne suis jamais allé(e) en Afrique, et j'aime les animaux sauvages. Je choisirai le deuxième voyage parce que j'aime les croisières et j'ai besoin de me détendre!

E. Change each sentence from présent to futur.

1. Il y aura un bon film au cinéma.
2. Tu sauras toutes les réponses.
3. Nous viendrons d'Europe.
4. Préférerez-vous habiter à Madrid ou à Paris?
5. Bernard nettoiera la maison pour ses parents.
6. En mangeant trop de chocolat, tu grossiras.
7. Je serai têtue.
8. Vous adorerez la maison des Caillebotte.

F. Des commandes.

1. Tu ne porteras pas cette veste démodée.
2. Vous ferez votre lit avant de partir.
3. Vous mangerez vos petits pois.
4. Tu seras sage!
5. Tu n'ouvriras la porte pour personne.
6. Vous ne vous disputerez pas.

G. Vos projets. *Answers will vary, but each should contain one of the verbs below.*

je trouverai . . . ; je me marierai . . . ; j'irai . . . ; je me coucherai . . . ; je serai . . . ; je voyagerai . . . ; je lirai . . . ; je préparerai . . . ; j'aurai . . . ; je travaillerai . . . ; j'achèterai . . . ; je prendrai . . .

Les mots croisés 11

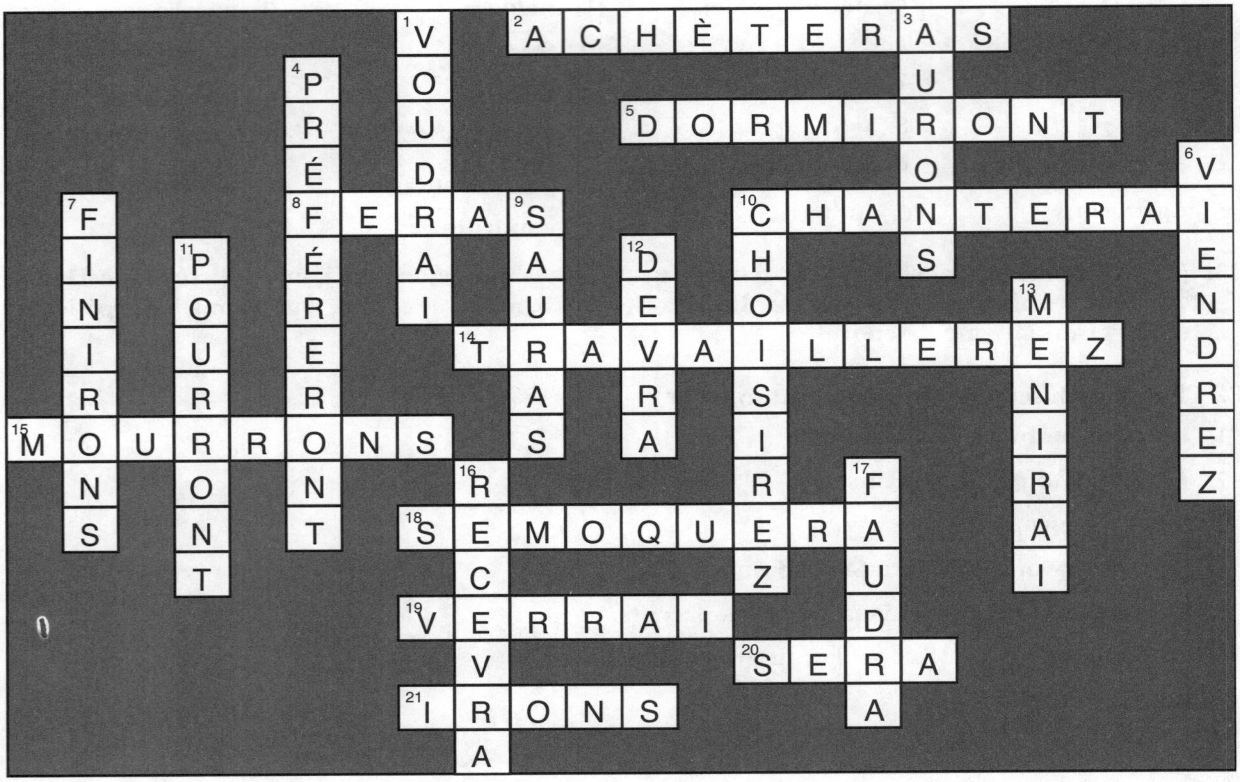
1 VOUDRAI
2 ACHÈTERAS
3 AURONS
4 PRÉFÉRERONT
5 DORMIRONT
6 VIENDREZ
7 FINIRONS
8 FERAS
9 SAURAS
10 CHANTERAI
10 CHOISIREZ
11 POURRONT
12 DEVRA
13 MENIRAI
14 TRAVAILLEREZ
15 MOURRONS
16 RECEVRA
17 FAUDRA
18 SEMOQUERA
19 VERRAI
20 SERA
21 IRONS

CHAPTER 12

A. Avant la soirée.

1. Mme Martin aura lu la recette pour le plat principal.

2. Mme Martin et Paul seront allés au marché.

3. M. Martin aura choisi le vin.

4. Paul aura acheté un gâteau.

5. On aura nettoyé la maison.

6. Les enfants auront rangé leurs jouets.

7. Nadine aura mis la table.

8. Je me serai douché(e).

9. Les Martin et moi, nous nous serons habillés élégamment.

10. Mme Martin se sera maquillée.

B. Now, write sentences of your own!

1. Le chien aura   répondu à la sonnette. (!?!)
                       aboyé aux invités.
                       reçu des fleurs. (!?!)

   Mme Martin aura   répondu à la sonnette.
                       aboyé aux invités. (!?!)
                       reçu des fleurs.

   Nous aurons   répondu à la sonnette.
                       aboyé aux invités. (!?!)
                       reçu des fleurs.

2. Vous   serez arrivé(e)(s).
                       aurez pris l'apéritif.
                       aurez mangé.

   Les invités   seront arrivés.
                       auront pris l'apéritif.
                       auront mangé.

   Tu   seras arrivé(e).
                       auras pris l'apéritif.
                       auras mangé.

3. Nous   aurons bu du vin.
                       aurons ri.
                       nous serons amusé(e)s.

   Je   J'aurai bu du vin.
                       J'aurai ri.
                       Je me serai amusé(e).

   On   aura bu du vin.
                       aura amusé.
                       se sera amusé.

4. **Les enfants**   auront dansé.
                          se seront ennuyé(e)s.
                          auront raconté des histoires.
    Je   J'aurai dansé.
                          Je me serai ennuyé(e).
                          J'aurai raconté des histoires.
    Élise   aura dansé.
                          se sera ennuyée.
                          aura raconté des histoires.

5. **Patrick**   aura dit au revoir.
                          sera parti avec une nouvelle amie.
                          aura fait une gaffe.
    Mes amis   auront dit au revoir.
                          seront parti(e)s avec une nouvelle amie.
                          auront fait une gaffe.
    Nadine   aura dit au revoir.
                          sera partie avec une nouvelle amie.
                          aura fait une gaffe.

C. Avant les vacances.

1. aura fait
2. sera allé
3. aura acheté
4. auront trouvé
5. aura réservé
6. aura obtenu
7. auront appris
8. auront feuilleté
9. auront fait
10. auront eu
11. sera sortie
12. se seront réveillées
13. aura pris
14. aura dit
15. auront appelé
16. seront partis

D. Avant de dormir demain.

j'aurai regardé . . . ; je serai allé(e) . . . ; je me serai douché(e); j'aurai reçu . . . ; je me serai amusé(e); j'aurai acheté . . . ; j'aurai pris . . . ; j'aurai fait . . . ; j'aurai lu . . . ; je me serai brossé les dents; j'aurai écrit . . . ; j'aurai mangé . . . ; j'aurai fini . . . ; je serai sorti(e)

E. Un gâteau spécial.

1. aura cassé; séparera
2. aura séparé; mélangera
3. aura mélangé; ajoutera
4. aura ajouté; tamisera
5. aura tamisé; incorporera
6. battera
7. aura battu; incorporera
8. aura incorporé; versera
9. aura versé; enfournera
10. éteindra; laissera
11. démoulera
12. aura préparé / préparera
13. décorera
14. aura décoré; placera
15. aura placé; posera
16. aura posé; disposera
17. aura disposé; servira

Les mots croisés 12

CHAPTER 13

A. What is the correct form?

1. voyagerait
2. essaierais
3. travaillerait
4. aimerions
5. voudriez
6. irais

B. Quel verbe?

1. pourrions
2. auraient ; achèteraient ; voudraient
3. mangerais ; voudrais ; ferais
4. feriez
5. resterais
6. iriez

C. Que feriez-vous? *Answers will vary, but each should include one of the following verbs.*

1–3. achèterais, irais, travaillerais, offrirais, partirais, apprendrais, trouverais, écrirais, enverrais, essaierais, voyagerais, serais, habiterais, quitterais, nettoierais

4. ils achèteraient, iraient, travailleraient, offriraient, partiraient, apprendraient, trouveraient, écriraient, enverraient, essaieraient, voyageraient, seraient, habiteraient, quitteraient, nettoieraient

5. il achèterait, irait, travaillerait, offrirait, partirait, apprendrait, trouverait, écrirait, enverrait, essaierait, voyagerait, serait, habiterait, quitterait, nettoierait

6. achèterais, irais, travaillerais, offrirais, partirais, apprendrais, trouverais, écrirais, enverrais, essaierais, voyagerais, serais, habiterais, quitterais, nettoierais

D. Plus poli?

1. Je voudrais un sandwich au jambon et une bière.
2. Mon ami voudrait un croque-monsieur et un verre de rouge.
3. Nous voudrions de l'eau.
4. Pourriez-vous me dire où sont les toilettes?
5. Il faudrait étudier plus.
6. Pourrais-tu m'emprunter (to loan) un peu d'argent?

E. Qu'est-ce qu'il a dit?

1. Yves a dit qu'il partirait en Hongrie mardi.
2. Mme Riband a dit qu'elle n'irait pas au mariage de Julien.
3. Thomas a dit que Quentin ne sortirait pas avec Gilberte.
4. Alice a dit qu'il ferait beau demain.
5. M. Menant a dit qu'il y aurait un examen vendredi.
6. Patrice a dit que Jules ne serait jamais professeur.

F. A la une.

1. Il y aurait une bombe à l'intérieur du Palais royal.

2. Les manifestants seraient prêts à aller en prison.

3. Le chocolat serait bon pour la santé.

4. Les employés de la RATP feraient grève.

5. Céline Dion aurait un nouveau bébé.

6. Les soldats seraient mécontents des conditions de guerre.

G. Quel verbe?

1. voudrait/ aimerait   3. irait   5. voudriez / aimeriez

2. aurais   4. parlerions   6. se nettoierait

H. Questions personnelles. *Answers will vary.*

1. Je serais avocat(e) (médecin, agent de police, coiffeur, etc.).

2. Je voudrais / J'aimerais un café et un croissant, s'il vous plaît.

3. Je parlerais probablement une langue différente et je m'habillerais différemment peut-être.

Les mots croisés 13

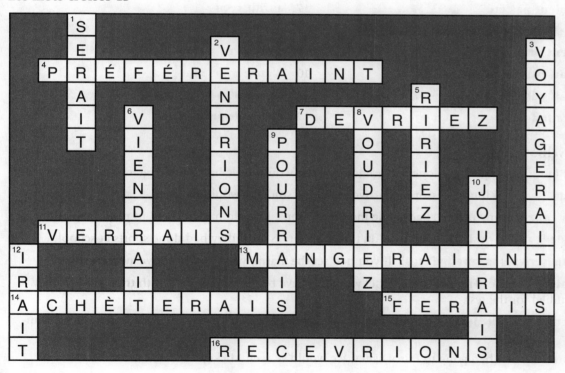

CHAPTER 14

A. Conjugaisons.

1. **aurais attendu;** You would have waited.

2. **aurait fait;** Marc would have made/done.

3. **serions parti(e)s;** We would have left.

4. **se seraient détendus;** They would have relaxed.

5. **auriez rempli;** You would have filled.

6. **aurais vu;** I would have seen.

7. **se serait douchée;** Rachel would have showered.

8. **auraient acheté;** They would have bought.

9. **seriez resté(e)(s);** You would have stayed.

10. **aurais été;** I would have been.

11. **aurais dû;** You should have.

12. **auraient pu;** They could have.

B. What is the correct form?

1. **n'auraient pas été**

2. **ne se seraient pas réveillés**

3. **auraient pris**

4. **n'aurait pas pu**

5. **n'aurait pas cru**

6. **se serait fâché**

7. **aurait reçu**

8. **auraient été**

9. **n'auraient pas emmené**

10. **n'aurait pas mangé**

11. **ne serait pas tombée**

12. **ne serait pas morte**

C. Which verb?

1. **aurait eu;** If Monique had done her homework, she would have had a better grade.

2. **seraient partis;** If the professor had arrived late, the students would have left.

3. **aurais appris;** If my parents had made me take lessons, I would have learned to play the piano.

4. **n'auraient pas grossi;** The girls wouldn't have gotten as fat if they had done sports at school.

5. **ne vous seriez pas réveillé(e)(s);** If you had set the alarm, you wouldn't have awakened late.

6. **n'auraient pas été;** Thomas and Michel wouldn't have been disappointed with their grade if they had studied for the test.

7. **auraient emmené(e)s;** Our parents would've taken us to EuroDisney if we had passed the bacalauréat.

8. **aurions vu;** If we had gone to EuroDisney, we would've seen Mickey.

9. **aurais reçu;** I would've gotten a raise if I had done the report in time.

D. Comment dit-on?

1. J'aurais dû téléphoner à (appeler) ma mère hier.

2. Si j'avais su la vérité, j'aurais parlé à la police.

3. Yves aurait pu arriver à l'heure s'il avait voulu.

4. Nous aurions gagné le match si seulement nous avions marqué un but.

5. Si elle avait vu la glace, elle l'aurait commandée.

6. Si vous aviez pu avoir les réponses, auriez-vous triché (est-ce que vous auriez triché)?

7. Elle aurait dû offrir un meilleur cadeau à son mari.

Les mots croisés 14

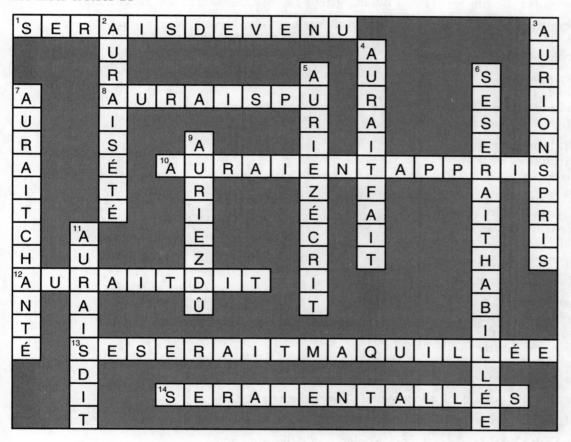

CHAPTER 15

A. What is the correct form?

1. **irons** ; If it's nice, we'll go to the beach.

2. **a** ; Patrick will make the trip to Senegal next year if he has enough money.

3. **ferez** ; What will you do if you win the lottery?

4. **écrit** ; If one writes an important book, one might win the Goncourt Prize.

5. **sera** ; If you feed the dog every day and you play with him, he will be happy.

6. **étudie** ; One (we) won't have good grades if one (we) doesn't (don't) study.

7. **connaissent** ; The girls won't find work in the music store if they don't know (about) Edith Piaf.

8. **achèterai** ; If my parents give me money, I will buy a birthday present for my sister.

B. Now, make sentences of your own!

1. **S'il neige demain . . .**
   je serai . . .
   les enfants seront . . .
   mon frère / ma sœur sera . . .

2. **S'il fait beau demain . . .**
   nous irons . . .
   vous irez . . .
   tu iras . . .

3. **Si on n'a pas cours demain . . .**
   mes amis feront . . .
   je ferai . . .
   nous ferons . . .

4. **Si j'ai assez d'argent j'achèterai . . .**

5. **J'irai en France si . . .**
   J'apprends le français.
   J'ai assez d'argent.
   Je gagne une bourse.

C. What is the correct form?

1. **savais** ; I would buy a book about Mali if I knew where to find it.

2. **dormirais** ; If I had a cat, I would sleep with it.

3. **se douchait** ; If Yves showered more, women would like him more.

4. **regarderaient** ; Children would watch television less if their parents played with them.

5. **serait** ; Jean would be happier if he weren't always on a diet.

6. **faisais** ; If I exercised, I would have more energy.

7. **aurais** ; If you worked more, you would have better grades.

8. **sortirais;** If you called me from time to time, I would go out with you.

9. **ferions** ; We would make fewer mistakes if we paid attention.

D. Que ferait-on?

1. **iraient . . . ; seraient ; feraient ; déménageraient ; joueraient . . . ; s'amuseraient ; démissionneraient ; se perdraient ; achèteraient . . . ; se préoccuperaient**

2. **irais . . . ; serais . . . ; ferais . . . ; déménagerais ; jouerais . . . ; m'amuserais ; démissionnerais ; me perdrais ; achèterais . . . ; me préoccuperais**

3. **iraient . . . ; seraient ; feraient ; déménageraient ; joueraient . . . ; s'amuseraient ; démissionneraient ; se perdraient ; achèteraient . . . ; se préoccuperaient**

4. **irais . . . ; serais . . . ; ferais . . . ; déménagerais ; jouerais . . . ; m'amuserais ; démissionnerais ; me perdrais ; achèterais . . . ; me préoccuperais**

5. **irait . . . ; serait . . . ; ferait . . . ; déménagerait ; jouerait . . . ; s'amuserait ; démissionnerait ; se perdrait ; achèterait . . . ; se préoccuperait**

E. What is the correct form?

1. **n'avait pas mangé;** If Richard hadn't eaten so many candies, he wouldn't have gotten fat.

2. **auriez fait;** What would you have done if your parents had left you at the age of 16?

3. **avais épargné;** I would've been able to buy a house if I had saved my money.

4. **ne nous serions pas mariés;** If we hadn't met, we wouldn't have gotten married.

5. **ne nous étions pas mariés;** If we hadn't gotten married, we wouldn't have gotten divorced.

6. **aurais réussi;** You would've passed the test if you had studied with me.

7. **n'était pas venue;** If Beatrice hadn't come to the party, we would've had fun.

8. **serais allé(e);** Where would you have gone to college if you could've chosen?

F. Which verb?

1. **me serais arrêté(e)**	4. **pouviez**	7. **aurait-elle recommandé**
2. **pleurera**	5. **étais**	8. **avions**
3. **pleuvra**	6. **n'étaient pas revenus**	

G. Comment dit-on?

1. **Si j'avais su que vous attendiez, je me serais dépêché(e).**

2. **Nous ferons du ski s'il neige.**

3. **Si tu te brossais les dents, tu n'aurais pas de caries.**

4. **Si Sylvain avait vu la voiture de police, il n'aurait pas ignoré le feu rouge.**

5. **Mangeras-tu (Est-ce que tu mangeras) le gâteau si je le fais?**

6. **Iriez-vous à Genève si votre patron payait le billet?**

7. **Si je n'avais pas lu le livre, j'aurais mieux aimé le film.**

Les mots croisés 15

							¹Ê				²V	
					³É	T	U	D	I	I	E	Z
		⁴M				E					N	
⁵S		⁶A	U	R	A	I	S	P	U		D	
E		M									R	
R	⁷V	O	U	L	A	I	S				A	
I		S				⁸A			¹⁰D		I	
E	⁹M	E				V			E		E	
Z	O	R		¹¹I	R	A	I	S	V		N	
P	U	A				O			R		T	
¹²A	U	R	A	I	¹³S	G	A	G	N	É		
R	R			E		S			O			
T	A			R	¹⁴D	E	V	I	E	N	S	
I	I			O		U			T			
	T			N								
	¹⁵S	E	S	E	R	A	I	T	F	Â	C	H	É

CHAPTER 16

A. What is the correct form?

1. **ne vienne pas;** We fear that Philippe will not come (is not coming) to the ceremony.

2. **neige;** It is possible that it will snow tomorrow.

3. **écrivent;** The professor demands that the students write their name on their project.

4. **aie;** Are you surprised that I have a small car?

5. **veniez;** Marie is delighted that you are coming (will come) to the party.

6. **finissions;** It is necessary that we finish this report. (We have to finish this report.)

7. **puissions;** I didn't think we could finish this work in time.

8. **ne fasse pas;** We are afraid that Josianne is not doing her best.

9. **travaillions;** It would be better that we work a great deal.

10. **veuillent;** We don't believe that our colleagues want to work on the weekend.

11. **nettoyions;** Our mother wanted us to clean our room.

12. **tolériez;** I don't want you to tolerate this insolence.

13. **aille;** It is impossible for me to go to Paris this summer.

14. **soyez;** I will come to the party, provided that you will be there.

15. **choisisse;** My boss asks that I choose a new assistant.

16. **lise;** The students prefer that the teacher read their essays right away.

17. **dise;** The Duponts wish that Thomas would tell the truth.

18. **allions;** Are you happy that we are going to France?

19. **soit;** René wants me to be at the museum with him.

20. **dorme;** The angry woman demands that her husband sleep on the couch.

21. **apprenne;** Ghislaine's boss wants her to learn Italian.

22. **boive;** I doubt that Mr. Troude is drinking lemonade.

23. **ait;** The doctor doesn't think that Sylvie has strep throat.

24. **dise;** I will tell you the news before I tell my parents.

B. Now, write sentences of your own!

1. **Maman veut que nous nettoyions la maison / fassions la vaisselle / soyons heureux.**
   Maman veut que vous nettoyiez la maison / fassiez la vaisselle / soyez heureux.
   Maman veut que ses enfants nettoient la maison / fassent la vaisselle / soient heureux.

2. **Je suis triste que tu attendes le bus / ailles à Tahiti sans moi / aies une pneumonie.**
   Je suis triste que mes amis attendent le bus / aillent à Tahiti sans moi / aient une pneumonie.
   Je suis triste que mon/ma collègue attende le bus / aille à Tahiti sans moi / ait une pneumonie.

3. **Il faut que je prenne des vacances / lise un bon livre / me détende.**
   Il faut que nous prenions des vacances / lisions un bon livre / nous détendions.
   Il faut que les employé(e)s prennent des vacances / lisent un bon livre / se détendent.

C. Subjonctif ou indicatif?

1. S	6. S	11. S	16. S	21. S	26. S	31. S
2. I	7. S	12. S	17. S	22. I	27. S	32. I
3. S	8. I	13. S	18. S	23. S	28. I	33. S
4. S	9. S	14. S	19. S	24. S	29. S	34. S
5. I	10. I	15. I	20. I	25. S	30. I	

D. What is the correct form?

1. jetions	6. a	11. vont	16. aie
2. recyclions	7. puisse	12. aillent	17. devienne
3. soit	8. veut	13. ne répondiez pas	18. fasse
4. lisent	9. fassent	14. devons	19. ait
5. vas	10. ne soient pas	15. fasse	20. rende

E.   Now, write sentences of your own!

1. **Il est possible que**   j'aille au restaurant / fasse du ski / m'amuse au parc.
       nous allions au restaurant / fassions du ski / nous amusions au parc.
       les enfants aillent au restaurant / fassent du ski / s'amusent au parc.

    Il est vrai que   je vais au restaurant / fais du ski / m'amuse au parc.
       nous allons au restaurant / faisons du ski / nous amusons au parc.
       les enfants vont au restaurant / font du ski / s'amusent au parc.

    Il faut que   j'aille au restaurant / fasse du ski / m'amuse au parc.
       nous allions au restaurant / fassions du ski / nous amusions au parc.
       les enfants aillent au restaurant / fassent du ski / s'amusent au parc.

2. **Je doute que**   le prof veuille de la glace / dorme jusqu'à midi / prenne le dîner à 22h.
       vous vouliez de la glace / dormiez jusqu'à midi / preniez le dîner à 22h.
       tu veuilles de la glace / dormes jusqu'à midi / prennes le dîner à 22h.

    Est-il vrai que   le prof veuille de la glace / dorme jusqu'à midi / prenne le dîner à 22h?
       vous vouliez de la glace / dormiez jusqu'à midi / preniez le dîner à 22h?
       tu veuilles de la glace / dormes jusqu'à midi / prennes le dîner à 22h?

    Je crois que   le prof veut de la glace / dort jusqu'à midi / prend le dîner à 22h.
       vous voulez de la glace / dormez jusqu'à midi / prenez le dîner à 22h.
       tu veux de la glace / dors jusqu'à midi / prends le dîner à 22h.

3. **Nous sommes content(e)s que** le patron soit malade / n'ait pas de rhume / achète un bateau.
       vous soyez malade(s) / n'ayez pas de rhume / achetez un bateau.
       les filles soient malades / n'aient pas de rhume / achètent un bateau.

    Nous sommes tristes que le patron soit malade / n'ait pas de rhume / achète un bateau.
       vous soyez malade(s) / n'ayez pas de rhume / achetez un bateau.
       les filles soient malades / n'aient pas de rhume / achètent un bateau.

    Nous sommes certain(e)s que le patron est malade / n'a pas de rhume / achète un bateau.
       vous êtes malade(s) / n'avez pas de rhume / achetez un bateau.
       les filles sont malades / n'ont pas de rhume / achètent un bateau.

F. Comment dit-on?

1. Nous voulons que tu ailles au magasin.

2. Il faut que (Il est nécessaire que) je vende la voiture.

3. Mon patron veut que je comprenne l'allemand.

4. Je pense (crois) qu'Alain est beau.

5. Penses-tu (Est-ce que tu penses) qu'il soit mignon?

6. Je ne pense (crois) pas qu'il ait une copine (petite amie).

7. Je souhaite qu'il sorte avec moi.

8. Il est évident que Roxanne veut plaire au patron.

9. J'espère que vous vous brossez les dents tous les jours.

10. Le dentiste exige que vous vous brossiez les dents tous les jours.

11. Élise étudie beaucoup bien qu'elle ne veuille pas aller à l'université.

12. Je ne serai pas content(e)/heureux(se) sans que (à moins que) vous vous excusiez.

G. Le rabat-joie.

1. Nous voulons aller au bord de la mer. Marc ne veut pas que nous allions au bord de la mer.

2. Vous voulez écrire un roman. Marc ne veut pas que vous écriviez un roman.

3. Hélène et Céline veulent faire un pique-nique. Marc ne veut pas qu'elles fassent un pique-nique.

4. Je veux être avocat. Marc ne veut pas que je sois avocat.

5. Les employés veulent demander une augmentation. Marc ne veut pas qu'ils demandent une augmentation.

6. Gérard veut finir ses devoirs. Marc ne veut pas que Gérard finisse ses devoirs.

7. Quentin veut rendre visite à sa grand-mère. Marc ne veut pas qu'il rende visite à sa grand-mère.

8. Je veux prendre un pot avec mes amis. Marc ne veut pas que je prenne un pot avec mes amis.

Les mots croisés 16

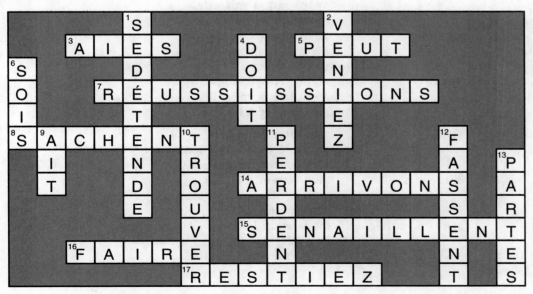

CHAPTER 17

A. What is the correct form?

1. **ne soit pas allé;** We fear that Philippe didn't go to the ceremony.
2. **ait neigé;** It is possible that it snowed last night.
3. **aient écrit;** The professor is happy that the students wrote their name on their project.
4. **aie acheté;** Are you surprised that I bought a small car?
5. **soyez venu(e)(s);** Marie is delighted that you came to the party.
6. **ayons fini;** Is it possible that we finished that report?
7. **ait pu;** I don't think Raoul could have finished that report.
8. **n'ait pas fait;** We are afraid that Josianne didn't do her best.
9. **ayons travaillé;** I am proud that we worked a great deal.
10. **aient vu;** We don't think our colleagues saw our report.
11. **te sois réveillé(e);** Your mother is surprised that you woke up early.
12. **soient parties;** I don't think the girls left without their parents.
13. **sois allé(e)** It is impossible that I went to Lise's last night. I was home all night long.
14. **aie choisi;** My boss is angry that I chose a new assistant.
15. **ait lu;** The students are shocked that their professor read their essays right away.
16. **ait dit;** The Duponts doubt that Thomas told the truth.
17. **soyons allé(e)s;** Are you happy that we went to France?
18. **se soit endormi;** The woman is horrified that her husband fell asleep during the opera.
19. **ait appris;** Ghislaine's boss doubts that she learned Italian.
20. **ait bu;** I am not sure that Mr. Troude drank lemonade at the party.

B. Now, write sentences of your own!

1. **Maman doute que**	**nous**	ayons nettoyé la maison.
		ayons fait la vaisselle.
		soyons allé(e)s à l'église.
	ses filles	aient nettoyé la maison.
		aient fait la vaisselle.
		soient allées à l'église.
	ses fils	aient nettoyé la maison.
		aient fait la vaisselle.
		soient allés à l'église.
2. **Je suis triste que**	**tu**	aies attendu le bus.
		sois allé(e) à Tahiti sans moi.
		aies eu une pneumonie.
	mes amis	aient attendu le bus.
		soient allés à Tahiti sans moi.
		aient eu une pneumonie.
	mon/ma collègue	ait attendu le bus.
		soit allé(e) à Tahiti sans moi.
		ait eu une pneumonie.

3. Il est possible que   Madeleine   soit partie en vacances.
                                              ait lu un bon livre.
                                              se soit couchée.
                     les Robichard   soient partis en vacances.
                                              aient lu un bon livre.
                                              se soient couchés.
                     Hervé   soit parti en vacances.
                                              ait lu un bon livre.
                                              se soit couché.

C. What is the correct form?

1.	aient jeté	6.	a causé	11.	sont allés
2.	se soient perdus	7.	a pu	12.	soient allés
3.	se sont perdus	8.	sois rentré(e)	13.	n'ayez pas réparé
4.	aient lu	9.	aient fait	14.	ont fini
5.	es allé(e)	10.	se soient fâchés	15.	ait fait

D. Now, write sentences of your own!

1. Il est possible que   je sois allé(e) au restaurant.
                                       j'aie fait du ski.
                                       je me sois amusé(e) au parc.
                                       nous soyons allé(e)s au restaurant.
                                       nous ayons fait du ski.
                                       nous nous soyons amusé(e)s au parc.
                                       les enfants soient allés au restaurant.
                                       les enfants aient fait du ski.
                                       les enfants se soient amusés au parc.

     Il est vrai que   je suis allé(e) au restaurant.
                                       j'ai fait du ski.
                                       je me suis amusé(e) au parc.
                                       nous sommes allé(e)s au restaurant.
                                       nous avons fait du ski.
                                       nous nous sommes amusé(e)s au parc.
                                       les enfants sont allés au restaurant.
                                       les enfants ont fait du ski.
                                       les enfants se sont amusés au parc.

     Il est clair que   je suis allé(e) au restaurant.
                                       j'ai fait du ski.
                                       je me suis amusé(e) au parc.
                                       nous sommes allé(e)s au restaurant.
                                       nous avons fait du ski.
                                       nous nous sommes amusé(e)s au parc.
                                       les enfants sont allés au restaurant.
                                       les enfants ont fait du ski.
                                       les enfants se sont amusés au parc.

2. Je doute que   le prof   ait mangé de la glace.
                                 ait dormi jusqu'à midi.
                                 ait pris le dîner à 22h.

                   vous   ayez mangé de la glace.
                                 ayez dormi jusqu'à midi.
                                 ayez pris le dîner à 22h.

                   tu   aies mangé de la glace.
                                 aies dormi jusqu'à midi.
                                 aies pris le dîner à 22h.

Est-il vrai que   le prof   ait mangé de la glace?
                                 ait dormi jusqu'à midi?
                                 ait pris le dîner à 22h?

                   vous   ayez mangé de la glace?
                                 ayez dormi jusqu'à midi?
                                 ayez pris le dîner à 22h?

                   tu   aies mangé de la glace?
                                 aies dormi jusqu'à midi?
                                 aies pris le dîner à 22h?

Je crois que   le prof a mangé de la glace.
                                 a dormi jusqu'à midi.
                                 a pris le dîner à 22h.

                   vous   avez mangé de la glace.
                                 avez dormi jusqu'à midi.
                                 avez pris le dîner à 22h.

                   tu   as mangé de la glace.
                                 as dormi jusqu'à midi.
                                 as pris le dîner à 22h.

3. Nous sommes content(e)s que   le patron   soit devenu malade.
                                                         se soit enrhumé.
                                                         ait acheté un bateau.

                                     vous   soyez devenu(e)(s) malade(s).
                                                         vous soyez enrhumé(e)(s).
                                                         ayez acheté un bateau.

                                     les filles   soient devenues malades.
                                                         se soient enrhumées.
                                                         aient acheté un bateau.

Nous sommes tristes que   le patron   soit devenu malade.
                                                         se soit enrhumé.
                                                         ait acheté un bateau.

                                     vous   soyez devenu(e)(s) malade(s).
                                                         vous soyez enrhumé(e)(s).
                                                         ayez acheté un bateau.

                                     les filles   soient devenues malades.
                                                         se soient enrhumées.
                                                         aient acheté un bateau.

Nous sommes certain(e)s que   le patron   est devenu malade.
                                                         s'est enrhumé.
                                                         a acheté un bateau.

                                     vous   êtes devenu(e)(s) malade(s).
                                                         vous êtes enrhumé(e)(s).
                                                         avez acheté un bateau.

                                     les filles   sont devenues malades.
                                                         se sont enrhumées.
                                                         ont acheté un bateau.

E. **Comment dit-on?**

1. **Il est bon que tu sois allé(e) au magasin.**
2. Mireille doute que j'aie vendu la voiture.
3. Il est vrai que je l'ai vendue.
4. Je pense (crois) qu'Alain est sorti avec Sophie hier soir.
5. Penses-tu (Est-ce que tu penses) qu'ils se soient amusés?
6. Je pense (crois) qu'ils ont aimé le film qu'ils ont vu.
7. Je ne pense (crois) pas qu'ils se soient embrassés.
8. Il est évident que Roxanne est arrivée tôt pour plaire au patron.
9. J'espère que vous vous êtes brossé les dents ce matin.
10. Le dentiste est content que vous vous soyez brossé les dents ce matin.

Les mots croisés 17

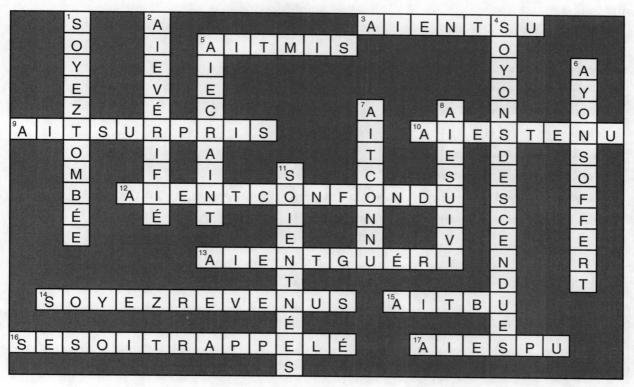

CHAPTER 18

A. Identifiez et changez.

1. ~~se fît~~; se fasse

2. ~~fût~~; soit

3. ~~fût~~; soit

4. ~~allât~~; aille

5. ~~s'en allât~~; s'en aille

6. ~~ne fussent~~; ne soient; ~~ne me nuisît~~; ne me nuise

7. ~~tournât~~; tourne

8. ~~partît~~; parte

9. ~~restât~~; reste

10. ~~eût~~; ait

11. ~~voulût~~; veuille

12. ~~se trouvât~~; se trouve

13. ~~s'en doutât~~; s'en doute

14. ~~restât~~; reste

15. ~~obtînt~~; obtienne; ~~s'assurât~~; s'assure

16. ~~ne fissions pas~~; ne fassions pas

17. ~~fût~~; soit

18. ~~ne profitât~~; ne profite

19. ~~tînt~~; tienne

20. ~~s'en ressouvînt~~; s'en ressouvienne

21. ~~ne vous en devînt~~; ne vous en devienne

22. ~~eussions~~; ayons

B. Identifiez et changez.

1. ~~s'y fût passé~~; s'y soit passé

2. ~~vous l'eusse dit~~; vous l'aie dit

3. ~~eussiez été~~; ayez été

4. ~~ne fût venu~~; ne soit venu

5. ~~l'eusse laissée~~; l'aie laissée

6. ~~ne se fussent point parlé~~; ne se soient point parlé; ~~n'y eût pas eu~~; n'y ait pas eu

7. ~~pût~~; puisse; ~~eusse remarqué~~; aie remarqué

CHAPTER 19

A. Une mère polie.

1. **Brosse-toi les dents! Brossez-vous les dents!**

2. **Aie de la patience! Ayez de la patience!**

3. **Aide-moi! Aidez-moi!**

4. **Sors la poubelle! Sortez la poubelle!**

5. **Fais les devoirs! Faites les devoirs!**

6. **Pense aux autres! Pensez aux autres!**

7. **Mange les petits pois! Mangez les petits pois!**

8. **Réveille-toi! Réveillez-vous!**

9. **Va au supermarché! Allez au supermarché!**

10. **Sois sage! Soyez sages!**

11. **Lis le journal! Lisez le journal!**

12. **Apprends à nager! Apprenez à nager!**

B. Des ordres négatives.

1. **Ne te bats pas avec ton frère! Ne vous battez pas!**

2. **N'écris pas sur les murs! N'écrivez pas sur les murs!**

3. **Ne dis pas de bêtises! Ne dites pas de bêtises!** (The word **des** changes to **de** in the negative.)

4. **Ne fume pas! Ne fumez pas!**

5. **Ne rentre pas après minuit! Ne rentrez pas après minuit!**

6. **Ne te fâche pas! Ne vous fâchez pas!**

7. **Ne vends pas ma voiture! Ne vendez pas ma voiture!**

8. **Ne perds pas les livres. Ne perdez pas les livres!**

9. **Ne me désobéis pas! Ne me désobéissez pas!**

10. **Ne maigris pas trop! Ne maigrissez pas trop!**

11. **Ne tutoie pas les professeurs. Ne tutoyez pas les professeurs!**

12. **Ne prends pas de drogues! Ne prenez pas de drogues!** (The word **des** changes to **de** in the negative.)

13. **Ne rouspète pas! Ne rouspétez pas!**

14. **Ne va pas en vacances sans moi! N'allez pas en vacances sans moi!**

15. **Ne te marie pas avant l'âge de 20 ans! Ne vous mariez pas avant l'âge de 20 ans!**

16. **Ne bois pas de bière avant l'âge de 21 ans! Ne buvez pas de bière avant l'âge de 21 ans!**

17. **Ne te moque pas de moi! Ne vous moquez pas de moi!**

18. **Ne deviens pas acteur médiocre! Ne devenez pas acteur médiocre!**

C. Des suggestions. *Answers will vary in order. The possible answers are:*

Voyons (ne voyons pas) un film.
Faisons (ne faisons pas) un pique-nique.
Allons (n'allons pas) au restaurant.
Finissons (ne finissons pas) notre travail.
Lisons (ne lisons pas) un bon livre.
Travaillons (ne travaillons pas) dur.
Reposons-nous (ne nous reposons pas).
Réfléchissons (ne réfléchissons pas).
Jouons (ne jouons pas) au football.
Détendons-nous (ne nous détendons pas).
Couchons-nous (ne nous couchons pas) tôt.
Mangeons (ne mangeons pas) au café.
Apprenons (n'apprenons pas) les leçons.
Étudions (n'étudions pas).
Prenons (ne prenons pas) un pot.

D. La soupe.

2. **mets; fais-y; ajoute-leur; sale; poivre; verse**

3. **Porte; laisse; retire**

4. **Bats; incorpore-les; ajoute**

5. **Dispose; saupoudre-les; recouvre**

6. **saupoudre-le; mets**

Les mots croisés 19

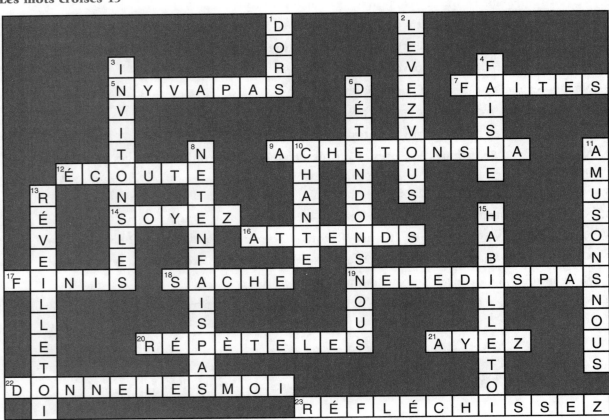

CHAPTER 20

A. À l'actif.

1. **La compagnie paie bien les employés.**

2. **Les étudiants feront les devoirs.**

3. **Guy a fait une gaffe.**

4. **Mes collègues ont vu ce film.**

5. **Mes grands-parents aimaient la Suisse.**

6. **Mon fils aurait perdu mes clés.**

7. **Ma fille trouvera mes clés.**

8. **Les filles comprennent les règles du jeu.**

9. **Paul a lu le nouveau roman de Laurent Gaudé.**

B. Au passif.

1. **Est-ce que l'espagnol est parlé au Brésil?**

2. **Les essais seront rendus aux étudiants par le professeur.**

3. **Les rues de Paris sont nettoyées chaque nuit.**

4. **La belle princesse a été ensorcelée par le magicien.**

5. **J'ai été suivi(e) dans la rue hier soir.**

6. **Les ordinateurs sont employés pour communiquer.**

7. **Ces poèmes ont été écrits par Arthur Rimbaud.**

8. **Les tee-shirts sont vendus partout.**

C. Comment dit-on?

1. **Le français est parlé au Cameroun.**
   Le français se parle au Cameroun.
   On parle français au Cameroun.

2. **Ce tableau a été créé par Paul Gauguin.**
   Paul Gauguin a créé ce tableau.

D. Réponses négatives.

1. **Non, il ne fait jamais beau en avril.**

2. **Non, Maman n'a pas encore acheté nos cadeaux de Noël.**

3. **Non, je n'aime pas du tout les pommes de terre.**

4. **Non, on n'a rien fait pour préparer notre voyage.**

5. **Non, personne n'aime chanter.**

6. **Non, nous n'avons vu personne à la soirée.**

7. **Non, rien ne m'intéresse.**

8. **Non, Mamie ne fume plus.**

E. Comment dit-on?

1. Nous n'aimons pas les pommes jaunes. Nous ne voulons que les rouges. (Nous voulons seulement les rouges.)

2. Personne ne fait ses propres tartes.

3. Je ne joue plus du violon.

4. Il ne fait jamais son lit.

5. On n'a rien fait hier. (Nous n'avons rien fait hier.)

6. Guy n'a pas encore fini ses devoirs.

F. Quelle préposition?

1. *X*; *X*; de	5. à	9. *X*	13. d'; de
2. à	6. *X*	10. à; à	14. *X*; *X*
3. de	7. *X*; à	11. à; d'	15. de; à; de
4. *X*	8. de	12. de	16. de; de

G. Now, write sentences of your own!

1. Maman	veut	jouer du piano / préparer le dîner / danser.
	hésite à	jouer du piano / préparer le dîner / danser.
	refuse de	jouer du piano / préparer le dîner / danser.
Papa	veut	jouer du piano / préparer le dîner / danser.
	hésite à	jouer du piano / préparer le dîner / danser.
	refuse de	jouer du piano / préparer le dîner / danser.
Les enfants	veulent	jouer du piano / préparer le dîner / danser.
	hésitent à	jouer du piano / préparer le dîner / danser.
	refusent de	jouer du piano / préparer le dîner / danser.
2. Je	rêve de	voyager en Chine / me marier / devenir célèbre.
	songe à	voyager en Chine / me marier / devenir célèbre.
	espère	voyager en Chine / me marier / devenir célèbre.
Vous	rêvez de	voyager en Chine / vous marier / devenir célèbre(s).
	songez à	voyager en Chine / vous marier / devenir célèbre(s).
	espérez	voyager en Chine / vous marier / devenir célèbre(s).
Nous	rêvons de	voyager en Chine / nous marier / devenir célèbres.
	songeons à	voyager en Chine / nous marier / devenir célèbres.
	espérons	voyager en Chine / nous marier / devenir célèbres.
3. Marie-Hélène	déteste	confronter son époux / se plaindre au patron / démissionner.
	a peur de	confronter son époux / se plaindre au patron / démissionner.
	hésite à	confronter son époux / se plaindre au patron / démissionner.
Mon ami	déteste	confronter son époux / se plaindre au patron / démissionner.
	a peur de	confronter son époux / se plaindre au patron / démissionner.
	hésite à	confronter son époux / se plaindre au patron / démissionner.
Tu	détestes	confronter ton époux(se) / te plaindre au patron / démissionner.
	as peur de	confronter ton époux(se) / te plaindre au patron / démissionner.
	hésites à	confronter ton époux(se) / te plaindre au patron / démissionner.

H. Comment dit-on?

1. Je refuse de travailler le dimanche.

2. J'apprends à jouer du piano.

3. Est-ce que tu veux utiliser l'ordinateur? (Veux-tu utiliser l'ordinateur?)

4. **Ils ont peur de parler au patron.**

5. **Est-ce que vous allez démissioner? (Allez-vous démissioner?)**

I. Un tyran implacable.

1. **Le patron fait taper les rapports aux secrétaires.**

2. **Le patron fait essuyer les fenêtres à Victor.**

3. **Le patron fait répondre au téléphone <u>par</u> Yves.** (The word **par** is used instead of à to avoid ambiguity.)

4. **Le patron fait examiner les budgets à Alex.**

5. **Le patron fait téléphoner aux clients <u>par</u> Hervé.** (The word **par** is used instead of à to avoid ambiguity.)

6. **Le patron fait vérifier les stocks à Xavier.**

J. Comment dit-on?

1. **Ma mère fait faire la vaisselle à mon père tous les soirs.**

2. **Faites (fais) fondre le beurre dans une petite casserole.**

3. **Le professeur a fait écrire un essai de cinq pages à ses étudiants.**

4. **Elle se fait couper les cheveux par Mme Siseaux.**

5. **Je me suis fait couper les cheveux.**

Les mots croisés 20

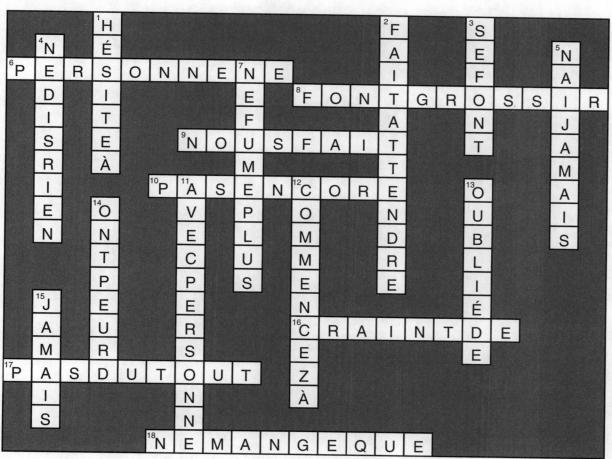

Answers to *Proverbs and Expressions*

1. When the cat's away, the mice will play.
2. The end justifies the means.
3. Once bitten, twice shy.
4. You made your bed, now lie in it.
5. Where there's smoke, there's fire.
6. Birds of a feather flock together.
7. Rome wasn't built in a day.
8. The more you eat, the more you want.
9. Two heads are better than one.
10. The road to hell is paved with good intentions.
11. Practice makes perfect.
12. There's no accounting for taste.
13. Lucky in cards, unlucky in love.
14. A bird in the hand is worth two in the bush.
15. Strike while the iron is hot.
16. Robbing Peter to pay Paul.
17. Out of sight, out of mind.
18. Cold hands, warm heart.
19. The first step is the hardest.
20. Better late than never.
21. Let sleeping dogs lie.
22. Forewarned is forearmed.
23. No news is good news.
24. A rolling stone gathers no moss.
25. The more the merrier.
26. Putting the cart before the horse.
27. Nothing ventured, nothing gained. (No pain, no gain.)
28. Like father, like son.
29. All roads lead to Rome.
30. He who laughs last laughs best.

Answers to *For More Practice*

CHAPTER 1

I.

1. <u>Elles</u> déjeunent au restaurant le dimanche.
2. <u>Tu</u> vends ta moto?
3. <u>Nous</u> mangeons de la dinde aux marrons à Noël.
4. <u>Vous</u> vouvoyez vos grands-parents?
5. <u>Tu</u> trouves intéressant le professeur d'histoire?
6. <u>Tu</u> pars en vacances bientôt?
7. <u>Nous</u> achetons notre pain dans cette boulangerie.
8. <u>Il</u> adore la classe de biologie.
9. <u>Nous</u> discutons des problèmes au Moyen Orient.
10. <u>Il</u> nettoie la cuisine pour ses parents.
11. <u>Nous</u> répondons aux courriels tout de suite.
12. <u>Elles</u> promènent leur chien tous les matins.
13. <u>Vous</u> parlez anglais, n'est-ce pas?
14. <u>Il</u> travaille beaucoup le matin.
15. <u>Nous</u> détestons les concombres.
16. <u>Il</u> dort souvent en classe.
17. <u>Elles</u> envoient des lettres au président.
18. <u>Tu</u> étudies à la bibliotheque?
19. <u>Il</u> désobéit à ses parents.
20. <u>Nous</u> finissons cet exercice.
21. <u>Elles</u> jouent au football avec leurs amis.
22. <u>Nous</u> essayons de comprendre nos enfants adolescents.
23. <u>Elles</u> sortent avec leurs amies le samedi soir.
24. <u>Tu</u> préfères le chocolat ou la vanille?
25. <u>Vous</u> aimez le cinéma italien?

II.

1. servir: tu <u>sers</u> = <u>you serve, you are serving, you do serve</u>
2. entrer: j'<u>entre</u> = <u>I enter, I am entering, I do enter</u>
3. travailler: ils <u>travaillent</u> = <u>they work, they are working, they do work</u>
4. dessiner: tu <u>dessines</u> = <u>you draw, you are drawing, you do draw</u>
5. obéir: il <u>obéit</u> = <u>he obeys, he is obeying, he does obey</u>
6. répondre: je <u>réponds</u> = <u>I answer, I am answering, I do answer</u>

7. **regarder: vous <u>regardez</u>** = <u>you watch, you are watching, you do watch</u>

8. **téléphoner: on <u>téléphone</u>** = <u>one calls, one is calling, one does call, we call, we are calling, we do call</u>

9. **souffrir: elle <u>souffre</u>** = <u>she suffers, she is suffering, she does suffer</u>

10. **vendre: tu <u>vends</u>** = <u>you sell, you are selling, you do sell</u>

11. **nager: nous <u>nageons</u>** = <u>we swim, we are swimming, we do swim</u>

12. **acheter: j'<u>achète</u>** = <u>I buy, I am buying, I do buy</u>

13. **finir: nous <u>finissons</u>** = <u>we finish, we are finishing, we do finish</u>

14. **entendre: on <u>entend</u>** = <u>we hear, we are hearing, we do hear</u>

15. **parler: il <u>parle</u>** = <u>he speaks, he is speaking, he does speak</u>

16. **ouvrir: nous <u>ouvrons</u>** = <u>we open, we are opening, we do open</u>

17. **exagérer: tu <u>exagères</u>** = <u>you exaggerate, you are exaggerating, you do exaggerate</u>

18. **demander: elles <u>demandent</u>** = <u>they ask for, they are asking for, they do ask for</u>

19. **attendre: nous <u>attendons</u>** = <u>we wait for, we are waiting for, we do wait for</u>

20. **balayer: tu <u>balaies</u>** = <u>you sweep, you are sweeping, you do sweep</u>

21. **couvrir: vous <u>couvrez</u>** = <u>you cover, you are covering, you do cover</u>

22. **sécher: elles <u>sèchent</u>** = <u>they dry, they are drying, they do dry</u>

23. **jouer: je <u>joue</u>** = <u>I play, I am playing, I do play</u>

24. **rougir: vous <u>rougissez</u>** = <u>you blush, you are blushing, you do blush</u>

25. **arriver: tu <u>arrives</u>** = <u>you arrive, you are arriving, you do arrive</u>

26. **jeter: je <u>jette</u>** = <u>I throw, I am throwing, I do throw</u>

27. **commencer: nous <u>commençons</u>** = <u>we start, we are starting, we do start</u>

28. **finir: ils <u>finissent</u>** = <u>they finish, they are finishing, they do finish</u>

29. **grossir: nous <u>grossissons</u>** = <u>we gain weight, we are gaining weight, we do gain weight</u>

30. **défendre: elle <u>défend</u>** = <u>she defends, she is defending, she does defend</u>

31. **chercher: on <u>cherche</u>** = <u>one looks for, one is looking for, one does look for, we look for, we are looking for, we do look for</u>

32. **tolérer: nous <u>tolérons</u>** = <u>we tolerate, we are tolerating, we do tolerate</u>

33. **danser: elles <u>dansent</u>** = <u>they dance, they are dancing, they do dance</u>

34. **finir: je <u>finis</u>** = <u>I finish, I am finishing, I do finish</u>

35. **effrayer: vous <u>effrayez</u>** = <u>you frighten, you are frightening, you do frighten</u>

36. **dormir: ils <u>dorment</u>** = <u>they sleep, they are sleeping, they do sleep</u>

37. **étudier: vous <u>étudiez</u>** = <u>they study, they are studying, they do study</u>

38. **partir: je <u>pars</u>** = <u>I leave, I am leaving, I do leave</u>

39. **servir: elles <u>servent</u>** = <u>they serve, they are serving, they do serve</u>

40. **employer: elles <u>emploient</u>** = <u>they use, they are using, they do use</u>

CHAPTER 2

I.

1. **Il** conduit très prudemment.

2. **Vous** suivez un cours de psychologie?

3. **Elles** sont assez perspicaces.

4. **Tu** vis avec tes parents?

5. **Nous** sommes ravis de vous voir!

6. **Nous** mourons de faim!

7. **Elles** vont à l'église tous les dimanches.

8. **Il** prend trop de médicaments à mon avis.

9. **Elles** lisent l'allemand et le français.

10. **Elles** font leurs devoirs après le dîner.

11. **Tu** apprends à danser le tango?

12. **Elles** ont un chien qui s'appelle Éros.

13. Qu'est-ce que **vous** buvez?

14. **Nous** devons rendre visite à notre grand-mère.

15. Est-ce que **tu** connais Richard François?

16. **Il** vaut mieux acheter une maison que louer un appartement.

17. **Il** rit trop facilement.

18. **Tu** ne crois pas que je t'aime?

19. **Elles** mettent du beurre sur leur pain.

20. **Nous** allons au théâtre. Veux-**tu** aller avec nous?

II.

1. **suivre: je suis** = I follow, I am following, I do follow

2. **être: je suis** = I am, I am being

3. **courir: tu cours** = you run, you are running, you do run

4. **faire: ils font** = they make/do, they are making/doing, they do make/do

5. **comprendre: elle comprend** = she understands, she is understanding, she does understand

6. **voir: vous voyez** = you see, you are seeing, you do see

7. **écrire: ils écrivent** = they write, they are writing, they do write

8. **avoir: j'ai** = I have, I am having, I do have

9. **lire: tu lis** = you read, you are reading, you do read

10. **aller: elles vont** = they go, they are going, they do go

11. **savoir: je sais** = I know, I am knowing, I do know

12. **croire: vous croyez** = you believe, you are believing, you do believe

13. **recevoir: ils reçoivent** = they receive, they are receiving, they do receive

302 FRENCH VERB WORKBOOK

14. **mettre: tu <u>mets</u>** = you put (on), you are putting (on), you do put (on)

15. **devoir: on <u>doit</u>** = one must, has to, we must, have to

16. **vouloir: tu <u>veux</u>** = you want, you are wanting, you do want

17. **pouvoir: nous <u>pouvons</u>** = we can, are able to

18. **venir: il <u>vient</u>** = he comes, he is coming, he does come

19. **dire: vous <u>dites</u>** = you say/tell, you are saying/telling, you do say/tell

20. **apprendre: j'<u>apprends</u>** = I learn, I am learning, I do learn

21. **boire: nous <u>buvons</u>** = we drink, we are drinking, we do drink

22. **connaître: vous <u>connaissez</u>** = you know, you do know

23. **mourir: il <u>meurt</u>** = he dies, he is dying, he does die

24. **prendre: elles <u>prennent</u>** = they take, they are taking, they do take

25. **rire: nous <u>rions</u>** = we laugh, we are laughing, we do laugh

CHAPTER 3

I.

je <u>m'habille</u> I get dressed, I am getting dressed, I do get dressed

nous <u>nous habillons</u> We get dressed, we are getting dressed, we do get dressed

elles <u>s'habillent</u> They get dressed, they are getting dressed, they do get dressed

vous <u>vous habillez</u> You get dressed, you are getting dressed, you do get dressed

tu <u>t'habilles</u> You get dressed, you are getting dressed, you do get dressed

Elle <u>s'habille</u> She gets dressed, she is getting dressed, she does get dressed

II.

Elle se détend She relaxes, she is relaxing, she does relax

Vous vous détendez You relax, you are relaxing, you do relax

Ils se détendent They relax, they are relaxing, they do relax

Tu te détends You relax, you are relaxing, you do relax

Je me détends I relax, I am relaxing, I do relax

Il se détend He relaxes, he is relaxing, he does relax

III.

Nous nous endormons We fall asleep, we are falling asleep, we do fall asleep

Ils s'endorment They fall asleep, they are falling asleep, they do fall asleep

Tu t'endors You fall asleep, you are falling asleep, you do fall asleep

Vous vous endormez You fall asleep, you are falling asleep, you do fall asleep

Je m'endors I fall asleep, I am falling asleep, I do fall asleep

Elle s'endort She falls asleep, she is falling asleep, she does fall asleep

IV.

1. **Je me souviens de Rachel. (Je me rappelle Rachel.)**
2. **Georges se lève, s'habille, se rase, et s'en va.**
3. **Couche-toi! (Couchez-vous!)**
4. **Nous nous parlons tous les jours. (On se parle tous les jours.)**
5. **Mes parents s'entendent bien.**
6. **Ne t'en fais pas! (Ne vous en faites pas!)**
7. **Yvonne s'occupe du chien.**
8. **Cécile et Rodrigue se marient samedi.**
9. **Tu t'intéresses à l'histoire? (T'intéresses-tu à l'histoire?)**
10. **Reposons-nous un peu.**
11. **Je m'ennuie dans la classe de philosophie.**

CHAPTER 4

I.

1. Il est minuit.

2. Il est trois heures du matin.

3. Il est quatre heures et demie du matin.

4. Il est neuf heures moins le quart du matin.

5. Il est onze heures moins dix du matin.

6. Il est midi. Il est douze heures.

7. Il est une heure cinq de l'après-midi. Il est treize heures cinq.

8. Il est deux heures et quart de l'après-midi. Il est quatorze heures quinze.

9. Il est cinq heures moins vingt de l'après-midi. Il est seize heures quarante.

10. Il est sept heures vingt du soir. Il est dix-neuf heures vingt.

11. Il est dix heures et demie du soir. Il est vingt-deux heures trente.

12. Il est minuit moins le quart. Il est vingt-trois heures quarante-cinq.

II.

1. Quel temps fait-il?

2. Il pleut à verse!

3. Il fait du brouillard et il gèle.

4. Il fait beau?

5. Non, il fait du vent et il pleut.

III.

1. Jérôme et ses parents viennent de manger.

2. Nous venons de faire la vaisselle.

3. Francine vient de partir.

4. Je viens d'aller au cinéma.

5. Vous venez de prendre des photos.

6. Tu viens d'écrire un poème.

IV.

1. Bertrand est en train de jouer au tennis.

2. Hervé et Alice sont en train de discuter de la politique.

3. Tu es en train de lire.

4. Nous sommes en train d'écrire.

5. Je suis en train d'apprendre le français.

6. Vous êtes en train d'écouter de la musique.

V.

1. **Les enfants vont se déguiser.**
2. **Robert va téléphoner à ses parents.**
3. **Nous allons faire une promenade.**
4. **Les Dupont vont divorcer.**
5. **Tu vas attendre le bus.**
6. **Vous allez faire de l'exercice.**
7. **Je vais aller au marché.**

CHAPTER 5

I.

1. Où est-ce que tu as ton cours de français?
   Où as-tu ton cours de français?

2. Quand (quels jours) est-ce que vous avez cours?
   Quand (quels jours) avez-vous cours?

3. Pourquoi est-ce que Marc est content?
   Pourquoi Marc est-il content?

4. Combien de chocolats est-ce qu'il y a dans la boîte?
   Combien de chocolats y a-t-il dans la boîte?

5. À quelle heure est-ce que Jérôme déjeune?
   À quelle heure Jérôme déjeune-t-il?

6. Qui est-ce qui aime chanter?
   Qui aime chanter?

7. Avec qui est-ce que tu dînes?
   Avec qui dînes-tu?

8. Qu'est-ce que vous étudiez?
   Qu'étudiez-vous?

9. Qu'est-ce que tu aimes faire?
   Qu'aimes-tu faire?

10. Où est-ce que tu vas ce weekend?
    Où vas-tu ce weekend?

11. Pourquoi est-ce que Suzanne est déçue?
    Pourquoi Suzanne est-elle déçue?

12. Qui est-ce qui est président de la France?
    Qui est président de la France?

13. Qui est-ce que Paul voit à la télé?
    Qui Paul voit-il à la télé?

14. À qui est-ce que Jacques Chirac téléphone?
    À qui Jacques Chirac téléphone-t-il?

15. De qui est-ce que vous avez (nous avons) besoin?
    De qui avez-vous (avons-nous) besoin?

16. Qu'est-ce qui donne peur aux enfants?

17. Qu'est-ce que les garçons aiment?
    Que les garçons aiment-ils?

18. Qu'est-ce que tu aimes faire?
    Qu'aimes-tu faire?

19. De quoi est-ce qu'Hélène a peur?
    De quoi Hélène a-t-elle peur?

20. À quoi est-ce qu'elle s'intéresse?
    À quoi s'intéresse-t-elle?

21. Quelles villes est-ce que tu visites?
    Quelles villes visites-tu?

22. Qui est-ce que tu admires?
    Qui admires-tu?

23. Qu'est-ce qu'elle est en train de regarder?
    Qu'est-elle en train de regarder?

24. Combien d'enfants est-ce que tu as?
    Combien d'enfants as-tu?

25. Est-ce tu es américaine?
    Es-tu américaine?

26. À quelle heure est-ce que vous dînez?
    À quelle heure dînez-vous?

27. Qu'est-ce que tes parents font le soir?
    Que tes parents font-ils le soir?

28. Pourquoi est-ce que tu aimes le français?
    Pourquoi aimes-tu le français?

29. Avec qui est-ce que ton fils joue?
    Avec qui ton fils joue-t-il?

30. Qu'est-ce que tu fais le soir?
    Que fais-tu le soir?

31. Qui est-ce qui aime le cinéma?
    Qui aime le cinéma?

32. Qu'est-ce que tu aimes faire?
    Qu'aimes-tu faire?

CHAPTER 6

I.

1. écouté	6. **eu**	11. **ri**	16. **chéri**
2. tombé	7. **né**	12. **lu**	17. **su**
3. fini	8. **chanté**	13. **attendu**	18. **connu**
4. entendu	9. **réussi**	14. **surpris**	19. **mangé**
5. venu	10. **pris**	15. **caché**	20. **descendu**

II.

1. **les garçons ont dansé** = the boys danced, the boys have danced, the boys did dance
2. **Isabelle a travaillé** = Isabelle worked, Isabelle has worked, Isabelle did work
3. **j'ai fini** = I finished, I have finished, I did finish
4. **tu as réfléchi** = you thought, you have thought, you did think
5. **nous avons attendu** = we waited, we have waited, we did wait
6. **vous avez téléphoné** = you phoned, you have phoned, you did phone
7. **les enfants ont dormi** = the children slept, the children have slept, the children did sleep
8. **j'ai pris** = I took, I have taken, I did take
9. **Mme Villard a lu** = Mme Villard read, Mme Villard has read, Mme Villard did read
10. **nous avons souri** = we smiled, we have smiled, we did smile
11. **tu as reçu** = you received, you have received, you did receive
12. **ma mère a offert** = my mother gave, my mother has given, my mother did give
13. **vous avez répondu** = you answered, you have answered, you did answer
14. **j'ai choisi** = I chose, I have chosen, I did choose
15. **Véronique a essayé** = Véronique tried, Véronique has tried, Véronique did try
16. **le beurre a fondu** = the butter melted, the butter has melted, the butter did melt
17. **nous avons cherché** = we looked for, we have looked for, we did look for
18. **vous avez perdu** = you lost, you have lost, you did lose
19. **j'ai vécu** = I lived, I have lived, I did live
20. **tu as écrit** = you wrote, you have written, you did write

III.

1. **elle est tombée** = she fell, she has fallen, she did fall
2. **nous sommes sorti(e)s** = we went out, we have gone out, we did go out
3. **Albert est devenu** = Albert became, Albert has become, Albert did become
4. **vous êtes venu(e)(s)** = you came, you have come, you did come
5. **ils sont arrivés** = they arrived, they have arrived, they did arrive
6. **tu es parti(e)** = you left, you have left, you did leave
7. **je suis descendu(e)** = I went down, I have gone down, I did go down

8. **vous êtes resté(e)(s)** = you stayed, you have stayed, you did stay

9. **je suis allé(e)** = I went, I have gone, I did go

10. **nous sommes entré(e)s** = we entered, we have entered, we did enter

11. **elle est née** = she was born, she has been born

12. **ils sont morts** = they died, they have died, they did die

IV.

1. **Elles se sont parlé** = They spoke, they have spoken, they did speak to each other
   (Note that the past participle does NOT agree because **se** is an indirect, not a direct, object.)

2. **Nous nous sommes réveillé(e)s** = We woke up, we have woken up, we did wake up

3. **Les acteurs se sont maquillés** = The actors put on, the actors have put on, the actors did put on makeup

4. **Je me suis lavé le visage** = I washed, I have washed, I did wash my face
   (Note that the past participle does NOT agree because **le visage** is the direct object; **me** is an indirect object.)

5. **Charles s'est douché.** = Charles took, Charles has taken, Charles did take a shower

6. **Marianne s'est brossé les dents** = Marianne brushed, Marianne has brushed, Marianne did brush her teeth
   (Note that the past participle does NOT agree because **les dents** is the direct object; **s'** is an indirect object.)

7. **Ils se sont embrassés** = They kissed, they have kissed, they did kiss (each other)

8. **Vous vous êtes amusé(e)(s)** = You had, you have had, you did have fun.

9. **Tu t'en es allé(e)** = You went away, you have gone away, you did go away

10. **Je me suis trompé(e)** = I made, I have made, I did make a mistake (was wrong)

11. **Ma grand-mère s'est évanouie** = My grandmother fainted, my grandmother has fainted, my grandmother did faint

12. **Nous nous sommes disputé(e)s** = We argued, we have argued, we did argue

13. **Elles se sont endormies** = They fell, they have fallen, they did fall asleep

14. **Ils se sont écrit** = They wrote, they have written, they did write (to) each other
    (Note that the past participle does NOT agree because **se** is an indirect, not a direct, object.)

15. **Elle s'est rasé les jambes** = She shaved, she has shaved, she did shave her legs
    (Note that the past participle does NOT agree because **les jambes** is the direct object; **s'** is an indirect object.)

CHAPTER 7

I.

1. **les garçons dansaient** = the boys danced, the boys were dancing, the boys used to dance

2. **Isabelle travaillait** = Isabelle worked, Isabelle was working, Isabelle used to work

3. **je finissais** = I finished, I was finishing, I used to finish

4. **tu étais** = you were, you used to be

5. **nous attendions** = we waited, we were waiting, we used to wait

6. **vous téléphoniez** = you phoned, you were phoning, you used to phone

7. **les enfants dormaient** = the children slept, the children were sleeping, the children used to sleep

8. **je prenais** = I took, I was taking, I used to take

9. **Mme Villard lisait** = Mme Villard read, Mme Villard was reading, Mme Villard used to read

10. **nous souriions** = we smiled, we were smiling, we used to smile

11. **tu recevais** = you received, you were receiving, you used to receive

12. **ma mère offrait** = my mother gave, my mother was giving, my mother used to give

13. **vous répondiez** = you answered, you were answering, you used to answer

14. **je choisissais** = I chose, I was choosing, I used to choose

15. **Véronique essayait** = Véronique tried, Véronique was trying, Véronique used to try

16. **le beurre fondait** = the butter melted, the butter was melting, the butter used to melt

17. **nous cherchions** = we looked for, we were looking for, we used to look for

18. **vous perdiez** = you lost, you were losing, you used to lose

19. **je vivais** = I lived, I was living, I used to live

20. **tu écrivais** = you wrote, you were writing, you used to write

II.

1. **Il faisait chaud le 14 juillet.**

2. **Nous allions à l'église tous les dimanches.**

3. **Élisabeth était très contente (heureuse).**

4. **Il commençait toujours à pleuvoir quand j'avais un jour de libre.**

5. **Quand j'étais jeune, je faisais la vaisselle tous les soirs.**

6. **Pauline courait dix kilomètres par jour.**

7. **Ils étaient de meilleurs amis.**

8. **Jouais-tu au football quand tu étais petit(e)?** or **Jouiez-vous au football quand vous étiez petit(e)?**

9. **Nous mangions des huîtres chaque année à Noël.**

10. **Il mangeait des bonbons.**

11. **Roxanne avait les yeux bleus quand elle était enfant.**

12. **Il pleuvait et il faisait du vent.**

CHAPTER 8

I.

Hier soir je <u>devais</u> appeler ma mère au téléphone, mais il <u>y a eu (y avait)</u> un problème . . . Mes chats <u>étaient</u> dehors pendant l'après-midi. Normalement, ils reviennent avant qu'il ne fasse noir. Hier, Gogo (la femelle) <u>est rentrée</u> pendant que nous <u>dînions</u>. Mais Didi (le mâle) <u>n'est pas rentré</u>. Après le dîner, on <u>a commencé</u> à s'inquiéter parce qu'on <u>ne savait pas</u> où il <u>était</u>. Jacques (mon mari) <u>est sorti</u> le chercher. Il <u>a appelé</u> Didi pendant dix minutes, mais il <u>n'a entendu aucune réponse</u>. Enfin, il <u>a su</u> où Didi <u>était</u>. Le chat <u>était</u> très haut dans un arbre, et il <u>ne pouvait pas</u> descendre. Normalement, il ne monte pas dans les arbres, mais un autre chat <u>a dû</u> l'effrayer (to scare). Le pauvre <u>miaulait</u> désespérément. Nous <u>avons téléphoné</u> aux pompiers, mais ils <u>ne voulaient pas</u> venir. Par contre, ils nous <u>ont donné</u> le numéro de téléphone d'un monsieur avec une grande échelle (ladder). Alors, on <u>a appelé</u> le monsieur. Il <u>ne voulait pas</u> venir parce qu'il <u>faisait</u> déjà nuit, mais on l'<u>a persuadé</u> de venir. Il <u>est arrivé</u> une demi-heure plus tard avec son échelle et sa femme. Pendant que le monsieur <u>tenait</u> l'échelle, la dame <u>est montée</u> chercher Didi. Mais Didi <u>ne voulait pas</u> aller vers la dame. Alors, Jacques <u>a monté</u> l'échelle, <u>a pris</u> Didi dans ses bras, et <u>est redescendu</u>. Nous <u>avons dû</u> payer le monsieur très cher. Quelle soirée! Et ma mère? Je lui <u>ai téléphoné</u> ce matin.

II.

1. Quand nous sommes arrivé(e)s au théâtre, il n'y avait plus de places.
2. Il pleuvait quand je suis parti(e) ce matin.
3. Puis il a commencé à neiger.
4. Elle s'appelait Rio et elle dansait sur le sable.
5. Où étais-tu (étiez-vous) quand j'ai appelé (téléphoné)?
6. Nous faisions de la pêche au lac.
7. Gisèle a attendu (pendant) une heure.
8. Paul était en retard.
9. Quand il s'est présenté, elle pleurait.
10. Puis elle a crié pendant cinq minutes.
11. Il s'est excusé et a dit qu'il l'aimait.
12. Elle a pris son manteau et est partie.

CHAPTER 9

I.

1. **les garçons avaient dansé** = the boys had danced
2. **Isabelle avait travaillé** = Isabelle had worked
3. **j'avais fini** = I had finished
4. **tu avais réfléchi** = you had thought
5. **nous avions attendu** = we had waited
6. **vous aviez téléphoné** = you had phoned
7. **les enfants avaient dormi** = the children had slept
8. **j'avais pris** = I had taken
9. **Mme Villard avait lu** = Mme Villard had read
10. **nous avions souri** = we had smiled
11. **tu avais reçu** = you had received
12. **ma mère avait offert** = my mother had given
13. **vous aviez répondu** = you had answered
14. **j'avais choisi** = I had chosen
15. **Véronique avait essayé** = Véronique had tried
16. **le beurre avait fondu** = the butter had melted
17. **nous avions cherché** = we had looked for
18. **vous aviez perdu** = you had lost
19. **j'avais vécu** = I had lived
20. **tu avais écrit** = you had written

II.

1. **elle était tombée** = she had fallen
2. **nous étions sorti(e)s** = we had gone out
3. **Albert était devenu** = Albert had become
4. **vous étiez venu(e)(s)** = you had come
5. **ils étaient arrivés** = they had arrived
6. **tu étais parti(e)** = you had left
7. **j'étais descendu(e)** = I had gone down
8. **vous étiez resté(e)(s)** = you had stayed
9. **j'étais allé(e)** = I had gone
10. **nous étions entré(e)s** = we had entered
11. **elle était née** = she had been born
12. **ils étaient morts** = they had died

III.

1. **Elles s'étaient parlé** = They had spoken to each other
   (Note that the past participle does NOT agree because **s'** is an indirect, not a direct, object.)

2. **Nous nous étions réveillé(e)s** = We had woken up

3. **Les acteurs s'étaient maquillés** = The actors had put on makeup

4. **Je m'étais lavé le visage** = I had washed my face
   (Note that the past participle does NOT agree because **le visage** is the direct object; **m'** is an indirect object.)

5. **Charles s'était douché** = Charles had taken a shower

6. **Marianne s'était brossé les dents** = Marianne had brushed her teeth
   (Note that the past participle does NOT agree because **les dents** is the direct object; **s'** is an indirect object.)

7. **Ils s'étaient embrassés** = They had kissed (each other)

8. **Vous vous étiez amusé(e)(s)** = You had had fun

9. **Tu t'en étais allé(e)** = You had gone away

10. **Je m'étais trompé(e)** = I had made a mistake (I had been wrong)

11. **Ma grand-mère s'était évanouie** = My grandmother had fainted

12. **Nous nous étions disputé(e)s** = We had argued

13. **Elles s'étaient endormies** = They had fallen asleep

14. **Ils s'étaient écrit** = They had written (to) each other
    (Note that the past participle does NOT agree because **se** is an indirect, not a direct, object.)

15. **Elle s'était rasé les jambes** = She had shaved her legs
    (Note that the past participle does NOT agree because **les jambes** is the direct object; **s'** is an indirect object.)

CHAPTER 10

passé simple	infinitif	passé composé
1. les garçons dansèrent	danser	les garçons ont dansé
2. Isabelle travailla	travailler	Isabelle a travaillé
3. je finis	finir	j'ai fini
4. tu réflechis	réfléchir	tu as réfléchi
5. nous attendîmes	attendre	nous avons attendu
6. vous téléphonâtes	téléphoner	vous avez téléphoné
7. les enfants dormirent	dormir	les enfants ont dormi
8. je pris	prendre	j'ai pris
9. Mme Villard lut	lire	Mme Villard a lu
10. nous sourîmes	sourire	nous avons souri
11. tu reçus	recevoir	tu as reçu
12. ma mère offrit	offrir	ma mère a offert
13. vous répondîtes	répondre	vous avez répondu
14. je choisis	choisir	j'ai choisi
15. Véronique essaya	essayer	Véronique a essayé
16. le beurre fondit	fondre	le beurre a fondu
17. nous cherchâmes	chercher	nous avons cherché
18. vous perdîtes	perdre	vous avez perdu
19. je vécus	vivre	j'ai vécu
20. tu écrivis	écrire	tu as écrit
21. nous eûmes	avoir	nous avons eu
22. je vins	venir	je suis venu(e)
23. elles furent	être	elles ont été
24. tu connus	connaître	tu as connu
25. nous tînmes	tenir	nous avons tenu
26. ils durent	devoir	ils ont dû
27. je pus	pouvoir	j'ai pu
28. il mourut	mourir	il est mort
29. elles naquirent	naître	elles sont nées
30. vous vous levâtes	se lever	vous vous êtes levé(e)(s)

CHAPTER 11

I.

1. <u>J'</u>achèterai mon billet d'avion demain.

2. <u>Il</u> chantera avec la chorale l'année prochaine.

3. <u>Elles</u> essaieront de tricher pendant l'examen.

4. <u>Tu</u> viendras au concert avec moi?

5. <u>Nous</u> serons ravis de vous voir.

6. Ferez-<u>vous</u> une promenade dimanche?

7. <u>Il</u> faudra se dépêcher.

8. <u>Je</u> pourrai éventuellement vous aider.

9. <u>Tu</u> auras du temps libre ce weekend?

10. <u>Nous</u> dirons la vérité au juge.

11. <u>Elles</u> partiront mardi pour le Japon.

12. Quand saurez-<u>vous</u> la réponse?

13. <u>Je</u> répéterai les directifs une fois seulement.

14. Écris-moi quand <u>tu</u> voudras.

15. <u>Nous</u> lirons ce roman pour la classe d'anglais.

16. <u>Vous</u> finirez les devoirs à temps?

II.

1. servir: tu serviras = you will serve

2. entrer: j'entrerai = I will enter

3. travailler: ils travailleront = they will work

4. venir: je viendrai = I will come

5. dessiner: tu dessineras = you will draw

6. obéir: il obéira = he will obey

7. aller: nous irons = we will go

8. répondre: je répondrai = I will answer

9. regarder: vous regarderez = you will watch

10. valoir: il vaudra = it will be worth

11. téléphoner: on téléphonera = one/we will phone

12. recevoir: je recevrai = I will receive

13. souffrir: elle souffrira = she will suffer

14. vendre: tu vendras = you will sell

15. devoir: on devra = one/we will have to

16. nager: nous nagerons = we will swim

17. voir: vous verrez = you will see

18. acheter: j'achèterai = I will buy

19. **finir: nous finirons** = we will finish

20. **entendre: on entendra** = one/we will hear

21. **avoir: elles auront** = they will have

22. **parler: il parlera** = he will speak

23. **ouvrir: nous ouvrirons** = we will open

24. **exagérer: tu exagéreras** = you will exaggerate

25. **être: je serai** = I will be

26. **demander: elles demanderont** = they will ask

27. **attendre: nous attendrons** = we will wait

28. **balayer: tu balaieras** = you will sweep

29. **couvrir: vous couvrirez** = you will cover

30. **sécher: elles sècheront** = they will dry

31. **vouloir: tu voudras** = you will want

32. **jouer: je jouerai** = I will play

33. **rougir: vous rougirez** = you will blush

34. **arriver: tu arriveras** = you will arrive

35. **jeter: je jetterai** = I will throw

36. **commencer: nous commencerons** = we will begin

37. **finir: ils finiront** = they will finish

38. **falloir: il faudra** = it will be necessary

39. **grossir: nous grossirons** = we will gain weight

40. **défendre: elle défendra** = she will defend

41. **chercher: on cherchera** = one/we will look for

42. **tolérer: nous tolérerons** = we will tolerate

43. **danser: elles danseront** = they will dance

44. **mourir: ils mourront** = they will die

45. **finir: je finirai** = I will finish

46. **effrayer: vous effraierez** = you will frighten

47. **dormir: ils dormiront** = they will sleep

48. **étudier: vous étudierez** = you will study

49. **faire: nous ferons** = we will make/do

50. **partir: je partirai** = I will leave

51. **servir: elles serviront** = they will serve

52. **employer: elles emploieront** = they will use

CHAPTER 12

I.

1. **les garçons auront dansé** = the boys will have danced
2. **Isabelle aura travaillé** = Isabelle will have worked
3. **j'aurai fini** = I will have finished
4. **tu auras réfléchi** = you will have thought
5. **nous aurons attendu** = we will have waited
6. **vous aurez téléphoné** = you will have phoned
7. **les enfants auront dormi** = the children will have slept
8. **j'aurai pris** = I will have taken
9. **Mme Villard aura lu** = Mme Villard will have read
10. **nous aurons souri** = we will have smiled
11. **tu auras reçu** = you will have received
12. **ma mère aura offert** = my mother will have given
13. **vous aurez répondu** = you will have answered
14. **j'aurai choisi** = I will have chosen
15. **Véronique aura essayé** = Véronique will have tried
16. **le beurre aura fondu** = the butter will have melted
17. **nous aurons cherché** = we will have looked for
18. **vous aurez perdu** = you will have lost
19. **j'aurai vécu** = I will have lived
20. **tu auras écrit** = you will have written

II.

1. **elle sera tombée** = she will have fallen
2. **nous serons sorti(e)s** = we will have gone out
3. **Albert sera devenu** = Albert will have become
4. **vous serez venu(e)(s)** = you will have come
5. **ils seront arrivés** = they will have arrived
6. **tu seras parti(e)** = you will have left
7. **je serai descendu(e)** = I will have gone down
8. **vous serez resté(e)(s)** = you will have stayed
9. **je serai allé(e)** = I will have gone
10. **nous serons entré(e)s** = we will have entered
11. **elle sera née** = she will have been born
12. **ils seront morts** = they will have died

III.

1. **Elles se seront parlé** = They will have spoken to each other
   (Note that the past participle does NOT agree because **se** is an indirect, not a direct, object.)

2. **Nous nous serons réveillé(e)s** = We will have woken up

3. **Les acteurs se seront maquillés** = The actors will have put on makeup

4. **Je me serai lavé le visage** = I will have washed my face
   (Note that the past participle does NOT agree because **le visage** is the direct object; **me** is an indirect object.)

5. **Charles se sera douché** = Charles will have taken a shower

6. **Marianne se sera brossé les dents** = Marianne will have brushed her teeth
   (Note that the past participle does NOT agree because **les dents** is the direct object; **se** is an indirect object.)

7. **Ils se seront embrassés** = They will have kissed (each other)

8. **Vous vous serez amusé(e)(s)** = You will have had fun

9. **Tu t'en seras allé(e)** = You will have gone away

10. **Je me serai trompé(e)** = I will have made a mistake (will have been wrong)

11. **Ma grand-mère se sera évanouie** = My grandmother will have fainted

12. **Nous nous serons disputé(e)s** = We will have argued

13. **Elles se seront endormies** = They will have fallen asleep

14. **Ils se seront écrit** = They will have written (to) each other
    (Note that the past participle does NOT agree because **se** is an indirect, not a direct, object.)

15. **Elle se sera rasé les jambes** = She will have shaved her legs
    (Note that the past participle does NOT agree because **les jambes** is the direct object; **se** is an indirect object.)

CHAPTER 13

I.

1. <u>Vincent</u> étudierait plus.
2. <u>Nous</u> passerions plus de temps avec notre famille.
3. <u>Je</u> jouerais avec mon chien.
4. <u>Vous</u> iriez au musée.
5. <u>Nicole et Thérèse</u> feraient le ménage.
6. <u>Nous</u> ferions du jardinage.
7. <u>Nous</u> achèterions une nouvelle voiture.
8. <u>Je</u> suivrais des cours de cuisine.
9. <u>Vincent</u> verrait tous les films au cinéma.
10. <u>Nicole et Thérèse</u> auraient plusieurs maisons.
11. <u>Vous</u> iriez en France tous les étés.
12. <u>Je</u> mangerais au restaurant tous les soirs.

II.

1. nous chanterions = we would sing
2. je trouverais = I would find
3. vous iriez = you would go
4. ils achèteraient = they would buy
5. nous achèterions = we would buy
6. tu prendrais = you would take
7. elle voyagerait = she would travel
8. je paierais = I would pay
9. il recevrait = he would receive
10. vous voudriez = you would want
11. on devrait = one/we would have to
12. nous attendrions = we would wait
13. tu finirais = you would finish
14. elle jetterait = she would throw
15. vous travailleriez = you would work
16. je ferais = I would make/do
17. tu courrais = you would run
18. il faudrait = it would be necessary
19. nous aurions = we would have
20. ils verraient = they would see
21. je serais = I would be
22. elle perdrait = she would lose
23. vous réfléchiriez = you would think
24. tu viendrais = you would come
25. ils prendraient = they would take

CHAPTER 14

I.

1. **les garçons auraient dansé** = the boys would have danced
2. **Isabelle aurait travaillé** = Isabelle would have worked
3. **j'aurais fini** = I would have finished
4. **tu aurais réfléchi** = you would have thought
5. **nous aurions attendu** = we would have waited
6. **vous auriez téléphoné** = you would have phoned
7. **les enfants auraient dormi** = the children would have slept
8. **j'aurais pris** = I would have taken
9. **Mme Villard aurait lu** = Mme Villard would have read
10. **nous aurions souri** = we would have smiled
11. **tu aurais reçu** = you would have received
12. **ma mère aurait offert** = my mother would have given
13. **vous auriez répondu** = you would have answered
14. **j'aurais choisi** = I would have chosen
15. **Véronique aurait essayé** = Véronique will have tried
16. **le beurre aurait fondu** = the butter would have melted
17. **nous aurions cherché** = we would have looked for
18. **vous auriez perdu** = you would have lost
19. **j'aurais vécu** = I would have lived
20. **tu aurais écrit** = you would have written

II.

1. **elle serait tombée** = she would have fallen
2. **nous serions sorti(e)s** = we would have gone out
3. **Albert serait devenu** = Albert would have become
4. **vous seriez venu(e)(s)** = you would have come
5. **ils seraient arrivés** = they would have arrived
6. **tu serais parti(e)** = you would have left
7. **je serais descendu(e)** = I would have gone down
8. **vous seriez resté(e)(s)** = you would have stayed
9. **je serais allé(e)** = I would have gone
10. **nous serions entré(e)s** = we would have entered
11. **elle serait née** = she would have been born
12. **ils seraient morts** = they would have died

III.

1. **Elles se seraient parlé** = They would have spoken to each other
   (Note that the past participle does NOT agree because **se** is an indirect, not a direct, object.)

2. **Nous nous serions réveillé(e)s** = We would have woken up

3. **Les acteurs se seraient maquillés** = The actors would have put on makeup

4. **Je me serais lavé le visage** = I would have washed my face
   (Note that the past participle does NOT agree because **le visage** is the direct object; **me** is an indirect object.)

5. **Charles se serait douché** = Charles would have taken a shower

6. **Marianne se serait brossé les dents** = Marianne would have brushed her teeth.
   (Note that the past participle does NOT agree because **les dents** is the direct object; **se** is an indirect object.)

7. **Ils se seraient embrassés** = They would have kissed (each other)

8. **Vous vous seriez amusé(e)(s)** = You would have had fun

9. **Tu t'en serais allé(e)** = You would have gone away

10. **Je me serais trompé(e)** = I would have made a mistake (would have been wrong)

11. **Ma grand-mère se serait évanouie** = My grandmother would have fainted

12. **Nous nous serions disputé(e)s** = We would have argued

13. **Elles se seraient endormies** = They would have fallen asleep

14. **Ils se seraient écrit** = They would have written (to) each other
    (Note that the past participle does NOT agree because **se** is an indirect, not a direct, object.)

15. **Elle se serait rasé les jambes** = She would have shaved her legs
    (Note that the past participle does NOT agree because **les jambes** is the direct object; **se** is an indirect object.)

CHAPTER 15

I.

1. Je serais venu(e) si ma sœur m'avait prêté sa voiture.

2. S'il avait 1000 euros, Martin ferait un voyage en Floride.

3. Si elle n'avait pas dormi en classe, Édith aurait réussi à l'examen.

4. Je n'irais pas si j'étais toi (vous).

5. Te serais-tu mariée si tu avais su que c'était un criminel?

6. Thomas mangerait tout le gâteau s'il n'était pas au régime.

7. Que feriez-vous si vous n'étiez pas obligé(e) de travailler?

8. Il faudrait acheter l'assiette si nous la cassions.

9. Ne voudrais-tu pas savoir?

10. N'aurais-tu pas voulu savoir?

CHAPTER 16

I.

1. que je finisse
2. que tu prennes
3. qu'il ai<u>t</u>
4. que nous quittions
5. que vous habitiez
6. que tu boives
7. que je sois
8. que nous donnions
9. qu'elle mette
10. que vous chantiez
11. qu'il attende
12. que je choisisse
13. que nous dormions
14. qu'elle appelle
15. que tu saches
16. qu'ils connaissent

II.

1. Nous voulons que vous chantiez.
2. Je doute qu'il boive du lait.
3. Ma mère a peur que (craint que) je ne fasse pas mes devoirs.
4. Marc est content (heureux) que ses sœurs puissent venir à la soirée.
5. Il est possible que Vivianne soit enceinte.
6. Il faut que nous rendions visite à Mme Thomas à l'hôpital.
7. La loi exige que nous portions une ceinture de sécurité.

CHAPTER 17

I.

1. que les garçons aient dansé
2. qu'Isabelle ait travaillé
3. que j'aie fini
4. que tu aies réfléchi
5. que nous ayons attendu
6. que vous ayez téléphoné
7. que les enfants aient dormi
8. que j'aie pris
9. que Mme Villard ait lu
10. que nous ayons souri
11. que tu aies reçu
12. que ma mère ait offert
13. que vous ayez répondu
14. que j'aie choisi
15. que Véronique ait essayé
16. que le beurre ait fondu
17. que nous ayons cherché
18. que vous ayez perdu
19. que j'aie vécu
20. que tu aies écrit

II.

1. qu'elle soit tombée
2. que nous soyons sorti(e)s
3. qu'Albert soit devenu
4. que vous soyez venu(e)(s)
5. qu'ils soient arrivés
6. que tu sois parti(e)
7. que je sois descendu(e)
8. que vous soyez resté(e)(s)
9. que je sois allé(e)
10. que nous soyons entré(e)s
11. qu'elle soit née
12. qu'ils soient morts

III.

1. qu'elles se soient parlé
   (Note that the past participle does NOT agree because se is an indirect, not a direct, object.)
2. que nous nous soyons réveillé(e)s
3. que les acteurs se soient maquillés
4. que je me sois lavé le visage
   (Note that the past participle does NOT agree because le visage is the direct object; me is an indirect object.)
5. que Charles se soit douché
6. que Marianne se soit brossé les dents
   (Note that the past participle does NOT agree because les dents is the direct object; se is an indirect object.)
7. qu'ils se soient embrassés
8. que vous vous soyez amusé(e)(s)
9. que tu t'en sois allé(e)
10. que je me sois trompé(e)
11. que ma grand-mère se soit évanouie
12. que nous nous soyons disputé(e)s

13. qu'elles se soient endormies

14. qu'ils se soient écrit
    (Note that the past participle does NOT agree because **se** is an indirect, not a direct, object.)

15. qu'elle se soit rasé les jambes
    (Note that the past participle does NOT agree because **les jambes** is the direct object; **se** is an indirect object.)

CHAPTER 19

I.

1.	**Sois sage.**	Be good.
2.	**Mange tes carottes.**	Eat your carrots.
3.	**Essuie la table.**	Wipe the table.
4.	**Mets la table.**	Set the table.
5.	**Range ta chambre.**	Clean up your room.
6.	**Habille-toi.**	Get dressed.
7.	**Lave-toi les mains.**	Wash your hands.
8.	**Peigne-toi.**	Comb your hair.
9.	**Fais tes devoirs.**	Do your homework.
10.	**N'embête pas ta sœur.**	Don't bother your sister.
11.	**Va dans ta chambre.**	Go to your room.
12.	**Viens avec moi.**	Come with me.
13.	**Ne chante pas à table.**	Don't sing at the table.
14.	**Aie de la patience.**	Be patient (have patience).

II.

1. **Soyez sages.**
2. **Mangez vos carottes.**
3. **Essuyez la table.**
4. **Mettez la table.**
5. **Rangez votre chambre.**
6. **Habillez-vous.**
7. **Lavez-vous les mains.**
8. **Peignez-vous.**
9. **Faites vos devoirs.**
10. **N'embêtez pas votre sœur.**
11. **Allez dans votre chambre.**
12. **Venez avec moi.**
13. **Ne chantez pas à table.**
14. **Ayez de la patience.**

FRENCH–ENGLISH GLOSSARY

A

à la mode   fashionable
à l'étranger   abroad
à l'heure   on time
à moins que   unless
à propos de   about
à temps   in time
aboyer   to bark
absent(e)   absent
accepter   to accept
accident (m)   accident
accompagner   to accompany
acheter   to buy
action (f)   share of stock
actuellement   currently
adorer   to adore
afin que   so that
s'agenouiller   to kneel down
agir   to act
aider   to help
aimable   nice
aimer   to love
ajouter   to add
alimentation (f)   food
allemand(e)   German
aller   to go
allumer   to turn on
alors   so, then
ami (m)   friend (male)
amie (f)   friend (female)
amusant(e)   funny
s'amuser   to have fun
angine (f)   strep throat
anniversaire (m)   birthday
annuler   to cancel
août (m)   August
apéritif (m)   before-dinner drink
appeler   to call
s'appeler   to be called/named
apprécier   to appreciate
apprendre   to learn
s'approcher   to approach
après-midi (m)   afternoon
arbre (m)   tree
argent (m)   money
arrêter   to arrest
arrêter   to stop

s'arrêter (de)   to stop (doing something)
arriver   to arrive
asile (m)   asylum
aspirateur (m)   vacuum cleaner
aspirine (f)   aspirin
s'asseoir   to sit down
attendre   to wait for
s'attendre à   to expect
aucun(e)   no, none
augmentation (de salaire) (f)   raise
autant   so much, as much, so many, as many
automne (m)   autumn
autostop (m)   hitchhiking
autre(s)   other
avancer   to advance
avant   before
avant que   until
avec   with
aveugle   blind
avion (m)   airplane
avis (m)   opinion
avoir   to have
avoir (x) ans   to be (x) years old
avoir besoin de/d'   to need
avoir chaud   to be hot
avoir du mal   to have a hard time
avoir envie de (+inf)   to feel like (doing something)
avoir faim   to be hungry
avoir froid   to be cold
avoir l'intention de   to intend to
avoir peur (de/d')   to be afraid (of)
avoir soif   to be thirsty
avril (m)   April

B

bague (f)   ring
se baigner   to bathe
bain (m) de soleil   sunbath

balayer   to sweep
balle (f)   ball
bande dessinée (f)   comic book
banlieue (f)   suburbs
basket (m)   basketball
bateau (m)   boat
battre   to beat
beaucoup   a lot, much, many
beaux-parents (m/pl)   (parents) -in-law
bête   silly, stupid
bêtise (f)   stupid, silly thing
beurre (m)   butter
bibliothèque (f)   library
bien entendu   of course
bien que   although
bientôt   soon
billet (m)   ticket
biscuit (m)   cookie
bistro (m)   bistro
blanc   white
bleu   blue
boire   to drink
bol (m)   bowl
bon marché   inexpensive
bon, bonne   good
bonbon (m)   candy
bonheur (m)   happiness
bord (m) de la mer   seashore
botte (f)   boot
boue (f)   mud
bouillir   to boil
bouillon (m)   broth
boulangerie (f)   bakery
bourse (f)   scholarship
bout (m)   end
bouteille (f)   bottle
bras (m)   arm
se brosser les cheveux   to brush one's hair
se brosser les dents   to brush one's teeth
bruit (m)   noise
brunir   to get brown
bureau (m)   desk
bureau (m)   office
but (m)   goal

C

ça   this, that
cadeau (m)   gift
café (m)   café
café (m)   coffee
se calmer   to calm (oneself) down
camarade de classe (m/f)   classmate
campagne (f)   countryside
canapé (m)   couch
cancre (m)   bad student
capable   able
carte de crédit (f)   credit card
casser   to break
casserole (f)   saucepan
ce, cet, cette, ces   this, that
célèbre   famous
célébrer   to celebrate
célibataire   single
centaine (f)   about a hundred
centre (m) commercial   mall
cesser   to cease
chaise (f)   chair
chambre (f)   room
changer   to change
chanson (f)   song
chanter   to sing
chantilly (m)   whipped cream
chaque   each, every
chat (m)   cat
chaud   hot, warm
chauffer   to heat
chaussette (f)   sock
chaussure (f)   shoe
chemise (f)   shirt
cher, chère   expensive
chercher   to look for
chérir   to cherish
cheveux (m/pl)   hair
chez   at the home/office of
chien (m)   dog
chimie (f)   chemistry
chocolat (m)   chocolate
choisir   to choose
cinéma (m)   movies
citron (m)   lemon
citron (m) pressé   lemonade
clé (f)   key
code (f) de la route   traffic laws
cœur (m)   heart
combien   how much/many
comme   as, for, like
commencer   to begin

comment   how
compléter   to complete
comprendre   to understand
compte (m) en banque   bank account
conduire   to drive
confondre   to confuse
congé (m)   time off from work
connaître   to know, to be familiar with
se connaître   to meet, make acquaintance
considérer   to consider
constamment   constantly
constitution (f)   constitution
coopérer   to cooperate
copain (m)   boyfriend
copier   to copy
copine (f)   girlfriend
corriger   to correct
Côte (f) d'azur   Riviera
côté (m)   side
se coucher   to go to bed
coup de fil (m)   phone call
course (f)   race
courir   to run
courriel (m)   e-mail
courrier (m)   mail
cours (m)   course
court(e)   short
couvert   silverware
couvrir   to cover
craindre   to fear
cravate (f)   tie
crème (f) fraîche   fresh cream
crier   to cry out
critique (f)   review
croire   to believe
croque-monsieur (m)   grilled ham and cheese sandwich
cuillère (f) à soupe   tablespoon
cuire   to cook
cuisine (f)   kitchen
cuisson (f)   cooking
curieux/se   curious

D

dangereux/se   dangerous
danser   to dance
de bonne heure   early
de l'   some
débrouillard(e)   resourceful
décapotable (f)   convertible
déchirer   to tear up

découper   to cut up
découvrir   to discover
déçu   disappointed
défendre   to defend
déjeuner   to have lunch
demain   tomorrow
déménager   to move (house)
démissionner   to resign
démouler   to remove from mold
se dépêcher   to hurry up
depuis   for, since
dernier, dernière   last
des   some
descendre   to descend
descendre   to stay (at a hotel, etc.)
se déshabiller   to get undressed
désirer   to desire
désobéir (à)   to disobey
se détendre   to relax
détester   to hate
devant   in front of
devenir   to become
devoir   to have to
devoir   to owe
devoirs (m, pl)   homework
d'habitude   usually
dictionnaire (m)   dictionary
Dieu (m)   God
dimanche (m)   Sunday
dîner   to have dinner
dîner (m)   dinner
dire   to say
directeur (m)   director
discuter   to discuss
disponible   available
disposer   arrange
se disputer   to quarrel
dissertation (f)   paper (essay)
dormir   to sleep
doucement   gently
se doucher   to take a shower
douter   to doubt
se douter de   to suspect
droit (m)   right
du   some
dur(e)   hard

E

eau (f)   water
échecs (m/pl)   chess
école (f)   school
écouter   to listen

écrire   to write
éditeur (m)   editor
effrayer   to frighten
église (f)   church
électricité (f)   electricity
élégant   elegant
élire   to elect
émission (f)   television show
empêcher   to prohibit
employer   to use
emprunter   to borrow
s'en aller   to go away
s'en faire   to be worried
en haut de   to the top of
en retard   late
encourager   to encourage
s'endormir   to fall asleep
enfant (m/f)   child
enfourner   to put in the oven
enlever   to remove
ennui (m)   trouble
ennuyer   to bore
s'ennuyer   to be bored
s'enrhumer   to catch a cold
enseigner   to teach
ensemble   together
ensorceler   to bewitch
entendre   to hear
s'entendre (avec)   to get along (with)
entrée (f)   appetizer
entreprendre   to attempt
entrer   to enter
entrouvert(e)   partly open
envoyer   to send
épargner   to save
épeler   to spell
éplucher   to peel
épouvanter   to frighten
époux (m), épouse (f)   spouse
erreur (f) de calcul   miscalculation
escalade (f)   rock climbing
escale (f)   port of call
escalier (m)   staircase
escargot (m)   snail
espérer   to hope
essai (m)   essay
essayer   to try
essuyer   to wipe
établir   to establish
été (m)   summer
éteindre   to turn off
étonné(e)   surprised
s'étonner   to be surprised
étranger, étrangère   foreign

être   to be
être en train de (+ inf)   to be (busy) doing something
études (f, pl)   studies
étudier   to study
s'évanouir   to faint
éveiller   to awaken
évidemment   obviously
éviter   to avoid
exagérer   to exaggerate
exiger   to require

F

fabriquer   to manufacture
fâché(e)   angry
facilement   easily
facture (f)   bill
faire   to do, to make
faire (la) grève   to go on strike
faire attention   to pay attention
faire bouillir   to boil
faire colorer   to sauté
faire cuire   to cook
faire de l'équitation   to go horseback riding
faire de son mieux   to do one's best
faire du vélo   to ride a bicycle
faire fondre   to melt
faire frire   to fry
faire gratiner   to brown (in the oven)
faire la cuisine   to cook
faire la fête   to party
faire la lessive   to do the laundry
faire la queue   to stand in line
faire la sieste   to take a nap
faire la tête   to pout
faire la vaisselle   to do the dishes
faire le lit   to make the bed
faire le ménage   to do housework
faire nuit   to get dark
faire revenir   to sauté
faire une gaffe   to make a mistake
faire une promenade   to take a walk
farine (f)   flour
fatigué(e)   tired
faute (f)   mistake
femme (f)   woman

fenêtre (f)   window
fêter   to celebrate
feuilleter   to leaf through
fier, fière   proud
fille (f)   daughter, girl
film (m) d'horreur   horror movie
film (m) policier   detective movie
fils (m)   son
fin (f)   end
fin(e)   thin
finir   to finish
fleur (f)   flower
fois (f)   time (occurrence)
fondre   to melt
fondu   melted
football (m)   soccer
forêt (f)   forest
fouetter   to whip
four (m)   oven
fraise (f)   strawberry
français(e)   French
frère (m)   brother
frigo (m)   refrigerator
frites (f, pl)   French fries
fromage (m)   cheese

G

gagner   to earn
gagner   to win
garçon (m)   boy
gâteau (m)   cake
gauche   left
glace (f)   ice cream
goût (m)   taste
goutte (f)   drop
grandir   to grow (up)
gratinée (f)   au gratin
grave   serious
grenier (m)   attic
grossir   to gain weight
guérir   to heal
guerre (f)   war
gymnase (m)   gym

H

s'habiller   to get dressed
habiter   to live
s'habituer à   to become accustomed to
haricot (m) vert   green bean
hésiter   to hesitate

heure (f) hour
heure (f) time of day
heureux, heureuse happy
hier yesterday
histoire (f) history
histoire (f) story
hiver (m) winter
honnête honest
horrifié(e) horrified
hurler to scream

I

il s'agit de it is about
il faut it is necessary
il vaut mieux (+ inf) it is better (to)
il y a there is, there are
imperméable (m) raincoat
important(e) important
imprimerie (f) printing house
inconnu(e) unknown
incorporer to incorporate
intégrer to integrate
intéresser to interest
s'intéresser à to be interested in
interférer to interfere
interpréter to interpret
invité(e) guest
inviter to invite

J

jamais never, ever
jambon (m) ham
jaune yellow
jaune (d'oeuf) egg yolk
jeter to throw
jeudi (m) Thursday
jeune young
joindre to join together
jouer to play
jouet (m) toy
jour (m) day
journal (m) newspaper
journaliste (m/f) reporter
journée (f) day
jupe (f) skirt
jusqu'à ce que until

L

là here, there
laisser to let
lancer to throw

langue (f) language, tongue
largement generously
laver to wash
se laver (le visage) to wash (one's face)
se laver (les mains) to wash (one's hands)
leçon (f) lesson
légume (m) vegetable
lettre (f) letter
leur their
se lever to get up
librairie (f) bookstore
libre free
licencier to lay off
limite (f) de vitesse speed limit
lire to read
lisse smooth
livre (m) book
logiciel (m) software
loterie (f) lottery
loup (m) wolf
lundi (m) Monday
lycée (m) high school

M

ma my
magasin (m) store
maigrir to lose weight
main (f) hand
mais but
maison (f) house, home
malade sick
malheureux, malheureuse unhappy
Maman (f) Mom
manger to eat
manifestant (m) protester
manquer to miss
se maquiller to put on makeup
marché (m) en plein air open-air market
mardi (m) Tuesday
mari (m) husband
marié(e) married
marier to unite in marriage
se marier to get married
marmite (f) dish, pot
marquer (un but) to score
matin (m) morning
méchant(e) mean
mécontent(e) discontented
médaille (f) medal

médecin (m) doctor
se méfier (de) to be suspicious (of)
meilleur(e) best
mélanger to mix
merci thank you
mercredi (m) Wednesday
mère (f) mother
mes my
météo (f) weather forecast
mettre to put
se mettre à to begin (to do something)
meubles (m, pl) furniture
mieux better
mignon, mignonne cute
moins less
moins de less/fewer
mois (m) month
mon my
Monsieur Mr.
montagne (f) mountain
se moquer de to make fun of
mordre to bite
moule (m) mold
mourir to die
moyen, moyenne middle/average
musée (m) museum
musique (f) music

N

nager to swim
naître to be born
ne ... jamais never
ne ... pas du tout not at all
ne ... pas encore not yet
ne ... personne nobody
ne ... plus no more
ne ... que only
ne ... rien nothing
négliger to neglect
neige (f) snow
neiger to snow
n'est-ce pas? is it not so?
nettoyer to clean
noces (f, pl) wedding
noir black
noix (f) de coco coconut
nos our
note (f) grade
notre our
nourriture (f) food
nouveau, nouvelle new
nouvelle (f) news

nuage (m)   cloud
nuit (f)   night

O

obéir (à)   to obey
occuper   to occupy
s'occuper de   to take care of
œuf (m)   egg
offrir   to offer, to give as a gift
oignon (m)   onion
on   one, we, people
onctueux/se   creamy
ordinateur (m)   computer
oreille (f)   ear
où   where
oublier   to forget
ours (m)   bear
ouvrier, ouvrière   worker
ouvrir   to open

P

pain (m)   bread
pain (m) grillé   toast
panneau (m)   sign
paquet (m)   package
paraître   to appear
parcourir   to examine
parler   to speak
partir   to leave
passer   to spend (time)
se passer   to happen
se passer de   to do without
pâte (f)   batter
patience (f)   patience
patinage (m)   ice skating
pâtisserie (f)   baking/bakery
patron, patronne   boss
pauvre   poor
payer   to pay
pêche (f)   peach
se peigner   to comb one's hair
pendant   during, for
pénible   tiresome
perdre   to lose
se perdre   to get lost
père (m)   father
permettre   to permit
Perrier (m)   Perrier (sparkling water)
personne (f)   person
petit déjeuner (m)   breakfast
petits pois (m/pl)   peas
petits-enfants (m/pl)   grandchildren

peu   little
photo (f)   photograph
piano (m)   piano
pièce (f)   coin
pièce (f)   play
pierre (f)   stone
pingouin (m)   penguin
pique-nique (m)   picnic
placer   to place
plage (f)   beach
plaindre   to pity
plaisanterie (f)   joke
planche à voile (f)   windsurfing board
plat (m)   plate, platter, dish
plat (m) principal   main dish/course
pleurnicher   to sniffle
pleuvoir   to rain
plus   more
plus de   more
plusieurs   several
poids (m)   weight
poisson (m)   fish
poisson (m) rouge   goldfish
poivre (m)   pepper
poivrer   to pepper
pomme (f)   apple
pomme (f) de terre   potato
portable (m)   cell phone
portefeuille (m)   wallet
porter à ébullition   bring to a boil
poser   to put, place
posséder   to possess
poubelle (f)   garbage can
poupée (f)   doll
pour   in order to, for
pourquoi   why
pourri(e)   rotten, spoiled
pourvu que   provided that
pouvoir   to be able to
pouvoir (m)   power
préalablement   beforehand, already
précéder   to precede
préchauffer   to preheat
se précipiter   to rush
préféré(e)   favorite
préférer   to prefer
premier, première   first
prendre   to take
prendre un pot   to have a drink
se préoccuper   to worry
préparer   to prepare

se préparer   to get ready
près (de)   near
prétendre   to claim
prêter   to loan
prêtre (m)   priest
prier   to request
printemps (m)   spring
probable   likely
prochain(e)   next
professeur (m)   professor, teacher
programme (m)   program
projeter   to project
propre   own, clean
prudemment   carefully, cautiously
puis   then
pull (m)   sweater
pupitre (m)   (student) desk

Q

quand   when
quart (m)   fourth
quartier (m)   neighborhood
que   what
québécois(e)   Quebecois
quel(s), quelle(s)   which
quelque chose   something
quelquefois   sometimes
question (f)   question
qui   who
quoi   what
quoique   although

R

rabat-joie (m)   spoilsport, party pooper
raisonnable   reasonable
randonnée (f)   hike
ranger   to arrange
ranger   to put away
râper   to grate
rappeler   to recall
se rappeler   to recall
rapport (m)   report
se raser   to shave
ratifier   to ratify
ravi(e)   delighted
rayer   to cross out
rayon (m)   section (of a store)
recette (f)   recipe
recevoir   to receive
recouvrir   to cover
rédaction (f)   composition

réfléchir (à) to think (about)
refroidi(e) cooled
refroidir to cool down
regarder to look at
régime (m) diet
règle (f) rule
régner to reign
regretter to regret
remarquer to notice
remercier to thank
remonter to come back up
remplacer to replace
remplir to fill
rendez-vous (m) meeting, date
rendre to give back
se rendre compte de to realize
rendre visite (à) to visit (a person)
renouveler to renew
renvoyer to fire
répéter to repeat
réponse (f) answer
répondeur (m) answering machine
répondre (à) to answer
se reposer to rest
respirer to breathe
restaurant (m) restaurant
rester to stay
retirer du feu remove from heat
retourner to go back
réussir to succeed
réveil (m) alarm (clock)
se réveiller to wake up
révéler to reveal
rêver (de) to dream (about)
rhume (m) cold
rire to laugh
robe (f) dress
roman (m) novel
rouge red
rouge (m) red wine
rougir to blush
rouspéter to grumble
rouspéteur, rouspéteuse grouchy
route (f) highway

S

sa his/her
sachet (m) packet
sage well-behaved

Saint Sylvestre (f) New Year's Eve
saison (f) season
sale dirty
saler to salt
salle (f) de bains bathroom
salle (f) de classe classroom
samedi (m) Saturday
sans que unless
saumon (m) salmon
saupoudrer to sprinkle
savoir to know
sécher to dry
séchoir (clothes) dryer
sel (m) salt
semaine (f) week
sembler to seem
sentir to feel
servir to serve
se servir de to use
ses his/her
seulement only
si if, yes
SIDA (m) AIDS
sieste (f) nap
situation (f) situation
skier to ski
sœur (f) sister
soigneusement carefully
soir (m) evening
soirée (f) party
soldat (m) soldier
soleil (m) sun
son his/her
songer à to think about
sonnette (f) doorbell
sortir to leave
se soucier (de) to worry (about)
souffrir to suffer
souhaiter to wish
soupe (f) soup
sourire to smile
se souvenir de to remember
souvent often
se spécialiser (en) to major (in)
stylo (m) pen
sucre (m) en poudre granulated sugar
sucre (m) glace confectioners' sugar
sucre (m) vanillé vanilla sugar
suggérer to suggest
suivant(e) next
suivre to follow

super terrific
surprendre to surprise
sympathique nice

T

ta your (informal)
tableau (m) painting
tableau (m) noir blackboard
tamiser to sift
tarte (f) tatin apple pie
télé (f) TV
télécharger to download
télégramme (m) telegram
téléphone (m) telephone
téléphoner to telephone
tellement so much
temps (m) time
tenir to hold
tenir à to insist on
tenter to attempt
se terminer to come to an end
tes your (informal)
thé (m) tea
tiers (m) third
tolérer to tolerate
tomber to fall
tomber amoureux/amoureuse de/d' to fall in love with
ton your (informal)
tôt early
toucher to touch
toujours always, still
tout de suite right away
tout(e)(s) all
train (m) train
traiter to treat
tranche (f) slice
travail (m) work
travailler to work
très very
tricher to cheat
triste sad
se tromper to be mistaken
tromper to deceive
trop too, too much
trouver to find
tuer to kill
tutoyer to address as "tu"

V

vacances (f, pl) vacation
vache (f) cow
vaisselle (f) dishes

valise (f)   suitcase
valoir   to be worth
veille (f)   the day before
vendre   to sell
vendredi (m)   Friday
venir   to come
venir de (+ inf)   to have just done something
vérifier les stocks   to check the inventory
vérité (f)   truth
verre (m)   glass
vers   about, around
verser   to pour
vert(e)   green
vêtements (m, pl)   clothes
viande (f)   meat
vie (f)   life
vieux, vieille   old

ville (f)   city
vin (m)   wine
violon (m)   violin
visiter   to visit (a place)
vite   quickly
vivre   to live
voir   to see
voisin(e)   neighbor
voiture (f)   car
voix (f)   voice
vol (m)   airplane flight
voler   to fly
voler   to steal
voleur (m)   thief
volontiers   gladly
vos   your (pl or formal)
votre   your (pl or formal)
vouloir   to wish, to want
vouvoyer   to address as "vous"

voyager   to travel
voyant(e)   fortune teller
voyou (m)   hoodlum
vraiment   really

W

week-end (m)   weekend

Y

yeux (m, pl)   eyes

Z

zoo (m)   zoo

ENGLISH–FRENCH GLOSSARY

A

a lot, much, many **beaucoup**
able **capable**
about **à propos de**
about a hundred **centaine (f)**
about, around **vers**
abroad **à l'étranger**
absent **absent(e)**
to accept **accepter**
accident **accident (m)**
to accompany **accompagner**
to act **agir**
to add **ajouter**
to address as "tu" **tutoyer**
to address as "vous" **vouvoyer**
to adore **adorer**
to advance **avancer**
afternoon **après-midi (m)**
AIDS **SIDA (m)**
airplane **avion (m)**
airplane flight **vol (m)**
alarm (clock) **réveil (m)**
all **tout(e)(s)**
although **bien que, quoique**
always, still **toujours**
angry **fâché(e)**
answer **réponse (f)**
to answer **répondre (à)**
answering machine **répondeur (m)**
to appear **paraître**
appetizer **entrée (f)**
apple **pomme (f)**
apple pie **tarte (f) tatin**
to appreciate **apprécier**
to approach **s'approcher**
April **avril (m)**
arm **bras (m)**
to arrange **ranger, disposer**
to arrest **arrêter**
to arrive **arriver**
as, for, like **comme**
aspirin **aspirine (f)**
asylum **asile (m)**
at the home/office of **chez**
to attempt **entreprendre, tenter**
attic **grenier (m)**

au gratin **gratinée (f)**
August **août (m)**
autumn **automne (m)**
available **disponible**
to avoid **éviter**
to awaken **éveiller**

B

bad student **cancre (m)**
baking/bakery **pâtisserie (f), boulangerie (f)**
ball **balle (f)**
bank account **compte (m) en banque**
to bark **aboyer**
basketball **basket (m)**
to bathe **se baigner**
bathroom **salle (f) de bains**
batter **pâte (f)**
to be **être**
to be (busy) doing something **être en train de (+ inf)**
to be (x) years old **avoir (x) ans**
to be able to **pouvoir**
to be afraid (of) **avoir peur (de/d')**
to be bored **s'ennuyer**
to be born **naître**
to be called/named **s'appeler**
to be cold **avoir froid**
to be hot **avoir chaud**
to be hungry **avoir faim**
to be interested in **s'intéresser à**
to be mistaken **se tromper**
to be surprised **s'étonner**
to be suspicious (of) **se méfier (de)**
to be thirsty **avoir soif**
to be worried **s'en faire**
to be worth **valoir**
beach **plage (f)**
bear **ours (m)**
to beat **battre**
to become **devenir**

to become accustomed to **s'habituer à**
before **avant**
before-dinner drink **apéritif (m)**
beforehand, already **préalablement**
to begin **commencer**
to begin (to do something) **se mettre à**
to believe **croire**
best **le/la meilleur(e)**
better **meilleur, mieux**
to bewitch **ensorceler**
bill **facture (f)**
birthday **anniversaire (m)**
bistro **bistro (m)**
to bite **mordre**
black **noir**
blackboard **tableau (m) noir**
blind **aveugle**
blue **bleu(e)**
to blush **rougir**
boat **bateau (m)**
to boil **bouillir, faire bouillir**
book **livre (m)**
bookstore **librairie (f)**
boot **botte (f)**
to bore **ennuyer**
to borrow **emprunter**
boss **patron, patronne**
bottle **bouteille (f)**
bowl **bol (m)**
boy **garçon (m)**
boyfriend **copain (m)**
bread **pain (m)**
to break **casser**
breakfast **petit déjeuner (m)**
breathe **respirer**
bring to a boil **porter à ébullition**
broth **bouillon (m)**
brother **frère (m)**
to brown (in the oven) **faire gratiner**
to brush one's hair **se brosser les cheveux**
to brush one's teeth **se brosser les dents**

but **mais**
butter **beurre (m)**
to buy **acheter**

C

café **café (m)**
cake **gâteau (m)**
to call **appeler**
to calm (oneself) down **se calmer**
to cancel **annuler**
candy **bonbon (m)**
car **voiture (f)**
carefully, cautiously **prudemment, soigneusement**
cat **chat (m)**
to catch a cold **s'enrhumer**
to cease **cesser**
to celebrate **célébrer, fêter**
cell phone **portable (m)**
chair **chaise (f)**
to change **changer**
to cheat **tricher**
to check the inventory **vérifier les stocks**
cheese **fromage (m)**
chemistry **chimie (f)**
to cherish **chérir**
chess **échecs (m/pl)**
child **enfant (m/f)**
chocolate **chocolat (m)**
to choose **choisir**
church **église (f)**
city **ville (f)**
to claim **prétendre**
classmate **camarade de classe (m/f)**
classroom **salle (f) de classe**
to clean **nettoyer**
clothes **vêtements (m, pl)**
cloud **nuage (m)**
coconut **noix (f) de coco**
coffee **café (m)**
coin **pièce (f)**
cold **rhume (m)**
to comb one's hair **se peigner**
to come **venir**
to come to an end **se terminer**
to come back up **remonter**
comic book **bande dessinée (f)**
to complete **compléter**
composition **rédaction (f)**
computer **ordinateur (m)**

confectioners' sugar **sucre (m) glace**
to confuse **confondre**
to consider **considérer**
constantly **constamment**
constitution **constitution (f)**
convertible **décapotable (f)**
to cook **cuire, faire cuire, faire la cuisine**
cookie **biscuit (m)**
cooking **cuisson (f)**
to cool down **refroidir**
cooled **refroidi(e)**
to cooperate **coopérer**
to copy **copier**
to correct **corriger**
couch **canapé (m)**
countryside **campagne (f)**
course **cours (m)**
to cover **couvrir, recouvrir**
cow **vache (f)**
creamy **onctueux/se**
credit card **carte de crédit (f)**
to cross out **rayer**
to cry out **crier**
curious **curieux/se**
currently **actuellement**
to cut up **découper**
cute **mignon, mignonne**

D

to dance **danser**
dangerous **dangereux/se**
daughter **fille (f)**
day **jour (m), journée (f)**
to deceive **tromper**
to defend **défendre**
delighted **ravi(e)**
to descend **descendre**
to desire **désirer**
desk **bureau (m)**
desk (in a classroom) **pupitre (m)**
detective movie **film (m) policier**
dictionary **dictionnaire (m)**
to die **mourir**
diet **régime (m)**
dinner **dîner (m)**
director **directeur (m)**
dirty **sale**
disappointed **déçu(e)**
discontented **mécontent(e)**
to discover **découvrir**
to discuss **discuter**

dish, pot **marmite (f)**
dishes **vaisselle (f)**
to disobey **désobéir (à)**
to do **faire**
to do housework **faire le ménage**
to do one's best **faire de son mieux**
to do the dishes **faire la vaisselle**
to do the laundry **faire la lessive**
to do without **se passer de**
doctor **médecin (m)**
dog **chien (m)**
doll **poupée (f)**
doorbell **sonnette (f)**
to doubt **douter**
to download **télécharger**
to dream (about) **rêver (de)**
dress **robe (f)**
to drink **boire**
to drive **conduire**
drop **goutte (f)**
to dry **sécher**
dryer (for clothes) **séchoir**
during, for **pendant**

E

each, every **chaque**
ear **oreille (f)**
early **de bonne heure, tôt**
to earn **gagner**
easily **facilement**
to eat **manger**
editor **éditeur (m)**
egg **œuf (m)**
egg yolk **jaune (d'oeuf)**
to elect **élire**
electricity **électricité (f)**
elegant **élégant(e)**
e-mail **courriel (m)**
to encourage **encourager**
end **bout (m), fin (f)**
to enter **entrer**
essay **essai (m)**
to establish **établir**
evening **soir (m)**
ever **jamais**
to exaggerate **exagérer**
to examine **parcourir**
to expect **s'attendre à**
expensive **cher, chère**
eyes **yeux (m, pl)**

F

to faint **s'évanouir**
to fall **tomber**
to fall asleep **s'endormir**
to fall in love with **tomber amoureux/amoureuse de/d'**
famous **célèbre**
fashionable **à la mode**
father **père (m)**
favorite **préféré(e)**
to fear **craindre**
to feel **sentir**
to feel like (doing something) **avoir envie de (+inf)**
to fill **remplir**
to find **trouver**
to finish **finir**
to fire **renvoyer**
first **premier, première**
fish **poisson (m)**
flour **farine (f)**
flower **fleur (f)**
to fly **voler**
to follow **suivre**
food **alimentation (f), nourriture (f)**
for, since **depuis**
foreign **étranger, étrangère**
forest **forêt (f)**
to forget **oublier**
fortune teller **voyant(e)**
fourth **quart (m)**
free **libre**
French **français(e)**
French fries **frites (f, pl)**
fresh cream **crème (f) fraîche**
Friday **vendredi (m)**
friend (female) **amie (f)**
friend (male) **ami (m)**
to frighten **effrayer, épouvanter**
to fry **faire frire**
funny **amusant(e)**
furniture **meubles (m, pl)**

G

to gain weight **grossir**
garbage can **poubelle (f)**
generously **largement**
gently **doucement**
German **allemand(e)**
to get along (with) **s'entendre (avec)**
to get brown **brunir**

to get dark **faire nuit**
to get dressed **s'habiller**
to get lost **se perdre**
to get married **se marier**
to get ready **se préparer**
to get undressed **se déshabiller**
to get up **se lever**
gift **cadeau (m)**
girl **fille (f)**
girlfriend **copine (f)**
to give **donner, offrir**
to give back **rendre**
gladly **volontiers**
glass **verre (m)**
to go **aller**
to go away **s'en aller**
to go back **retourner**
to go out **sortir**
to go to bed **se coucher**
to go horseback riding **faire de l'équitation**
to go on strike **faire (la) grève**
goal **but (m)**
God **Dieu (m)**
goldfish **poisson (m) rouge**
good **bon, bonne**
grade **note (f)**
grandchildren **petits-enfants (m/pl)**
granulated sugar **sucre (m) en poudre**
to grate **râper**
green **vert(e)**
green bean **haricot (m) vert**
grilled ham and cheese sandwich **croque-monsieur (m)**
grouchy **rouspéteur, rouspéteuse**
to grow (up) **grandir**
to grumble **rouspéter**
guest **invité(e)**
gym **gymnase (m)**

H

hair **cheveux (m/pl)**
ham **jambon (m)**
hand **main (f)**
to happen **se passer**
happiness **bonheur (m)**
happy **heureux, heureuse**
hard **dur(e)**
to hate **détester**
to have **avoir**

to have a drink **prendre un pot**
to have a hard time **avoir du mal**
to have dinner **dîner**
to have fun **s'amuser**
to have just done something **venir de (+ inf)**
to have lunch **déjeuner**
to have to **devoir**
to heal **guérir**
to hear **entendre**
heart **cœur (m)**
to heat **chauffer**
to help **aider**
here, there **là**
to hesitate **hésiter**
high school **lycée (m)**
highway **route (f)**
hike **randonnée (f)**
his/her **son, sa, ses**
history **histoire (f)**
hitchhiking **autostop (m)**
to hold **tenir**
homework **devoirs (m, pl)**
honest **honnête**
hoodlum **voyou (m)**
to hope **espérer**
horrified **horrifié(e)**
horror movie **film (m) d'horreur**
hot, warm **chaud(e)**
hour **heure (f)**
house, home **maison (f)**
how **comment**
how much/many **combien**
to hurry up **se dépêcher**
husband **mari (m)**

I

ice cream **glace (f)**
ice skating **patinage (m)**
if **si**
important **important(e)**
in front of **devant**
in order to, for **pour**
in time **à temps**
to incorporate **incorporer**
inexpensive **bon marché**
to insist on **tenir à**
to integrate **intégrer**
to intend to **avoir l'intention de**
to interest **intéresser**
to interfere **interférer**

to interpret **interpréter**
to invite **inviter**
is it not so? **n'est-ce pas?**
it is about **il s'agit de**
it is better (to) **il vaut mieux (+ inf)**
it is necessary **il faut**

J

to join together **joindre**
joke **plaisanterie (f)**

K

key **clé (f)**
to kill **tuer**
kitchen **cuisine (f)**
to kneel down **s'agenouiller**
to know **savoir**
to know, to be familiar with **connaître**

L

language **langue (f)**
last **dernier, dernière**
late **en retard**
to laugh **rire**
to lay off **licencier**
to leaf through **feuilleter**
to learn **apprendre**
to leave **partir, sortir**
left **gauche**
lemon **citron (m)**
lemonade **citron (m) pressé**
less **moins**
less/fewer **moins de**
lesson **leçon (f)**
to let **laisser**
letter **lettre (f)**
library **bibliothèque (f)**
life **vie (f)**
likely **probable**
to listen **écouter**
little **peu**
to live **habiter, vivre**
to loan **prêter**
to look at **regarder**
to look for **chercher**
to lose **perdre**
to lose weight **maigrir**
lottery **loterie (f)**
to love **aimer**

M

mail **courrier (m)**
main dish/course **plat (m) principal**
to major (in) **se spécialiser (en)**
to make **faire**
to make a faux pas **faire une gaffe**
to make fun of **se moquer de**
to make the bed **faire le lit**
mall **centre (m) commercial**
to manufacture **fabriquer**
many **beaucoup (de)**
married **marié(e)**
mean **méchant(e)**
meat **viande (f)**
medal **médaille (f)**
to meet, make acquaintance **se connaître**
meeting, date **rendez-vous (m)**
to melt **fondre, faire fondre**
melted **fondu(e)**
middle/average **moyen, moyenne**
miscalculation **erreur (f) de calcul**
to miss **manquer**
mistake **faute (f)**
to mix **mélanger**
mold **moule (m)**
Mom **Maman (f)**
Monday **lundi (m)**
money **argent (m)**
month **mois (m)**
more **plus**
more (of something) **plus de**
morning **matin (m)**
mother **mère (f)**
mountain **montagne (f)**
to move (house) **déménager**
movies **cinéma (m)**
Mr. **Monsieur**
Mrs. **Madame**
much **beaucoup (de)**
mud **boue (f)**
museum **musée (m)**
music **musique (f)**
my **mon, ma, mes**

N

nap **sieste (f)**
near **près (de)**

to need **avoir besoin de/d'**
to neglect **négliger**
neighbor **voisin(e)**
neighborhood **quartier (m)**
never **ne ... jamais**
new **nouveau, nouvelle**
New Year's Eve **Saint Sylvestre (f)**
news **nouvelle (f)**
newspaper **journal (m)**
next **prochain(e), suivant(e)**
nice **aimable, sympathique**
night **nuit (f)**
no more **ne ... plus**
no, none **ne ... aucun(e)**
nobody **ne ... personne**
noise **bruit (m)**
not at all **ne ... pas du tout**
not yet **ne ... pas encore**
nothing **ne ... rien**
to notice **remarquer**
novel **roman (m)**

O

to obey **obéir (à)**
obviously **évidemment**
to occupy **occuper**
of course **bien entendu**
to offer, to give as a gift **offrir**
office **bureau (m)**
often **souvent**
old **vieux, vieille**
on time **à l'heure**
one, we, people **on**
onion **oignon (m)**
only **ne ... que, seulement**
to open **ouvrir**
open-air market **marché (m) en plein air**
opinion **avis (m)**
other **autre(s)**
our **notre, nos**
oven **four (m)**
to owe **devoir**
own, clean **propre**

P

package **paquet (m)**
packet **sachet (m)**
painting **tableau (m)**
paper (essay) **dissertation (f)**
parents-in-law **beaux-parents (m/pl)**

partly open **entrouvert(e)**
party **soirée (f)**
to party **faire la fête**
patience **patience (f)**
to pay **payer**
to pay attention **faire attention**
peach **pêche (f)**
peas **petits pois (m/pl)**
to peel **éplucher**
pen **stylo (m)**
penguin **pingouin (m)**
pepper **poivre (m)**
to pepper **poivrer**
to permit **permettre**
Perrier (sparkling water) **Perrier (m)**
person **personne (f)**
phone call **coup de fil (m)**
photograph **photo (f)**
piano **piano (m)**
picnic **pique-nique (m)**
to pity **plaindre**
to place **placer**
plate, platter, dish **plat (m)**
play **pièce (f)**
to play **jouer**
poor **pauvre**
port of call **escale (f)**
to possess **posséder**
potato **pomme (f) de terre**
to pour **verser**
to pout **faire la tête**
power **pouvoir (m)**
to precede **précéder**
to prefer **préférer**
to preheat **préchauffer**
to prepare **préparer**
priest **prêtre (m)**
printing house **imprimerie (f)**
professor, teacher **professeur (m)**
program **programme (m)**
to prohibit **empêcher**
to project **projeter**
protester **manifestant (m)**
proud **fier, fière**
provided that **pourvu que**
to put **mettre**
to put away **ranger**
to put in the oven **enfourner**
to put on makeup **se maquiller**
to put, place **poser**

Q

to quarrel **se disputer**
Quebecois **québécois(e)**
question **question (f)**
quickly **vite**

R

race **course (f)**
to rain **pleuvoir**
raincoat **imperméable (m)**
raise **augmentation (de salaire) (f)**
to ratify **ratifier**
to read **lire**
to realize **se rendre compte de**
really **vraiment**
reasonable **raisonnable**
to recall (call back) **rappeler**
to recall (remember) **se rappeler**
to receive **recevoir**
recipe **recette (f)**
red **rouge**
red wine **(vin) rouge (m)**
refrigerator **frigo (m)**
to regret **regretter**
to reign **régner**
to relax **se détendre**
to remember **se souvenir de**
to remove **enlever**
remove from heat **retirer du feu**
to remove from mold **démouler**
to renew **renouveler**
to repeat **répéter**
to replace **remplacer**
report **rapport (m)**
reporter **journaliste (m/f)**
to request **prier**
to require **exiger**
to resign **démissionner**
resourceful **débrouillard(e)**
to rest **se reposer**
restaurant **restaurant (m)**
to reveal **révéler**
review **critique (f)**
to ride a bicycle **faire du vélo**
right **droit (m)**
right away **tout de suite**
ring **bague (f)**
Riviera **Côte (f) d'azur**
rock climbing **escalade (f)**

room **chambre (f)**
rotten, spoiled **pourri(e)**
rule **règle (f)**
to run **courir**
to rush **se précipiter**

S

sad **triste**
salmon **saumon (m)**
salt **sel (m)**
to salt **saler**
Saturday **samedi (m)**
saucepan **casserole (f)**
to sauté **faire colorer, faire revenir**
to save **épargner**
to say **dire**
scholarship **bourse (f)**
school **école (f)**
to score **marquer (un but)**
to scream **hurler**
seashore **bord (m) de la mer**
season **saison (f)**
section (of a store) **rayon (m)**
to see **voir**
to seem **sembler**
to sell **vendre**
to send **envoyer**
serious **grave**
to serve **servir**
several **plusieurs**
share of stock **action (f)**
to shave **se raser**
shirt **chemise (f)**
shoe **chaussure (f)**
short **court(e), petit(e)**
sick **malade**
side **côté (m)**
to sift **tamiser**
sign **panneau (m)**
silly, stupid **bête**
silverware **couvert (m)**
to sing **chanter**
single **célibataire**
sister **sœur (f)**
to sit down **s'asseoir**
situation **situation (f)**
to ski **skier**
skirt **jupe (f)**
to sleep **dormir**
slice **tranche (f)**
to smile **sourire**
smooth **lisse**
snail **escargot (m)**
to sniffle **pleurnicher**

snow **neige (f)**
to snow **neiger**
so much **tellement**
so much, as much, so many, as many **autant**
so that **afin que**
so, then **alors**
soccer **football (m)**
sock **chaussette (f)**
software **logiciel (m)**
soldier **soldat (m)**
some **du, de la, de l', des**
something **quelque chose**
sometimes **quelquefois**
son **fils (m)**
song **chanson (f)**
soon **bientôt**
soup **soupe (f)**
to speak **parler**
speed limit **limite (f) de vitesse**
to spell **épeler**
to spend (time) **passer**
spoilsport, party pooper **rabat-joie (m)**
spouse **époux (m), épouse (f)**
spring **printemps (m)**
to sprinkle **saupoudrer**
staircase **escalier (m)**
to stand in line **faire la queue**
to stay **rester**
to stay (at a hotel, etc.) **descendre**
to steal **voler**
stone **pierre (f)**
to stop **arrêter**
to stop (doing something) **s'arrêter (de)**
store **magasin (m)**
story **histoire (f)**
strawberry **fraise (f)**
strep throat **angine (f)**
student desk **pupitre (m)**
studies **études (f, pl)**
to study **étudier**
stupid, silly thing **bêtise (f)**
suburbs **banlieue (f)**
to succeed **réussir**
to suffer **souffrir**
to suggest **suggérer**
suitcase **valise (f)**
summer **été (m)**
sun **soleil (m)**
sunbath **bain (m) de soleil**
Sunday **dimanche (m)**
to surprise **surprendre**

surprised **étonné(e)**
to suspect **se douter de**
sweater **pull (m)**
to sweep **balayer**
to swim **nager**

T

tablespoon **cuillère (f) à soupe**
to take **prendre**
to take a nap **faire la sieste**
to take a shower **se doucher**
to take a walk **faire une promenade**
to take care of **s'occuper de**
taste **goût (m)**
tea **thé (m)**
to teach **enseigner**
to tear up **déchirer**
telegram **télégramme (m)**
telephone **téléphone (m)**
to telephone **téléphoner**
television show **émission (f)**
terrific **super**
to thank **remercier**
thank you **merci**
that (adj) **ce, cet, cette, ces**
that (pron) **ça**
the day before **veille (f)**
to the top of **en haut de**
their **leur**
then **puis**
there is, there are **il y a**
thief **voleur (m)**
thin **fin(e)**
to think (about) **réfléchir (à), songer (à)**
third **tiers (m)**
this (adj) **ce, cet, cette, ces**
this (pron) **ça**
to throw **jeter, lancer**
Thursday **jeudi (m)**
ticket **billet (m)**
tie **cravate (f)**
time **temps (m)**
time (occurrence) **fois (f)**
time of day **heure (f)**
time off from work **congé (m)**
tired **fatigué(e)**
tiresome **pénible**
toast **pain (m) grillé**
together **ensemble**
to tolerate **tolérer**
tomorrow **demain**

tongue **langue (f)**
too, too much **trop**
to touch **toucher**
toy **jouet (m)**
traffic laws **code (f) de la route**
train **train (m)**
to travel **voyager**
to treat **traiter**
tree **arbre (m)**
trouble **ennui (m)**
truth **vérité (f)**
to try **essayer**
Tuesday **mardi (m)**
to turn off **éteindre**
to turn on **allumer**
TV **télé (f)**

U

to understand **comprendre**
unhappy **malheureux, malheureuse**
to unite in marriage **marier**
unknown **inconnu(e)**
unless **à moins que, sans que**
until **avant que, jusqu'à ce que**
to use **employer, se servir de**
usually **d'habitude**

V

vacation **vacances (f, pl)**
vacuum cleaner **aspirateur (m)**
vanilla sugar **sucre (m) vanillé**
vegetable **légume (m)**
very **très**
violin **violon (m)**
to visit (a person) **rendre visite (à)**
to visit (a place) **visiter**
voice **voix (f)**

W

to wait for **attendre**
to wake up **se réveiller**
wallet **portefeuille (m)**
war **guerre (f)**
to wash **laver**
to wash (one's face) **se laver (le visage)**

to wash (one's hands) **se laver (les mains)**
water **eau (f)**
weather forecast **météo (f)**
wedding **noces (f, pl)**
Wednesday **mercredi (m)**
week **semaine (f)**
weekend **week-end (m)**
weight **poids (m)**
well-behaved **sage**
what **que, quoi**
when **quand**
where **où**
which **quel(s), quelle(s)**
to whip **fouetter**
whipped cream **chantilly (m)**
white **blanc**
who **qui**

why **pourquoi**
to win **gagner**
window **fenêtre (f)**
windsurfing board **planche à voile (f)**
wine **vin (m)**
winter **hiver (m)**
to wipe **essuyer**
to wish **souhaiter**
to wish, to want **vouloir**
with **avec**
wolf **loup (m)**
woman **femme (f)**
to work **travailler**
work **travail (m)**
worker **ouvrier, ouvrière**
to worry **se préoccuper**

to worry (about) **se soucier (de)**
to write **écrire**

Y

yellow **jaune**
yes **oui, si**
yesterday **hier**
young **jeune**
your (informal) **ton, ta, tes**
your (pl or formal) **votre, vos**

Z

zoo **zoo (m)**